"Creighton Horton's account of h
powerful, and authentic tale that shc
Prosecutors are supposed to be mini
they often fall short of that standard. But Creighton Horton walked the
walk. He was one of the most noble prosecutors I have ever met, and his
memoir is essential reading for those of us concerned with and committed
to justice."

> ~ **DANIEL S. MEDWED,** author of *Prosecution Complex – America's Race
> to Convict and Its Impact on the Innocent,* and Professor at Northeastern
> University School of Law

"You'll be hooked instantly by this riveting insider look at prosecutors
and their surprising power for good. Wow!"

> ~ **BARBARA OAKLEY,** author of the New York Times science bestseller
> *A Mind for Numbers* and instructor of *Learning How to Learn* from Coursera,
> the world's largest and most popular online course

"I couldn't put it down. It inspired me. I am certain it will inspire many
who find themselves drawn to the law and public service in the future.
It will have a significant impact on anyone who aspires to be a thinking
person of action in his or her community."

> ~ **DAVID SCHWENDIMAN,** lead prosecutor of the European Union's
> Special Investigative Task Force investigating crimes against humanity in
> Kosovo

"Creighton Horton is a natural – and national – leader among prosecutors.
His genuine interest in putting fairness, truth, and justice first resonates
throughout his memoir and his life."

> ~ **KATIE MONROE,** leading innocence advocate, former director of the
> Rocky Mountain Innocence Center, and current director of the Healing
> Justice Project

"I have little doubt that my and my family's ordeal ever would have occurred if the Rhode Island State Police's single and focused investigation had landed on Creighton's desk for review."

~ **SCOTT HORNOFF,** former Rhode Island Police Officer, who was wrongfully convicted of murder and sent to prison in 1996, and exonerated six year later when the actual murderer came forward and confessed to the crime

---

"*A Reluctant Prosecutor* chronicles the journey of a law school graduate whom fate casts in the role of criminal prosecutor of high-profile murder cases. A consummate storyteller, Horton takes us behind the scenes in this fascinating and compelling glimpse into the everyday drama of the criminal justice system."

~ **JAY C. MUNNS**, Deputy City Attorney, City of Los Angeles

---

"This book is a profound look at the internal work of a prosecutor driven by a passion to do justice and make the world a better place."

~ **MICHAEL D. WIMS**, author of *How to Try a Murder Case, Pretrial and Trial Guidelines for Prosecution and Defense*, and former Utah Assistant Attorney General, prosecutor, appellate defense counsel, and judge

A RELUCTANT PROSECUTOR

My Journey

*Creighton during capital murder trial of serial killer Arthur Gary Bishop, 1984.
Judge Jay Banks in background, defense counsel and Bishop in foreground.*

A RELUCTANT PROSECUTOR

My Journey

Creighton C. Horton II

Wild ginger Press

A Reluctant Prosecutor: My Journey
© 2016 Creighton C. Horton II

News articles on page 158, 159 and 160 are used by permission of the Salt Lake Tribune.

Printed in the USA
ISBN: 978-1-943190-03-4

Wild Ginger Press
www.wildgingerpress.com

For My Dad,
Creighton C. Horton, M.D.,
and for
Paul Boland, my UCLA Law School Professor

CONTENTS

CITY NIGHT

From the northern hills in summer
Above the Capitol at nightfall
The city stretches seamlessly
On a terrain of miniature sparkling lights
From dense to sparse to faint as distant stars
Like a shimmering fairyland world

If you are quiet and listen
Through the warm wind you hear
Wondrous far-away trains
Or muted sirens in the distance
Or see toy-colorful flashing lights
Move slowly on tiny streets below
Where uniformed attendants rush dutifully into a tragedy

They lie side by side
The two worlds

One man nurtures a dream
Another squats and shivers
The children are safe and warm
But a baby lies dead in the river

From the hill you watch in silence
While just here, to the south or west
The city stages a moment of tenderness or outrage
Redemption
Or an assault on the heart and the senses

Quiet breezes and murdering fires
Compassion and cruelty
Laughter and hope and gaping wounds
Blood hosed from the street
And spent casings on the floor
The birth of a child

City night,
A cacophony of dreams and nightmares
Of fantasy and burglary, magic and mayhem
From the hills you soothe us
With silence and beauty
That only distance and darkness can bring

And as the horizon softens and fades
With the falling of the light,
The city shimmers
Through a hundred thousand pin-prick beacons
Sending up undulating waves of light,
Signaling in the dark

Creighton Horton

SALT LAKE CITY
Summer 1983

"I believe that I have been able to do more as a prosecutor to prevent innocent people from being caught up in the criminal justice system than I ever could have as a defense attorney."
~ GEORGE OAKES,
Deputy District Attorney for Los Angeles County, 1977

"Between the private life of the citizen and the public glare of criminal accusation stands the prosecutor. That state official has the power to employ the full machinery of the state in scrutinizing any given individual. Even if a defendant is ultimately acquitted, forced immersion in criminal investigation and adjudication is a wrenching disruption of everyday life. For this reason, we must have assurance that those who would wield this power will be guided solely by their sense of public responsibility for the attainment of justice."
~ *Young v. U.S. ex rel. Vuitton et Fils S.A.*, 481 U.S. 787, 814 (1987)

FOREWORD

A RELUCTANT PROSECUTOR is based on personal experiences I had in more than 30 years as a prosecutor in the Salt Lake County District Attorney's Office and the Utah Attorney General's Office. The path I followed in my career led me to be involved in a series of high-profile cases, most of them murder cases. They involved defendants who were serial killers, child killers, sexually deviant killers, religious fanatic killers, and mentally deranged killers.

While others have written comprehensive books about cases I prosecuted, such as John Krakauer's *Under the Banner of Heaven: A Story of Violent Faith* (Doubleday, 2013) and Barbara Oakley's *Cold-Blooded Kindness: Neuroquirks of a Codependent Killer, or Just Give Me a Shot at Loving You, Dear, and Other Reflections on Helping That Hurts* (Prometheus Books, 2011), I set out to write a different kind of book – one that focuses on the things I found most fascinating during my thirty years as a prosecutor.

Throughout those years, when I encountered something that fascinated me or that I found particularly meaningful, I jotted down notes and threw them into a file with the thought that one day I might write a book. This book is the result of those experiences. While it's about bombings, murders, political intrigue, public corruption, religious fanatics, imperious and eccentric judges, capital cases, con men, innocent people convicted of crimes they didn't commit, overreaching cops, and venal public officials – more than anything else, it's the story of my personal odyssey through the criminal justice system.

During my years as a prosecutor, I was repeatedly in the right place at the right time to become involved in the most interesting cases of the day.

As a result, the book highlights cases which at the time commanded a great deal of press interest and attention, both locally and nationally.

When I was assigned my first murder case, it was to assist in the prosecution of Joseph Paul Franklin, an avowed racist and prolific serial killer.

A few years later, just as I developed expertise in countering bogus mental defenses, Arthur Gary Bishop confessed to kidnapping, sexually abusing, and killing five young boys over a 4-year period, and I was assigned to rebut his mental defense.

Within three months of my joining the Attorney General's Office, a group of polygamist extremists bombed a Mormon church building and then engaged in a thirteen-day armed standoff with law enforcement officers that culminated in a shootout and the death of an officer. I was assigned the case, which was later made into a TV movie, *In the Line of Duty: Siege at Marion* (1992).

When Ron Lafferty's capital murder convictions for the brutal slayings of his sister-in-law and her baby were reversed on appeal, I was assigned to re-try the case, which became the subject of Jon Krakauer's book, *Under the Banner of Heaven*.

I also became involved in major murder cases which I did not personally try. I was picking a jury in a triple capital murder case when notorious serial bomber and master forger Mark Hofmann set off his first bomb in Salt Lake City, so I was not assigned the case, and yet I was the only prosecutor who ever cross-examined Hofmann on the stand.

I did not participate in the trials of multiple murderer Ronnie Lee Gardner or serial killer Roberto Arguelles, but when their lawyers raised mental claims in post-conviction proceedings, I was called in to counter those claims.

When my colleague Mike Wims retired from the Attorney General's Office, I stepped in to take his place and assist Pat Nolan and Pat Finlinson in the prosecution of Carole Alden, whose case later became the subject of Barbara Oakley's book, *Cold-Blooded Kindness*.

I wrote the book for my own satisfaction and enjoyment, without giving too much thought to its marketability, but I have received such enthusiastic feedback from those with whom I have shared the draft that I think the book may have general appeal, even to those who have never heard of the high-profile defendants I prosecuted.

The process of selecting the topics to include in this book was simple. I have always loved to write, and I had stories I wanted to tell. Many of the chapters touch on aspects of the high-profile cases I handled which were never publicly reported, and I tell those stories just as I remember them.

AUTHOR'S NOTE

THE EPISODES DESCRIBED IN THIS BOOK are my best recollection of events that actually happened. I have not created any fictional characters or altered events for dramatic effect. Where I have included dialogue in quotes, it represents my best recollection of what was said. I didn't record the conversations as the events were unfolding.

My intention in writing the book was to chronicle my personal experiences in the criminal justice system, not to produce a tell-all exposé that might embarrass others, and so I have frequently used pseudonyms where it seemed not central to the narrative to identify people by name. Similarly, I changed the names of several crime victims out of privacy concerns for them and their family members.

In picking pseudonyms, I've realized it's difficult to come up with names no living person has, so I apologize in advance if your name is, for example, "Len Scooter." I trust that time, place, and context will make it clear that I am not referring to you.

In some instances, it didn't make sense to use pseudonyms. For example, I have not changed the names of high-profile defendants whose cases are highlighted, or of many of my colleagues, or of some people who were so prominent in the public eye that they would be readily identifiable from the context.

In telling these stories, I have relied on sources other than my memory to enhance the accuracy of what I relate – notes I made at the time, legal memos and pleadings from the cases, correspondence, news reports of events as they were unfolding, and feedback from some of the colleagues who shared the experiences with me in real time. This book represents my best attempt at "telling it like it was."

CHAPTER 1

Taking a Different Path:
From Aspiring Defense Attorney
to Prosecutor

I FELL INTO PROSECUTION through the back door, which might seem strange for someone who, for almost 30 years, prosecuted high-profile murders in Utah, including serial killers, child killers, sexually deviant killers, religious fanatic killers, and mentally deranged killers. About a dozen of those were capital cases, and some of the murderers I helped convict have been executed or are presently on death row. I also prosecuted elected officials, police officers, judges, attorneys – even other prosecutors – during my 22 years in the Utah Attorney General's Office.

But as a kid, the last thing I contemplated was being a prosecutor. I grew up in a Los Angeles suburb in the 60s, and the primary public image for prosecutors was Hamilton Burger of *Perry Mason* fame. Not only was Burger mistaken in virtually every one of his cases, he was also portrayed as not too bright by an actor who was physically unattractive. It all had little appeal to a young kid growing up in the shadow of Hollywood, especially one whose uncle was the dashing scout Flint McCullough on the TV show *Wagon Train*. In those days, there were a handful of lawyer shows on television besides *Perry Mason*, but the heroes were always defense attorneys, and the prosecutors were generally portrayed as either dim-witted or politically ambitious and unscrupulous.

The first time I got the notion of going into law was my junior year of college as an English major at the University of Utah, when I wandered over to the student union building one Saturday night. They happened to be showing the movie *To Kill a Mockingbird*. I was inspired by the story of Atticus Finch, a principled Southern lawyer charged with the responsibility of defending a black man, Tom Robinson, who was falsely accused of raping a white woman.

The story was set in the Deep South during the Depression, and Atticus faced insurmountable odds trying to defend his innocent client. While he was ultimately unsuccessful and Tom Robinson was wrongfully convicted on scant evidence by yet another unscrupulous prosecutor, Atticus Finch's efforts were noble and his words inspiring. The idea of fighting for justice deeply appealed to me, and sparked my interest in becoming a lawyer.

And then there was the influence of my father. He was a doctor, a specialist in internal medicine who had a close relationship with his patients. I remember when I was about 10 or 11 going with him on a house call to visit an elderly lady who had been a patient for many years, and who lived in a stately home up in Pasadena. While I usually stayed in the car when I accompanied my dad on house calls, this time he asked me if I wanted to come inside with him.

We walked up to the front door and rang the doorbell, and an elderly lady opened it, who smiled when she saw Dad on her front porch. We went inside and Dad introduced me to her. Her name was Mrs. Randolph. I remember that she seemed very nice, but I was struck by how old and frail she was. Dad spent a good deal of time with her, talking not just about medical things but also about other things that she wanted to discuss. By the time we left, it seemed to me that she felt better just because Dad had come to her house with his medical bag, and was there to help her.

When we left the house and got back in the car, Dad mentioned that the lady was quite ill and would probably not live very much longer. We drove home in silence, but when we pulled into the driveway and he turned off the key to the Oldsmobile, he turned to me and said, "Crate,[1] there are lots of ways to make money in this world, and everybody has to make a living, but I hope you will choose some type of work where you'll be helping people, rather than just making money."

Years later, when I watched Atticus Finch defend Tom Robinson, his quest for justice resonated with me. *"Choose work where you'll be helping people, rather than just making money."* What could be more meaningful than working to bring about justice?

So I applied to law school, and attended the UCLA College of Law from 1973 to 1976. Even though Atticus Finch had inspired me to study law, I couldn't quite see how I was going to get from here to there. Deep down, I didn't feel like I was capable of actually becoming a courtroom lawyer, since I was rather introverted and shy, disinclined to volunteer in class and afraid of being called on for fear of looking stupid to my fellow classmates. If I was too timid to do that, how could I ever stand up in court, question witnesses, and make arguments to a judge or jury? So I spent a good deal of time during law school wondering what I was going to do after I graduated.

THE POWER OF ENCOURAGEMENT

During my second year of law school, I took a clinical course called "Neighborhood Legal Services." As part of the class, I worked two hours twice a week manning the UCLA Student Legal Services Office on campus, helping students with things like consumer and landlord-tenant problems. It was my good fortune that year to have Paul Boland as my instructor. In addition to teaching the second-year clinical course, Paul taught a course called "Trial Advocacy" to third-year students. I enjoyed

---

[1] This was my nickname when I was a kid.

the clinical course experience during my second year, but really gave no serious thought to applying for the trial advocacy program during my third and final year of law school.

So the fall of my third year, I intentionally let the deadline pass to apply to take the trial advocacy class. Paul, who was one of four trial advocacy teachers, caught me in the hallway on the first day of school and said he hadn't seen my name on the list of students who were signed up for the course. I told him that I hadn't applied, and hastened to point out that the deadline had already passed. Paul encouraged me to apply anyway, and to get on the waiting list. He said he thought I would be good at trial work, which seemed highly unlikely to me.

Paul's only exposure to me at the time was my work in the Student Legal Services Office the year before, and what did that have to do with trial skills? I figured that the "hot dogs" – the students who asserted themselves in class and seemed self-confident – they were the types to take that course, not me. I remember wondering: How could Paul possibly know that I might make a good trial lawyer? I was mystified, and figured he just didn't really know me. Still, I agreed to go down to the office and apply for the trial advocacy program, although I did it without any real intent of getting into the class.

A few days later, I learned that I had gotten into the program, and had been assigned to Paul Boland's section. I had no idea at the time that this would change the entire course of my professional career. For reasons I still don't quite understand, Paul Boland believed in me long before I believed in myself.

Early in my third year, I approached Paul about a scheduling problem. I played the banjo in a ragtime musical group, "Jay C. Munns & His Boys," and we had a gig that was going to conflict with one of Paul's lectures. I approached him rather tentatively, unsure of what his reaction would be. After all, wasn't law school supposed to be my first priority, not some frivolous musical distraction?

To my surprise, Paul's reaction was totally positive. He told me not to worry about it, that he would record the lecture and I could listen to it later. More than that, he wanted to know all about the group, and when I mentioned that we had recorded an album, he wanted to hear it. When I brought him a copy, he was so enthusiastic about it that he even encouraged me to take our album down to the record store in Westwood Village to see if they'd sell it on consignment.

As part of the trial advocacy course, we as third-year students were able to conduct actual trials under the supervision of "real attorneys" like Paul. We were assigned to represent parents who had been accused of neglecting or abusing their children, and it was a high-stakes deal. I remember being told that, the year before, a student had successfully represented a parent in court, and the child had been returned to the parent's home. A few months later, the parent had killed the child, and the student had been devastated. We were told that if any of us didn't feel comfortable representing a parent in court, we didn't have to do it, and another attorney would be assigned to the case. For a while, I wondered what I had gotten myself into.

A lot of what we did in the program were things like mock trials, mock direct and cross-examinations, and mock interviewing of witnesses. At the law school, they had a room that was set up to resemble a real courtroom, which gave us the chance to get used to the feel of a courtroom, and lessened the intimidation factor.

About three-quarters of the way through the school year, the students at the law school got to vote on whether to do away with the awards ceremony at graduation. It was an easy decision for me. Who needed to sit through a long drawn-out process at graduation while a bunch of hot dogs got awards? Most of the students felt the same way, and we voted down the awards ceremony by a landslide.

A few weeks later, I got a call at home from Paul Boland. He told me that, each year, the clinical professors nominated one student from each of the four sections to be the Trial Advocacy Student of the Year, and that he was going to submit my name. I was surprised, flattered, and a bit confused. I thought I had done all right up to that point in the course, although I hadn't yet done my "real trial." But I couldn't help thinking that, at least in part, Paul was nominating me because he liked me and liked the way I played the banjo.

While it was nice of Paul to nominate me, I didn't expect to win, and didn't think much more about it. After all, there were four clinical Trial Advocacy professors, and each of them could nominate one student, so at best my odds were one in four. Besides, there were probably some truly outstanding students in the other sections – students who were better than me.

A short time later, Paul called again. He said that of the four clinical professors, one hadn't nominated anyone, which left just three students in the running. In the end, they'd just put our names in a hat, and my name was the one they'd drawn out, so I was going to be awarded the honor of UCLA Trial Advocacy Student of the Year! I had a fleeting thought that maybe I shouldn't have voted against the awards ceremony after all.

While I was astonished that I would be getting the award, I felt a lot of pressure, because I hadn't yet done my actual case in court. The case involved allegations that parents were unable to adequately supervise their four children. The juvenile court petition cited a whole litany of purported problems, and the County was trying to remove the kids from the home. The mother had spent some time in a mental hospital, the oldest boy had committed theft and vandalism, the younger kids frequently played hooky from school and occasionally stole, and the father was abusive and had allegedly kicked the oldest boy with his boots. It was quite a list of allegations.

As a regular practice, two students were assigned to each case, but as the trial approached, the student assigned as my partner had a problem and had to pull out of the case. No one else in the clinical class volunteered to help me because they had their own assigned cases to worry about, so

I told Paul I didn't mind handling it alone. That was probably a good thing, because I had to rely on myself. I spent a lot of time preparing for trial, interviewing witnesses, going out to the mental hospital, and planning out how to defend the case.

Finally the day of the trial came, and I was pretty nervous – all the more so because I had already been chosen as Advocate of the Year and I knew some of the other students in the program had more actual trial experience under their belts than I did. Paul was acting as the supervising attorney, which meant he would be there to watch me if I bombed.

The trial lasted most of the day, and once it began, I got into it and wasn't too nervous. I objected to a lot of the questions put to witnesses by the attorney for the County, and most of the objections were sustained by the judge, meaning he was ruling in my favor.

Midway through trial, the County offered a settlement, but the parents didn't want to accept it. In the end, the judge ruled in favor of the parents. I tried to explain to the family afterwards that winning in court didn't mean they didn't have some serious problems, and that the judge's ruling was not an endorsement of their behavior. All it meant was that the judge had found insufficient evidence of neglect or abuse to remove the kids from the parents' custody.

It was a good feeling that day riding home with Paul, not just because we had won in court and I thought the judge had made the right decision, but also because I had faced the challenge of handling an actual court case and had done well. The pressure was now off, and I hadn't embarrassed myself or done anything to show Paul that he'd nominated the wrong guy for the award.

More importantly, I had learned two invaluable things: First, that I could stand up in court against an actual attorney in an actual case and hold my own, if I was sufficiently prepared. Second, that while being in a trial was intimidating and put a knot in my stomach, it was also exciting and more interesting than anything else I had experienced in law school.

As graduation approached, I learned that even though most awards would not be announced because of the student vote, there were four awards, including the one I was going to receive, that Dean Bauman considered his special awards, and he was determined to announce them anyway. It all seemed a bit surreal, and I felt almost like an imposter. I felt that I was OK, but not exceptional, as a trial advocacy student – probably not within the top dozen in the school. I was certainly not in the hot dog category academically, and I hadn't particularly distinguished myself in law school in any other respect. I thought back on my three years of law school. The only accomplishment I really felt, other than just running the law school gauntlet and getting through the experience, was overcoming my fear of being called on by professors and being put on the spot.[2]

GRADUATION AND BEYOND

But now it was all coming to an end, and more than 300 students would be graduating with me in June. The idea that I was going to be one of only four students recognized as exceptional seemed almost absurd to me.

On graduation day, I sat next to a guy in my class who started grousing when the Dean said he would be announcing four special awards. One was for the student with the highest GPA overall. One was for the student who had done the most public service. There was another I can't recall, and then there was the Trial Advocacy award. When my name was announced, the guy sitting next to me turned with a look of disbelief. "You?" he said incredulously. I totally understood his point of view.

As I walked to the front of the stage to receive my award, I couldn't suppress a broad grin, and was almost laughing. The thought that went through my mind was, "I'm getting this award because Paul Boland likes the way I play the banjo." I still didn't really believe in my own potential as a trial lawyer.

---

[2] For more about this, see Chapter 9.

After graduation, as I was studying for the Bar exam, I was invited to attend a meeting of the American Board of Trial Advocates to receive the plaque they were giving in connection with the Trial Advocacy award. It was to be held at the swanky Jonathan Club, a private club in downtown Los Angeles. They would be giving out plaques to the Trial Advocacy award winners from four local law schools: USC, Southwestern, Loyola and UCLA. I was studying for the bar exam every day and not that excited about taking the time to go down to a highfalutin event, so I hoped it wouldn't take long to pick up the plaque and run.

After the event, I penned this description of it to a friend: "I went down to the Jonathan Club and was introduced to the other students as well as attorneys who belonged to the American Board of Trial Advocates. They were all big-time civil trial lawyers and, frankly, they seemed mostly like blowhards with big egos. I didn't feel particularly good about regarding them as the cream of the legal profession, which they supposedly were. But they gave a good plaque, as well as a check for $100. At the end of the presentation, I was eager to take off and get back to my apartment to study, when the little fireball from Southwestern popped up unsolicited to make a speech toasting all the big wheels. Gee whiz, kid, I thought, sit down and pipe down."

FINDING MEANINGFUL WORK

I took the bar exam in July, but didn't get the results until December. I knew that a lot of students failed their first bar exam, and I wasn't that confident that I had done well enough to pass it. I had taken it with my ragtime bandmate, Jay Munns, who had attended Loyola Law School, and Jay found out that a certain newspaper in central California always got the bar exam results first.

As the time neared for the results to be announced, Jay checked with the paper daily, and when the day came, he reported back to me that both of our names were on the list of new lawyers! It was fortunate that Jay had taken the proactive approach, because the following day, the *Pasadena Star-News* published its list of new lawyers, and my name wasn't on it. I called the California State Bar, just to be sure, and was relieved to hear that I had in fact passed the bar.

Now it was time to find a job. I suppose the seeds Paul Boland sowed by orchestrating my award made me feel some need to at least try to become a trial lawyer, now that I was out of law school and had no better idea for my legal career. I quickly learned that the best way to get trial experience fast was to get into a public defender's office or a prosecutor's office. I gave very little thought to the second option, since I saw nothing at the time that would draw me to prosecution. I had no interest in being Hamilton Burger when I could be Atticus Finch. Besides, I had grown up feeling a strong identification with the underdog, and whatever else you could say about Hamilton Burger, he certainly wasn't a champion of the underdog.

I had started the process of applying to a number of public defender's offices when a friend suggested that I go down to the L.A. District Attorney's Office and speak with George Oakes, a prosecutor who, I was told, had a different perspective on prosecution. While I was only mildly interested, I figured it couldn't hurt, so I called and arranged to go down and meet with George in his office.

Just as Paul Boland had a big influence on my becoming a trial lawyer, George Oakes played a similar role in influencing me to consider prosecution as a career. He told me about the tremendous power and discretion of the prosecutor to decide when, and against whom, to bring criminal charges. He told me he thought he had been able to do more as a prosecutor to prevent innocent people from being caught up in the criminal justice system than he ever could have as a defense attorney. He pointed out that defense attorneys can only react to what prosecutors charge. Prosecutors, on the other hand, stand between the police and the public in making charging decisions, and if they don't rush to judgment and are careful about the way they do their jobs, they can prevent injustices by not bringing charges against the wrong people.

To make his point, he told me about a high-profile case he had been assigned and had refused to prosecute – one where the police had pushed hard for criminal charges, but where he felt that the investigation was infused with ethnic bias, and that there was insufficient evidence of the man's guilt. He said that the police were unhappy with his decision not to prosecute, but that he held his ground, feeling it was the right thing to do.

George went on to say, "If you were devising a system of justice and were able to pick young lawyers to be either prosecutors or defense attorneys, you would want to pick the people most concerned about justice to be prosecutors, because they are the most powerful players in the system." He ended on the point that, while the money is scant compared to what you can make in private practice, as a prosecutor you get to make decisions based on what you think is the right thing to do, a luxury in the practice of law, and you have the satisfaction of knowing that you're working for the public good – in essence, for justice. While I was soon to learn that things weren't always that black and white, and that certain influences can impinge upon the prosecutor's ability to make decisions guided solely by what is just, I left George Oakes' office that day with a new perspective.

The next day, I expanded my job search and began applying for positions both as a defense attorney and as a prosecutor. Although criminal law was now my primary focus, I also applied for other positions in government and private practice. Since jobs were hard to come by for new law school graduates, I figured I should cast a pretty broad net and see what developed. I even put an ad in the local LA legal newspaper to see if I got any bites.

I started getting some offers from private law firms, but nothing that really interested me. I remember a partner in one of the law firms that offered me a job walking me around his office, introducing me to the other lawyers there. He told me that they were a diverse group, but that they all came together for one common purpose – to make as much money as possible. It was not inspiring.

Another person I interviewed with was a prominent personal injury lawyer whose office was not far from downtown L.A. He had made a fortune representing plaintiffs in personal injury lawsuits, taking large contingency fees. I went for the interview, and he offered me a job on the spot. His office building was grand and looked like a Colonial mansion – Monticello came to mind – and his personal office resembled Thomas Jefferson's drawing room, complete with ornate furniture and a riser for his desk so you looked up at him while he asked you questions. He told me that the law was a jealous mistress, that my time would no longer be my own, but that if I worked hard, I could make a lot of money and in five years be driving a fancy car and living in a big house with a swimming pool, just like him.

The guy struck me as having a huge ego, a lot like those lawyers at the Jonathan Club. I wasn't at all sure I wanted to work for him. I asked if I could have some time to think about the offer, and he bristled, "What is there to think about?" Here was this rich lawyer offering a young law school grad in a poor job market a golden opportunity, with a hefty starting salary and the chance to make a million bucks, and I was balking. He asked me if I didn't think the starting salary was high enough, and I told him the money was fine, but that I'd still like some time to think it over. He seemed frustrated with my hesitancy, but said he'd give me three hours to think it over.

As I left his office, I noticed that almost all the cars in the parking lot were Mercedes Benzes. I jumped into my VW bus and headed home.

By the time I got there, I had made up my mind. I just couldn't see carrying this guy's briefcase around for five years in the pursuit of riches, even if I didn't have any other prospects at the moment. If that was all law was about, I preferred to find another, less contentious way to make a living. So I called the guy back and turned him down. He sounded shocked,

and in a whole different tone of voice than I'd heard when he was interviewing me, a quieter voice, he almost stammered, "I ... don't understand."
I just told him the job wasn't really what I was looking for, and thanks
anyway.

While I was applying for jobs, I continued to play banjo with "Jay C.
Munns & His Boys." We had some fun gigs – played for Ronald Reagan
when he was Governor of California, played on the *Queen Mary* in Long
Beach Harbor, played for the crowd waiting for President Ford's plane to
land at the Burbank Airport, played for the guy who played Father Mulcahy
on the TV show *M*A*S*H*. It was a lot of fun, but I figured I couldn't
keep turning down legal offers forever. I was also getting lots of rejection
letters from firms and government offices I had applied to. I kind of enjoyed
getting them, and figured that someday I'd use them to wallpaper a bathroom or something.

By late summer of 1977, I had a wad of rejection letters and a handful
of offers, but I couldn't get excited about any of them. They were all from
private law firms, offering positions in insurance defense work, personal
injury work, and other things I couldn't really see myself doing. I figured
it was time to either accept one of the offers or strike out in a different
direction.

My younger brother Joe was in his last year of undergraduate studies
at the University of Utah, and he suggested that I come with him to Salt
Lake City in the fall, and look for work there. The idea of living and
working in Salt Lake rather than L.A. appealed to me, but taking another
bar exam didn't sound like any fun at all. I had gone through that once
already in California, and it was a tough gauntlet to run.

But after mulling my options, I decided to go for it anyway. I really
didn't want to stay in L.A., and Salt Lake with Joe, who was not only my
brother but also my best friend, sounded like it had some promise. I had
lived in Salt Lake during my junior year of college and had enjoyed it,
and I was drawn to the natural beauty of the state. While I had grown up

in the Mormon Church in Southern California, that wasn't what propelled me to Utah, as I had always been skeptical of the Church's claim that it was the one true church, and I had an uneasy relationship with it at best.[3]

Joe and I found a little upstairs apartment to rent in an old house near the University of Utah, and I studied for and took the Utah Bar Exam while working as a law clerk for a downtown firm. I passed the Bar and was admitted to practice in Utah, but had no contacts in the legal community, and no job prospects. The year before I moved to Utah, I had gone into the Salt Lake County Attorney's office to ask about job prospects there. One of the prosecutors in the office had told me that unless I knew somebody or had clerked for the office, my chances of getting hired were slim. Similarly, I had no contacts in the Legal Defender Association office in Salt Lake. Still, I applied to both offices in hopes of getting a position either as a prosecutor or a public defender.

Around the time I passed the bar, I learned that the Salt Lake County Attorney's Office had funding for a temporary position that would only last three months. Although I was already an attorney and it was a law clerk's position, I decided to apply for the job to get my foot in the door. I started working there in the spring of 1978. Right away, I met several prosecutors I liked and related to – people like John T. Nielsen, Dick Shepherd, Bill Hyde and John Soltis. These were people who were interested in working for justice, rather than using their law degrees primarily to make money. It was a stark contrast to the lawyers I had met who were purely focused on financial gain. I felt a kinship with the attorneys there, and when I got an offer to work as an attorney in a private law firm the week after I started clerking for the County Attorney's Office, I turned it down, hoping that I'd be able to parlay the clerkship into a regular position once the County Attorney's Office had an opening.

By September, as the grant was running out, a position opened up at

---

[3] For more on my ties to and relationship with the Mormon Church, see footnote 71 on page 207.

the County Attorney's Office for an entry-level prosecutor. Having clerked there for a few months, I had an inside track, and got the position. I was assigned to the satellite office, which was located in Murray, about 10 miles south of the main downtown office where I had worked as a law clerk. At the satellite office, I handled misdemeanor cases in the justice courts throughout the county.[4]

At that time, justices of the peace conducted their business out of their living rooms, basements, trailers, and, occasionally, a building containing a room that somewhat resembled a courtroom. There were a lot of traffic cases, most notably DUIs, domestic cases, neighborhood disputes, simple assaults, dogs running at large, and the like. It was a good training ground, with a heavy caseload and plenty of jury trials.

About a year later, I was transferred to the downtown office to start handling felony cases, and almost immediately was assigned to assist Bob Stott, a seasoned prosecutor, who had filed two counts of capital murder against a serial killer named Joseph Paul Franklin. I was on my way.

---

[4] In 1994, the Salt Lake County Attorney's Office became known as the "Salt Lake County District Attorney's Office." For simplicity and continuity, I will generally refer to that office throughout the rest of this book as the "District Attorney's Office."

___

CHAPTER 2

Holding My Ground

AFTER I WAS ASSIGNED to help Bob Stott with the prosecution of serial killer Joseph Paul Franklin, I was also given the assignment of working on a case that had not yet been filed, but was under investigation. It involved a woman named Debbie Gladstone, who had died under suspicious circumstances. She had first been reported missing by her husband Kyle in early January of 1981, but after being interviewed by the police several times and flunking a polygraph test on the issue of knowing her whereabouts, he admitted he knew where she was, and directed the officers to a location in the mountains where they discovered her body in the snow.

Kyle Gladstone's story to the police was that he had found his wife dead at their home, where she had hanged herself and left a suicide note in which she asked him to take her body to the mountains because she didn't want her parents to know that she had committed suicide. The police strongly suspected that she had died at Kyle's hands. They had interviewed him several times, and details of his story had changed over time, reinforcing their suspicions.

On January 28, I met with the Chief Deputy of the D.A.'s Office and four detectives from the Salt Lake Police Department's homicide squad – an experienced and impressive cadre of detectives. They said that from the outset of the investigation, officers had been suspicious of Kyle Gladstone, an odd man who had displayed neither affection for his wife nor any real grief at her death. Everyone's hunch was that he had killed her.

But the case was weak on hard evidence, and the autopsy, which I had attended, was inconclusive. The State Medical Examiner could not rule out suicide by the method Gladstone described. So had he killed his wife, or had he carried out this bizarre scheme to take her body and leave it in the mountains after she killed herself?

The detectives and I talked over the case for some time, and then formulated a plan to try to develop further evidence. I wrote in my notes: "My position – right now investigation must continue – too weak to file at this point."

The lead detective assigned to the case was Dale Bartlett, a bright and charismatic officer, and someone I had only known a few months, but had immediately liked. He came to my office alone a few days after the first meeting with all the detectives, and we discussed the case. Bartlett told me that nothing new had been developed, but that Gladstone, who appeared to be quite willing to be interviewed whenever the police asked him to come in, was going to come in again that night for a follow-up interview.

Bartlett went on to say that he was sure that if Gladstone were to be arrested for murder, he would crack and confess to the crime. He wanted me to file murder charges and issue an arrest warrant. I told Bartlett that based on the evidence developed so far, I felt we had insufficient evidence to convict, and that I wasn't at all confident that Gladstone would confess if arrested. So I refused to file charges, and told Bartlett not to arrest Gladstone unless he confessed during the interview.

I also told him that as long as Gladstone was willing to talk, we should encourage him to keep talking, as his changing versions of what happened might ultimately be the best evidence we could develop to establish his guilt. As Bartlett left my office that afternoon without the warrant, my understanding was that he would hold off arresting Gladstone unless he confessed during the interview that evening.

That night, I saw a TV news report that Gladstone had been arrested for murder, and assumed he must have confessed.

The next day, Detective Bartlett came to the office. When he sat down across from my desk, I asked, "So how did it go? I'm curious to hear about the confession."

To my surprise, Bartlett said, "Well, he didn't actually confess."

I took a deep breath and said, "I'm confused. Yesterday we talked about this and you agreed not to arrest him unless he confessed."

Bartlett replied, "Yeah, well I was pretty sure that if I arrested him, he'd break. I took a calculated risk, but he didn't confess. I figured it really didn't matter because the evidence isn't going to get any better by waiting, and we all know he killed his wife."

So Bartlett had in effect decided that the case was ready to be filed. Damn!

I leaned back in my chair and said nothing. I'm sure Bartlett knew I wasn't pleased.

He went on, "We need you to file charges. Gladstone's been arrested and it's been all over the news. We need you to back us up on this one."

The bottom line was that the evidence was no better than it had been earlier, when I had declined to file charges. Detective Bartlett now was sitting in my office, waiting for me to file charges anyway.

He shifted in his seat, and I pondered my options, not doubting that if I turned him down, there would be repercussions. The brass at the police department weren't going to bear easily the public embarrassment of making an arrest on a murder charge and then having the suspect released the next day because the D.A. refused to file charges.

While I believed we would probably file against Gladstone at the point

19

the investigation was complete, I didn't think we were there yet, and I wasn't willing to file charges just to avoid embarrassment to the police department. Nor did I think it was a good precedent to set, because it would effectively allow – even encourage – the police to usurp the prosecutor's vital role in deciding when, and against whom, to bring criminal charges.

Bartlett was waiting for my answer. I couldn't do it.

"No," I said, "the case wasn't ready to file yesterday and it hasn't gotten any better overnight. I don't think we have sufficient evidence yet to bring charges against him. We can always file later if we get more evidence."

Bartlett looked incredulous. "I can't believe this," he said. "You're not really going to hang us out to dry? You know as well as I do that the son-of-a bitch is guilty, and it's time to wrap up the investigation, which could go on forever if we just dawdle around. We have everything we need right now, and the case isn't going to get any better with time."

"I'm sorry, but I told you yesterday I didn't think we had enough evidence, and I'm not comfortable filing charges now. You can take my decision up the chain of command if you want, but I'm not going to file on the evidence we have so far."

As he realized he wasn't going to talk me out of my position, Bartlett, who was a very decent guy, just shrugged and said "O.K. I'll go back and tell my captain."

As he left my office, I wondered how this was going to play out. It couldn't be good.

As I suspected, my decision not to file charges after a high-profile arrest in a murder case started a firestorm, and high-ranking officials at the police department immediately contacted my boss, Ted Cannon, to demand that we file charges. Ted had recently been elected Salt Lake County Attorney, campaigning as the policeman's best friend – complete with commercials of him in a trench coat standing beside a police car with its emergency lights flashing. I suspected that he wasn't about to turn them down, particularly since it had already been reported on the news that the cops had solved the case and arrested the murderer.

I was a rookie prosecutor, but the circumstances of the case soon circulated among the more experienced prosecutors in the office, and many felt, as I did, that the filing of charges was premature and that we shouldn't allow the police to force us to file a case that wasn't ready.

We were told that all prosecutors were to attend a meeting with Cannon and a high-ranking police official to discuss the situation and what was going to happen next. We gathered in the conference room, expecting a group discussion, when Captain D.J. Thornton of the Salt Lake City Police Department walked in with Ted. Thornton was smiling, and told us that he "knew damn well" that our office would stand behind the P.D. and ratify the arrest by filing homicide charges. We wouldn't hang them out to dry. Ted readily agreed, announcing almost jokingly that of course our office would stand behind the police. Ted did not invite any discussion among his staff of prosecutors. It was clear that the staff was just there to listen, not to discuss the merits of whether we should or should not file charges against Gladstone.

As we walked out of the meeting, I could tell by their demeanor that many of the prosecutors weren't happy with the way it had been handled. While I wasn't that surprised with the result, I was surprised that Ted had convened a meeting of the entire staff and then essentially shut down any discussion about what our office should do. He seemed eager to curry favor with the police, even if it meant turning over to them the power to decide who would be charged with crimes – an essential role of the prosecutor.

After the staff meeting, I was called in to meet with Ted Cannon and his chief deputy. They acknowledged that I had given good direction and advice to Detective Bartlett, and that even a more experienced prosecutor would likely have done the same. What had happened was regrettable, they said, but they had made the decision to proceed with the case, and they wanted me to handle it. I said no.

Ted then suggested that the case could be reassigned to a more experienced prosecutor, and that I could assist as "second chair," which would give me good experience in how to try a murder case. He also told me that the police would respect me more if I stayed on the case. I told them that I didn't want to be assigned to the case at all – not even as second chair.

It clearly wasn't what they wanted to hear, so they told me again that they wanted me to remain on the case as second chair, this time adding "unless you feel it's a moral issue." I told them I did feel it was a moral issue, because we were either prosecuting an innocent man or, more likely, a guilty one whom we probably could not convict on the evidence we had. Either way, I did not see the justice in it, and so I told them I would not handle the case in any capacity.

Being a young prosecutor, and having caused the boss this kind of angst, I wasn't sure how he would respond, but I knew what I wasn't willing to do. I wondered if I would be assigned to any other murder cases, or whether there might be other negative repercussions because of my unwillingness to "play ball."

I did receive encouragement from one of the most experienced prosecutors in the office – Richard "Shep" Shepherd – advice I have always appreciated. When I shared with him how I felt and my reluctance to be part of the prosecution team in the *Gladstone* case, he told me, "Well, if you feel that strongly about it, I'd just stick to your guns. And as for the police, I think they'll respect you more if you hold your ground and don't just go along."

While Ted Cannon was clearly not pleased with my recalcitrance, he went ahead and assigned the case to another prosecutor, and essentially left me alone.[5] I continued to work on my other cases, and soon built a reputation among the police as a prosecutor who would take tough cases

---

[5] Gladstone's case never went to trial. He pled guilty to less serious charges, which spared the prosecution the risk of his being found "not guilty" had the case gone to trial. The plea bargain also spared Gladstone the risk of being convicted of murder.

and handle them well, so when major cases came into the office, I got my share.

And Shep was right – by refusing to file charges until I felt we had sufficient evidence to convict, I actually gained more, not less, respect from the officers I worked with, including Detective Bartlett, who eventually became a good friend throughout the many years we worked together.[6]

I also felt that by holding my ground, I was being true to George Oakes' vision of what a prosecutor should be: a person who, despite political pressure, is willing to say no and take the heat for making a decision that's unpopular with the "powers that be." It was a scenario that not only happened to me at other times in my career, but one that I saw play out in the careers of other prosecutors as well – in some cases, at great personal cost. For me, the ability to withstand outside pressures in making charging decisions is central to the ethical conduct of prosecutors, and it's one of the things I like to emphasize in ethics presentations to young prosecutors.

Shortly after I retired in 2009, Mark Nash, Director of Utah Prosecution Council, asked me if I would be willing to write an article for that group's publication, *The Utah Prosecutor*. He said I could pick any topic that interested me, anything I wanted to say to Utah's prosecutors – something along the lines of, "Reflections of a Senior Prosecutor." After more than 30 years as a prosecutor, here's what I told them:

Reflections of a Senior Prosecutor
Creighton Horton, Former Assistant Attorney General
July 2010

THE "TOUGH PROSECUTOR"
Having spent over 30 years as a prosecutor, I want to share with you my

---

[6] A few years later, I worked with Bartlett on another murder case. He was the principal detective in the case against Arthur Gary Bishop, a serial murderer who killed five young boys over a four-year period.

perspective on what it means to be a tough prosecutor. That's a term I've often heard to describe a hard-working and tough-minded prosecutor who will take hard cases and see them through without caving in when things get rough.

Several years ago I remember becoming aware of an up-and-coming young attorney who was building a reputation as a tough prosecutor. He carried a large caseload, was a tough negotiator, and was particularly well-thought-of among the police officers with whom he regularly worked. It was clear they held him in high regard because he was willing to take cases others might decline, and to vigorously pursue them. I later learned that this prosecutor filed all cases the police brought to him, and had never declined a case.

I knew another prosecutor about the same time who was not so well-regarded by the officers with whom he worked. I heard comments that he would sometimes decline cases, that he was soft on crime, that he hid behind "prosecutorial discretion," and that he ought to be a social worker instead of a prosecutor.

Looking at these two prosecutors throughout the years, I came to regard the second one as the "tougher" prosecutor, because one of the most difficult things you must do as a prosecutor is be willing to decline a case if it's not there, despite the considerable pressure that can be brought to bear to induce you to file. The first prosecutor, the one who never declined a case and who was viewed as "tough," was in a way taking the path of least resistance by never risking disappointing the police officers with whom he worked. While he may have been a tough prosecutor in the sense of being willing to tackle difficult cases, the other part of the equation seemed to be missing – the toughness to say no when needed.

Prosecutors stand between the police and the citizenry in performing a vital and unique function, because the prosecutor, and only the prosecutor, has the power and authority to decide who to charge, what to charge, and when to charge. The U.S. Supreme Court explained the unique role of the prosecutor this way:

"Between the private life of the citizen and the public glare of criminal accusation stands the prosecutor. That state official has the power to employ the full machinery of the state in scrutinizing any given individual. Even if a defendant is ultimately acquitted, forced immersion in criminal investigation and adjudication is a wrenching disruption of everyday life. For this reason, we must have assurance that those who would wield this power will be guided solely by their sense of public responsibility for the attainment of justice." Young v. U.S. ex rel. Vuitton et Fils S.A., 481 U.S. 787, 814 (1987)

Former U. S. Supreme Court Justice Robert Jackson put it this way: "The prosecutor has more control over the life, liberty and reputation than any other person in America." That's a strong statement, but if you think about it, it's true. While the police have the power to arrest, only prosecutors can authorize criminal charges.

So the short version is this — if you take your role as a prosecutor seriously, you must be willing to exercise your independent prosecutorial discretion and at times disappoint officers you work closely with and with whom you want to maintain good relationships. It's not easy to do, particularly with officers you work with on an ongoing basis, but you cannot delegate such decisions to the police without abrogating your responsibility as a prosecutor.

I've seen a number of instances, usually in high-profile cases, when prosecutors have been under tremendous pressure to file cases where emotions were running high, but the evidence was just too thin. That pressure can often come not only from the police but also from the press and public, who are frustrated with the amount of time it takes to identify and charge a suspect. I've heard such prosecutors characterized as soft on crime for not bringing charges quickly enough, and have even seen elected prosecutors voted out of office because of this perceived weakness. To me, paradoxically, these were "tough prosecutors." They had the right stuff because they were willing to take the heat of criticism rather than abrogate their responsibility to bring their best judgment to bear in the exercise of prosecutorial discretion. That takes courage, but it's rarely lauded at the time.

So while it's important to foster good relationships with the police, and I certainly recommend that you do, being the policeman's best friend is not the proper role of the prosecutor. There are times when you have to make tough decisions, and while it may be the easier course to file cases for officers who are in your office forcefully advocating for it, there are times when you simply have to say no, not yet, or in some instances, not at all.

Lest I be misunderstood, I need to tell you that there were officers I worked with during my career who I thought the world of, and whom I counted and still count as true friends. But those friendships were never grounded on the idea that I would file a case for them based on friendship rather than upon an independent review of the strengths and weaknesses of a case. I do remember one instance in which a screening officer came in asking me for "a favor." My antenna went up, as I assumed he was going to ask me to file a case that wasn't really ready to go. And that's in fact what did happen. I declined the case, and referred it back for additional investigation.

Although there were cases I declined through the years, I think that overall I had good relationships with most officers, partly because I worked hard with them on the cases I did file, and partly because when I declined cases I tried to do so respectfully. That sometimes involved brainstorming with them what additional evidence we would need to file, or going over with them admissibility problems, if they existed. I also tried to emphasize that while we have different roles in the system, prosecutors are not superior to police officers, or smarter, for that matter. I hope that message made it through, because I truly believe if I were subject to the day-to-day stressors and pressures that officers face, I'd make my share of "mistakes" for someone to "Monday morning quarterback"[7] when the danger was over. So while saying no to the police at times comes with the job, so should respect for them and what they do.

---

[7] Most football games used to be played on weekends, and so the term "Monday morning quarterback" refers to someone who criticizes a quarterback's or coach's decisions after a game is over, which is easy to do once one has the benefit of hindsight.

Over the course of thirty years, you see a lot of things. I have seen cases that were declined over the objection of the police get better over time, and result in solid convictions of suspects who became defendants when the cases were ready to go. I have also seen the rush to file result in acquittals where the "better evidence" anticipated at the time of screening simply never materialized. And I have seen several cases which were declined for insufficient evidence, resulting in strong public criticism against prosecutors, where it turned out later that someone other than the original suspect actually committed the crimes. In those cases, had the prosecutors caved in to the pressure to file prematurely, it would not only have resulted in the prosecution of innocent persons, but the likelihood of bringing the actual perpetrators to justice would have gone way down, since the police would have considered the cases solved and, consequently, closed.

In conclusion, I think prosecutors need to have both the toughness to prosecute difficult cases which are ripe for prosecution and the toughness to say no to cases that are not. Knowing which is which is not always easy to determine, and the stakes are often high. For those who aspire to be "tough prosecutors," I hope this perspective is helpful.

Oh, and that "social worker" prosecutor I mentioned, the one who was characterized as soft on crime – he went on to distinguish himself in his career, and a few years later received an award for "prosecutorial excellence." Sounds like a tough prosecutor to me.

Good luck in the trenches.

CHAPTER 3

Devastating Crime, Nagging Doubts

SANDY CITY, IN THE SOUTHEAST CORNER of the Salt Lake Valley, was a quiet little town in 1979, a place where people felt safe. Kids rode their bikes down tree-lined streets and people didn't worry too much about locking their doors. Twenty minutes away from Salt Lake City, people who lived in Sandy felt insulated from the crime they heard about on the evening news, things that happened in the city. But Sandy would soon become the setting of a vicious crime, a crime that was to shock the community and lead to my first felony trial – one of the most personally challenging of my career.

What started as a routine day for Linda Curry ended as the most horrific day of her life, and one that almost ended her life. It was a pleasant fall morning in late September, and, as usual, her husband Tom had left to go to work in downtown Salt Lake. Linda had spent some time that morning at the house and was preparing to leave when someone knocked on the door. As she came to the front of the house, she saw a man standing on the porch. He spoke to her through the screen door and asked her if she knew where a woman named Renee Reed lived. There was nothing about the man that particularly concerned her, and she answered that she didn't know anyone by that name.

The man then asked if he could use the phone book, and Linda retrieved one from a drawer in the kitchen and handed it out to him through the screen door. The man looked inside the phone book for a minute, then asked Linda if he could come inside and use her telephone. She wasn't comfortable with allowing a man she didn't know inside her home, and told him no. He said he understood, and reached out to hand the phone book back to her through the screen door.

She took the phone book and went to close the door, but in a sudden flash of force and confusion the man was in her home, standing behind her with his arm around her neck, telling her not to scream. She was terrified. The next thing she could later recall was waking up in the hospital.

That day at work, Tom received a very strange call. He didn't recognize the voice on the other end of the line, and couldn't understand a word the person was saying. Was it a crank call? Was the person drunk? A wrong number? Just as Tom was about to hang up the phone, he heard the person on the other end of the line say his name, and suddenly a cold shudder went through his body. He knew instinctively that something had happened to Linda.

He ran out of his office, jumped into his car and started to drive home like a maniac. His thoughts were racing and his heart pounding, and he hoped his car would catch the attention of the police as he sped down I-15 towards Sandy, but he didn't see any police cars. When he arrived in front of the house, he jumped out of the car and ran inside, calling for his wife. He wasn't prepared for what he found.

Linda had been beaten so severely that her face was swollen and disfigured to the point that she was almost unrecognizable. He couldn't fathom what had happened to her, and she was too battered to tell him. In a rush of panic, he carried his wife to the car and raced to the hospital.

Six months after the crime occurred, when Sandy Police Department

Detective George McCamrick came to my office to screen the case, the police had a suspect, but no physical evidence and no positive identification. Not even the motive was clear. Was it a robbery? No property was taken from the house or the victim. Was it a sexual assault? There was no medical evidence of sexual assault. Had the attacker initially intended to commit a sexual assault, but changed his mind after beating the victim so savagely? Perhaps. Did he hate women? Was he mentally unstable, a sadist, a monster? Who could have done such a horrendous thing to another human being? And why? No one could say, and the victim couldn't remember what had happened to her after the assault began.

As was standard practice, the police had shown "photo spreads" to the victim. Generally, each photo spread would consist of a sheet of paper with eight photographs – photographs of people who matched the description of the suspect. The first time Linda was shown photos was at her parents' house, where she was still recovering from her serious injuries, and she was not able to identify anyone as her attacker from among the several photos she was shown.

One of the only clues the police had about Linda's attacker was that he had asked about a woman by the name of Renee Reed. During the investigation, Detective McCamrick happened to be discussing the case with a detective from South Salt Lake, who told him that he was familiar with that name. He said that Renee Reed was the former girlfriend of a man named Clayton Rudiger. Her body had been discovered in an apartment in South Salt Lake, and the circumstances of her death were ambiguous. Had she died by her own hand, or had someone killed her?

McCamrick pulled mug shots of Rudiger, who generally matched the description of the attacker given by Linda, and decided to show her another photo spread that included Rudiger's picture. On the day officers showed her the photo spread, Linda looked carefully at all the pictures, then identified Rudiger as the person who most resembled her attacker. Still, it wasn't a positive ID, as she couldn't say for sure that the person she picked out of the photos was her actual attacker. Officers later showed her another photo spread which contained a different picture of Rudiger, and once again, she thought he looked most like her attacker, but couldn't make a positive identification.

After discussing the case with Detective McCamrick, I decided to do an in-person lineup at the Metropolitan Hall of Justice in Salt Lake, to see if Linda could make a positive ID if she saw Rudiger in person. On the day of the lineup, eight people walked across the stage, and Linda unequivocally identified Rudiger as the man who had nearly beaten her to death. I was busy conducting the lineup, so I wasn't focusing on it at the time, but my friend and fellow prosecutor Lee Dever told me that Linda was visibly shaken when Rudiger walked into the room.

The case was solved, the defendant was charged, and we were on the road to trial. I wasn't worried about presenting my case in court, although I knew that cases based primarily on eyewitness identification could be tricky. This was to be my first felony trial, but I had tried dozens of more difficult cases, including DUIs. The old saying that "if you can try a difficult DUI case, you can try anything" is pretty much true.

What made this case problematic for me was not its technical difficulty, but my own level of confidence as more information came in. As we prepared for trial, Rudiger's attorney, an able young public defender named Trevor Hamasaki, raised issues casting doubt on the accuracy of Linda's eyewitness identification of the defendant, and some of his points made me question how solid our case was.

Hadn't the victim initially described an assailant who was taller than the defendant? What if she had identified Rudiger at the lineup, not because he was her true assailant, but because he was the person whose pictures she had been repeatedly shown who most resembled her attacker? What about the fact that another woman in the neighborhood had said that a larger man had come to her door that same day asking about Renee Reed – a man who she said was definitely not Rudiger? And what about the polygraph expert hired by the defense, who said that he gave Rudiger two polygraph tests, and while the first was inconclusive, the second tended to show truthful responses? I knew that polygraph results were inadmissible in court, being deemed not sufficiently reliable to be presented to a jury. But I also knew that police and prosecutors often themselves relied on polygraphs to make decisions in close cases.

As we approached the date of trial, I struggled with whether I was sure enough that we had the right man. I wasn't too troubled by the polygraph results – I knew enough about the fallibility of polygraphs not to be too swayed by them – but the eyewitness identification issue was more troubling.

I felt a pull in two different directions: I knew that the case was based almost entirely on eyewitness identification, and that while Linda seemed certain that Rudiger was her attacker, another woman with a similar opportunity to view the man who came to her door asking about Renee Reed seemed just as certain that it wasn't Rudiger. Could there possibly have been two men walking around the neighborhood asking about Renee Reed that day? Could we even convict with that conflicting evidence? And most concerning, given the fallibility of eyewitness identification – could Linda simply be mistaken?

I wished we had more circumstantial evidence to bolster our case. While circumstantial evidence is sometimes derided as "weak evidence," it's often more reliable and compelling than eyewitness identification, and I wished we had just one fingerprint of the defendant at the scene.

On the other hand, Linda, who had undergone almost unimaginable trauma at the hands of her assailant, was absolutely convinced that Rudiger was the one who had so brutally assaulted her.

Didn't she have the right to have the case presented to a jury? And, after all, we did have some circumstantial corroboration of identity, through the connection between Rudiger and Renee Reed.

As I often did when confronted with difficult circumstances, I sought out veteran prosecutor Dick Shepherd to ask his advice. I told Shep that I was concerned that the evidence wasn't stronger. Should I dismiss the case or go ahead and take it to trial? What if, at the end of the case, I myself still had doubts about whether Rudiger was the attacker? What would I do then? How could I argue to the jury that the evidence proved beyond a reasonable doubt that he was guilty, if I myself had doubts? This wasn't just a game or academic debate. Yes, I knew that lawyers played various roles in the system, and served as advocates, but I felt that a prosecutor whose primary responsibility was to do justice should not just be playing a role when arguing a defendant's guilt to a jury.

Shep listened to the facts of the case and to my concerns, mulled it over for a moment, and then told me that, all things considered, he thought the victim should have her day in court. I agreed to take his advice, but wondered how the case would play out, and if I would be presented with a moral dilemma before it ended.

The case was tried in May of 1980 before Third District Judge Christine Durham. The trial took place in Salt Lake, in a courtroom in the old City and County Building, which at that time had ornate courtrooms with carved wood ceilings and chandeliers. It rivaled the opulence of the courtrooms found in the Federal District Court building a few blocks away. More to the point, the courtroom had windows, which distinguished it from the drab courtrooms in the Metropolitan Hall of Justice a block to the east, where most Third District Court business was conducted. Unbeknownst to us all as the trial began, those windows were to play a part in what was to follow.

It was a mild spring day when Linda Curry entered the courtroom on the third floor of the courthouse to face the man she believed had shattered not only her face, but her life. She had never been back to her house in Sandy since the day she had almost been beaten to death there eight months earlier, nor would she ever return. This was her chance to tell her story to the jury, to identify the defendant as her attacker, to get him convicted and sent away forever so she could move beyond the horror of what had happened to her and start rebuilding her life.

Although Rudiger had been in jail since his arrest, he was seated at counsel table, wearing a suit. (All prisoners were dressed in civilian clothes, so juries would not be prejudiced against them.) By now, the jury had heard our opening statements and knew something of Linda's terrible ordeal. They also knew from Trevor Hamasaki that the defense would be mistaken identity. Finally, in his opening statement, Hamasaki had told the jury that Rudiger would produce an alibi witness.

This case represented the first and last time two things happened in my career. It was the first and only time I started a trial uneasy about my own level of confidence that we had the right person on trial. And it was the only time I called a victim to the stand and the skies darkened, the wind raged, and the victim testified while lightning and thunder and torrential rains punctuated her testimony. And when she finished with her testimony, the storm ended.

On cross-examination, Hamasaki did his best to assail the circumstances of Linda's identification of his client, but she was unshakable: Rudiger was the man who beat her so severely that her own doctor didn't recognize her at the hospital. Linda's testimony was powerful, and seemed to affect almost everyone in the courtroom – the jurors, the judge, the court personnel, and the spectators. I myself was affected by hearing her account of what happened that day, even though I knew the details of the case inside and out. The only person in the courtroom who appeared unaffected was the defendant, who showed no reaction either to Linda's description of her ordeal or to her identification of him as her attacker.

After I presented the rest of the State's evidence and witnesses – Detective McCamrick to establish the Renee Reed connection and the identification procedures, Tom to recount the nightmare he experienced that day, the doctors to describe the seriousness of Linda's injuries – I rested my case. Then it was the defense's turn.

This was one of those instances where evidence of a defendant's guilt actually increases during the defense's own case. Neither of the two witnesses they put on the stand helped their defense, and the second witness, the alibi witness, not only didn't help, but actively hurt them. In my experience, juries do not react favorably to defendants who call alibi witnesses that the jury believes are lying, and I think that's what happened here. The alibi witness, one of Rudiger's friends with whom he allegedly spent time that day, was inconsistent, evasive, and generally appeared to be fabricating his entire story.

Once his alibi witness backfired, it was probably a tactical mistake for Rudiger not to take the stand and deny that he was the man who had so cruelly devastated Linda Curry's life. While a defendant has the constitutional right to remain silent, and the jury was instructed that the decision not to testify could not be used against him, Rudiger's silence in this case left the jury with only the alibi witness asserting that Rudiger hadn't done it – a witness who had no credibility in their eyes.

Perhaps the biggest surprise of the case was the defense's star witness, Sharon Gibbs, who was called to establish that the man she saw in the neighborhood that day asking about Renee Reed was not Clayton Rudiger – hence, the implied argument went, Linda must be mistaken about her attacker. On the stand, Gibbs recounted her story to Hamasaki: On the same day Linda was attacked, a man came to her door asking for Renee Reed, and it was not the defendant. Sharon, who was a very tall woman, substantially taller than Linda, described the man as being very big, much taller than she was, and muscular – in fact, on cross-examination, she agreed that he was built like a pro football linebacker.

What was striking was this: At the time the police first spoke with Linda in the hospital, they had already been contacted by Gibbs, who had given them a description of the man she saw. They told Linda that another witness had come forward who had also seen her attacker that day, and so they already knew that the suspect was tall and muscular. Although Linda could hardly speak, she told the officers that they were wrong. She said that her attacker was not that big – in fact, he was not much larger than she was. Why would she minimize the size of the man who had almost beaten her to death? If anything, having been brutalized as she was, one might expect her to exaggerate her attacker's size. And Rudiger was of average size and build, consistent with Linda's description of the man who attacked her.

The discrepancy between Linda's description and Sharon Gibbs' was so great that it became clear that, if someone did come to Gibbs' door that day, it could not have been the same man who assaulted Linda. What I never knew for sure was Gibbs' motivation for testifying as she did: Did a man really come to her door that day, or, as the police suspected, did she have some ulterior motive for claiming it had happened? Or could it have been that the defendant and a larger man were in Sandy that day working together, casing the neighborhood for some unknown purpose? In the end, it didn't matter, because Gibbs' testimony did not undermine Linda's identification of the defendant as her attacker.

By the time the defense rested, I was convinced that we had the right man. I argued, and I believed, that the evidence had established Rudiger's guilt beyond a reasonable doubt, although his motive for attacking Linda remained a mystery. The jury went out late in the afternoon to start deliberations. I went back over to the office, grabbed a quick bite, and waited for the phone call letting me know that the jury had returned a verdict. I felt good about the case, but wasn't sure what the jury would do. It could go either way.

A few hours later, the word came over that the jury was ready to announce its verdict. I walked quickly back to the courthouse, eager to find out what the verdict would be. Hamasaki was there, and we waited for the jailors to bring Rudiger back to court. We all stood as the jury re-entered the courtroom, and when Judge Durham asked the jury if they had reached a verdict, the foreman said yes. He said that they had found Rudiger guilty as charged on all counts.

When I walked back to my office from court that night, I felt a great sense of relief. I called the Curry home to give them the news, and Tom answered. I told him that Linda's attacker had been brought to justice and would be going to prison. Their nightmare was over, and they could now move on with their lives. What Tom told me that night has stayed with me to this day: "Thank you. This is the first time since Linda was attacked that we will be able to sleep at night."

My first felony jury trial was over, and while I was to try many cases in the three decades that followed, this one remained unique. When I retired from the Attorney General's Office in 2009, I was interviewed by Chris Vanocur, a local television reporter, who was interested in doing a story about my career, primarily because of the high-profile murder cases I had handled. When he asked me if there was a case that particularly stood out in my mind, I think he expected me to mention one of the capital murder cases I tried, something that had commanded a lot of press attention at the time. For some reason, the Rudiger case came to mind instead, and in explaining the kind of satisfaction you can have as a prosecutor, I told him what Tom had told me the night the jury returned its verdict.

CHAPTER 4

When Polygraphs Lie

IN THE FALL OF 1982, a transient was found stabbed to death lying under a tree in Pioneer Park, then a well-known drug trafficking zone just a few blocks west of the heart of Salt Lake City. The victim was a Native American in his 40s who lived on the streets, and when the police came in to screen the case with me, they had identified and arrested 22-year-old Danny Austin as the killer.

Austin, who was from Arkansas, had been seen walking around the park that day, along with two tag-along friends, who were also transients. The trio had ridden together from Las Vegas to Salt Lake in a boxcar, stayed a short time and then left town. All three were young and had blond hair.

The only person who may have witnessed the crime was a woman who was driving her car past Pioneer Park. She thought she saw a struggle taking place between an older Native American man and a younger man with blond hair. She didn't get a very good look at what was going on, wasn't able to make a confident ID of Austin – although she thought he "looked like" the younger man she saw that day – and she wasn't even sure if a knife was involved in the struggle.

During the investigation, the police learned about the three young transients, at least one of whom was a juvenile, and eventually located and interrogated Austin, who admitted that he and his friends had been at the park that afternoon, but denied knowing anything about a struggle or a murder. The police felt that he was holding something back, and asked if he would take a polygraph test. He readily agreed.

When they came in to screen the case with me, the officers emphasized that Austin had flunked two polygraph tests, and they were sure he was the murderer. They had also received information from police authorities in Arizona that Austin's two companions had been picked up on a robbery charge there, and when questioned about the murder in Salt Lake, the 17-year-old juvenile named Jack had pointed to Austin as the killer. Plus, there was blood on a shirt Austin had in his possession when he was arrested in Wyoming, two days after the crime.

I filed the case, but told the officers that I wanted to listen to the tape recordings of Austin's interviews, including the polygraph interviews. I went into the office over the weekend to listen to the tapes. What I heard was Austin denying any involvement, followed by the police informing him that he had flunked the polygraph, followed by Austin again denying his involvement and asking to take another polygraph test, and so it went.

In the course of the interviews, the police used all sorts of tactics to get Austin to admit that he had stabbed the victim – suggesting that the victim had probably attacked him, playing good cop/bad cop, using the father confessor approach (confession is good for the soul), and telling him that "you're facing the death penalty unless you come clean." Despite all the psychological pressures the police used to get him to confess, Austin just kept up his plaintive refrain: "But God, I didn't do it! Give me another test!"

I knew that polygraph results were not deemed reliable enough to be admitted in court, and I had already done some research on them, but now I became interested in delving deeper. I went up to the University of Utah and spent time at the library finding out whatever I could about the polygraph machine – how it worked, how it was interpreted, its defenders and detractors. I learned that there are no physiological responses unique to lying, and that the things measured by the polygraph, such as sweating, faster breathing, and elevated heart rate, can be caused by things other than lying. And I learned about false positives, which occur when innocent people are considered to be lying, as well as false negatives, which occur when guilty people are deemed to be truthful.

After doing my research, I came away feeling that the polygraph results in the Austin case proved nothing, and that, while polygraphs can be useful in cases where people confess after failing tests, they tell us nothing we can rely on when people continue to maintain their innocence after failing them.

So however strongly the polygraph tests may have seemed to indicate Austin's guilt, to me that indication of guilt was neutralized by Austin' continual denials, which he maintained even in the face of the substantial psychological techniques the police used to get him to confess.

In the meantime, the blood test results had come back on the blood-stained shirt Austin had had in his possession when he was arrested. The blood didn't appear to be the victim's, or otherwise tie Austin to the crime.

Now came the fun part: telling the officers that I didn't believe the polygraph was a reliable indicator of guilt. I met with the case agent, Detective Roy Westphall, and told him my concerns. Not long afterwards, the police polygrapher, Ben Krupp, came to my office, and he wasn't pleased. How could I doubt his findings? Did I doubt his competence as an examiner? How could I think Austin might not be the killer? After all, not only did we have the polygraph results, but we also had the statements of Austin's buddy who had been arrested in Arizona.

When Krupp left my office, it was clear he was not happy, and I figured he would take it up the chain of command if I didn't continue on with the case. If I were to dismiss it, I knew it would be an embarrassment to him personally as well as to the department, which had publicly declared the case "solved."

In the meantime, the police department was planning to fly the case agent, Detective Westphall, to Arizona to get a taped statement from Jack, who would then be brought back to Utah as a material witness to testify against Austin.

Before he left, Westphall came to my office, and we discussed the case. I was leery of criminal informants – "snitches," as we referred to them – and so I was skeptical about whether Jack was telling the truth. This was especially true because the officers in Arizona had already told Jack that Austin had been arrested for the murder before Jack claimed to have witnessed it. Jack had a strong incentive to become an important witness in order to save his own skin, since he was facing serious felony charges in Arizona. I was also aware that he matched the eyewitness' description of the assailant as much as Austin did.[8]

I knew Detective Westphall was convinced that Austin was guilty, and I was concerned he might telegraph to Jack what he wanted him to say. So I told Westphall that when he interviewed Jack, he needed to emphasize that all we wanted was for him to tell the truth. Westphall should be careful not to suggest or intimate in any way what he wanted Jack to say. We went over the approach several times, and Westphall said he understood what I was asking him to do, and would do it. As he was leaving my office, he repeated it – "Just tell the kid that all we want him to do is tell the truth; that's all we're after." Right.

The next day, Westphall called from Arizona with "good news" – Jack had indeed pointed to Austin as the killer. There was no question that we had charged the right man. When I asked him if he had been careful to tell Jack that all we wanted from him was the truth, he said, "Yes, that's exactly what I told him."

Well … , not exactly. Later, when I listened to the tape of the interview,

---

[8] Sometimes "snitches" implicate others in crimes that they themselves have committed. In the case of Ronnie Williamson and Dennis Fritz, who were convicted of capital murder and later exonerated by DNA evidence, it turned out that Glen Gore, a police informant, was the actual murderer. (See Chapter 24.)

I just shook my head. What Westphall had actually said was, "Jack, all I want is for you to tell me the truth. And I know you've talked to officers here in Arizona and I know you've told them the truth about what you saw in Utah, and it's important that you keep telling us the truth, and if you do, everything will be OK."

Oh, man – so now I had a highly suspect "snitch" witness, an inadmissible (and unreliable) polygraph result, and a shaky eyewitness identification at best. And no physical evidence that pointed to Austin as the killer.

I decided I needed to pull the plug and dismiss the case. By this point, we had already arranged to extradite Jack so he could testify against Austin at the preliminary hearing.[9] As I tended to do when confronted with thorny issues, I ran the case by senior prosecutor Dick Shepherd. I told Shep I wasn't going to take the case to trial, since in my opinion neither polygraphs nor criminal "snitches" provided solid enough evidence of guilt. Shep said he understood, but suggested that I take the case through preliminary hearing, and then decide what to do if the judge bound the defendant over to stand trial. I think he suspected that the case wouldn't survive prelim, and probably thought it preferable to have a judge dismiss the case rather than for me go to war with the police over it. I agreed, but knew that one way or the other, the case would never go to trial, because either the judge would pull the plug, or I would.

The morning of the preliminary hearing, I was approached by Westphall, who informed me that Jack, who had been flown in from Arizona the night before, had just taken a polygraph test about his statements that Austin was involved in the murder, and his responses had appeared to be deceptive, indicating that he might be lying.

---

[9] A preliminary hearing is a hearing at which a judge decides whether there is sufficient evidence to require a defendant to stand trial for a felony offense. If so, the defendant is "bound over" to the district court, where felony cases are tried. If the judge finds there is not probable cause to believe that a crime has been committed and that the defendant committed it, the judge can dismiss the case. It's a safeguard – a mechanism for a judge to rein in prosecutors who bring charges on flimsy evidence.

While this appeared to take the officers by surprise, it seemed entirely predictable to me. People facing serious charges such as robbery are often desperate to get out from under them by cooperating with the police, and in this case, Austin's juvenile companion had told the cops what he thought they wanted to hear, after they had informed him that Austin had been arrested for murder in Salt Lake. And again, it wasn't lost on me that, based on the physical description given by the witness who had been driving by Pioneer Park, the assailant might just as well have been any of the three young blond men who were at the park that day, including Jack.

In court, the case was called and I put on the evidence, such as it was, after notifying Austin's attorney that Jack had flunked the polygraph test. After hearing the evidence, Judge William Rawson, who presided over the preliminary hearing, was about to issue his ruling. While I had hoped the judge was paying close attention to the evidence during the hearing, my impression was that he was just going through the motions. Since the standard for binding a defendant over for trial was relatively low, only requiring probable cause to believe a person may have committed a crime, judges rarely failed to bind cases over, especially murder cases. So I was quite sure it would fall to me to give the bad news to the police that the case wouldn't fly – which would be all the more difficult once Judge Rawson bound the defendant over for trial.

To my surprise (and with apologies to Judge Rawson for assuming he wasn't carefully performing his judicial function), he dismissed the case for insufficient evidence, and released the defendant. By doing so, he diverted my collision course with the police. Because the judge threw out the case, I didn't have to bring a motion to dismiss it – and since Ted Cannon was still the elected county attorney, who knows how it would have played out if the brass at the police department had objected to my decision to dismiss the case, and gone directly to Ted? This time, unlike in the *Gladstone* case, I would have insisted that the charges be dismissed, because I didn't think the evidence was anywhere near sufficient to prove that Austin had committed the murder. In my judgment, continuing to prosecute him would have been a travesty of justice.

But it didn't come to that. The case *was* dismissed, the police went back to the drawing board in their investigation, and I was not the focus of their wrath.

The case reinforced my skepticism about polygraph tests. I don't know what insights, if any, the police polygrapher gleaned from the *Austin* case. But less than a year later, serial killer Arthur Gary Bishop confessed to kidnapping, sexually abusing, and murdering five young boys between 1979 and 1983, and led the police to the victims' bodies. In three of the five cases, the police had concluded prior to Bishop's confession that the victims' parents were somehow responsible for the disappearance of their own children, based on the fact that they had failed polygraph tests administered by the police polygrapher.

Two years later, master forger and murderer Mark Hofmann passed a polygraph test after delivering bombs that killed two people, Steven Christensen and Kathleen Sheets. Hofmann later described the techniques he used to fool the polygraph machine, admitted his crimes, and pled guilty.

After that, no police officers came to my office advocating that a polygraph test could reliably identify either the innocent or the guilty. By then, the evidence suggesting otherwise had become too strong to ignore.

CHAPTER 5

Was Mont Rawley Framed?

IN 1983, WHEN I WAS A YOUNG PROSECUTOR in the D.A.'s Office, I was handed a stack of files and sent over to court to handle a number of "routine matters," or so I was told – including one involving a man who had spent decades in the state mental hospital after allegedly killing a woman.

I looked down at the name on the file. It said "Mont Rawley." I glanced through the file and saw that the crimes he committed dated back to the mid-1950s, and that he had been found "not guilty by reason of insanity" and committed to the state mental hospital. As I walked over to the court-house, I wondered what this hearing was going to be about, having never handled a mental review hearing before.

In court, Judge Lester Lee called the case and said that he needed to schedule a hearing to take testimony on the issue of Rawley's current mental condition. Was he still mentally ill and dangerous, requiring continued confinement in the Utah State Hospital? Or was he no longer mentally ill, or no longer a danger to himself or others, and therefore eligible for release? The judge set a hearing date and told me to bring in the mental health experts from the hospital to testify about Rawley's current mental condition, and his potential dangerousness.

Back in my office, I contacted Dr. Van Gellar, the psychiatrist most directly involved in Rawley's care at the hospital. Van Gellar was known among lawyers at the D.A.'s Office for his tendency to slip away from the hospital and go up to the ski slopes when you needed him as a witness in a hearing. When I explained the circumstances of Rawley's case, he wasn't too eager to show up for this one either.

And so he told me he was very busy (he didn't say doing what), which didn't surprise me, but then he told me something that did. He said he doubted that Mont Rawley had ever killed anyone – that the chief of police at the time, Edgar Carlisle, had needed a scapegoat to pin the crime on, and that Mont was probably innocent. He also said that he doubted that Mont had ever been mentally ill – only mentally retarded – even though he had been at the Utah State Hospital for more than 20 years on a commitment of "not guilty by reason of insanity."

When I pressed Van Gellar for information supporting the theory that Rawley might be innocent, he couldn't provide specifics, but he did say he wondered if Mont had even been in the area when the murder occurred. He said he'd heard Mont had been confined in some secure facility at the time, so how could he have committed the murder?

When I hung up the phone, I started going through all the documents in the file. I found an old press clipping from the 1950s, showing a then-19-year-old Mont Rawley being led into court in handcuffs. In the article, he was described as a "hulking, illiterate teenager." I noticed that in the photograph above the article he looked huge, literally towering head and shoulders above the officer standing beside him.

As I dug deeper into the file, I learned that the saga dated back to 1955, when a man who was hiking with his son made a grisly discovery in a ravine at the base of Parley's Canyon, on the east side of the Salt Lake Valley. He noticed something unusual protruding from the ground, and when he moved closer to see what it was, he was shocked to see a decomposing human arm. He ran and called the police, who came to the scene. From a shallow grave, they recovered the decomposed body of 23-year-old Rosaline Ledbetter, a mentally retarded woman who had been reported missing nineteen days earlier.

As I read through the file, it became clear that the Ledbetter murder had profoundly unsettled the Salt Lake community, and jolted its sense of security. Parents were afraid to let their children go outside to play, particularly anywhere near the scene of the murder, a ravine that was otherwise a natural playground for children. Adding to the horror, an autopsy had shown that not only had Ledbetter been strangled, bludgeoned over the head, and raped – she had also been buried alive.

Months passed, and the police had no clues and no suspects. Even a year after the grisly discovery, and on into the following year, the perpetrator of this notorious crime was still at large.

The crime went unsolved for two years. Then, in 1957, the police finally got a break. Mont Rawley, a mentally retarded 19-year-old, was picked up on a charge of raping a 4-year-old girl named Anna Carter. While being questioned, he confessed to the police that he had also killed Ledbetter, whom he had known two years before, when they were both in an institution for the mentally retarded.

It was, of course, front-page news when the police apprehended Rawley, and in the photograph that accompanied the newspaper article, he looked big and frightening – the sort of person one might think capable of committing such a grisly crime. And with his arrest, Chief Carlisle (who did in fact later rise to greater prominence in the community) could assure the public that the streets of Salt Lake were once again safe.

I finished reading through the file, closed it, and placed it on the credenza behind my desk. There was enough about the circumstances of the case to catch my attention, and to make me wonder. Could Van Gellar be right? Could Mont Rawley be an innocent man, at least as far as the murder of Rosaline Ledbetter was concerned?

A number of aspects of the case troubled me: that there would have been tremendous pressure to solve such a grisly and notorious crime; that the case seemed to be based largely on Rawley's confession – the confession of a mentally retarded man who could have been susceptible to suggestion during police questioning; and that even Rawley's appearance may have worked against him. He was hulking, looked dim-witted and, well, kind of like a monster – the perfect bogeyman. But was he really a "monster" who bludgeoned a young woman and buried her alive, or could he have been Boo Radley?[10] Under the circumstances, could the officers involved with the case have rushed to judgment?

And then there was one more red flag – Rawley had never been tried for the murder of Rosaline Ledbetter. The case had been dismissed in 1957, the same year it was filed, and as a result, no evidence of Rawley's involvement in the murder had ever been presented to a judge or jury. Yet somehow he had ended up at the state mental hospital for almost three decades, and his potential release was being impacted by the fact that "everybody knew" he had killed Rosaline.

I decided I needed to find out the truth by investigating the case anew, almost thirty years after the fact. I would take a fresh look at whatever evidence I could find – not with the goal of proving that Mont Rawley had killed Rosaline Ledbetter, but to try to determine whether he really had.

This was before DNA testing and the advent of innocence advocates or programs, and I wasn't Mont Rawley's attorney. But I considered it as much my job to exonerate him as it was to prove his guilt, depending on what the evidence showed. I felt compelled to find out if a mistake had been made and a great injustice done to an innocent man – one who, by

---

[10] The benevolent bogeyman in "To Kill a Mockingbird"

virtue of his mental problems, was particularly powerless in the system that had institutionalized him for his entire adult life. As I think back on it, I believe I kind of wanted that to be true, because I was in a position to do something about it — to correct the injustice.

So I started my investigation by looking into why the murder charge would have been dismissed. Here's what I was able to piece together:

In 1957, Mont Rawley was charged with both the murder of Rosaline Ledbetter and the rape of Anna Carter. The District Attorney decided to try the child rape case first, since he had a surviving victim and an open-and-shut case. But the case stalled when a judge found that Rawley was incompetent to stand trial, meaning that because of mental disease or defect, he did not have "sufficient present ability to consult with his lawyer with a reasonable degree of rational understanding," nor did he have "a rational as well as factual understanding of the proceedings against him."[11]

In short, Rawley couldn't be tried unless he could be restored to competency, and given his mental retardation, it was unlikely that he would ever recover from the combination of mental problems that prevented him from being competent. The prosecution had hit a brick wall.

The District Attorney was now faced with a huge problem. He had brought charges against one of the most notorious criminal defendants in Utah history, and he couldn't move forward on either of the cases against that defendant. The cases were effectively stalled in their tracks.

So Rawley was committed to the Utah State Hospital for "treatment," and I believe the D.A., after consulting with the doctors at the state hospital, made the assumption that, given his mental retardation, Rawley would never be competent to stand trial for either the rape of Anna Carter or the murder of Rosaline Ledbetter. The only consolation was that Rawley would likely remain at the state mental hospital indefinitely, which would

---

[11] This was the legal standard for competency, established in by the U.S. Supreme Court in *United States v. Dusky*, 362 US 402 (1960).

keep him off the streets and at least go some distance in allaying public fears. And so, after Rawley was committed to the Utah State Hospital based on his incompetency to stand trial on the child rape charge, the D.A. dismissed the murder charge against him.

Then, in 1972, the legal landscape changed abruptly. The United States Supreme Court, in *Jackson v. Indiana*,[12] ruled that it violates due process to indefinitely commit a criminal defendant to a mental facility on the basis of his permanent incompetency to stand trial. The upshot? Mont Rawley had to either be civilly committed (and there was no secure facility in Utah for the mentally retarded), or he had to be released outright into the community.

I'm sure the specter of Rawley's release would have literally terrified the community, as well as the authorities. How could they release a man who had committed two heinous crimes, and then so publicly confessed? After all, this was the man who, according to news reports at the time, had taken police to the crime scene, and, in front of reporters and photographers, reenacted the killing of Rosaline Ledbetter while standing in her grave.

Perhaps, then, it was not surprising that shortly after the Supreme Court decision in 1972, the Superintendent of the Utah State Hospital wrote a letter to the court in Salt Lake, stating that in his opinion, Rawley was now competent to stand trial. It was, after all, either that or releasing him back into the community.[13]

So in December of 1972, Rawley went to trial on the charge of raping Anna Carter. A judge found him "not guilty by reason of insanity," finding that Rawley had committed the rape but had done so while he was insane. As a result, Rawley was once again committed to the Utah State Hospital.

The judge's findings did not specify the nature of Rawley's insanity, and I noticed from reading through the file that during review hearings throughout the years, the psychiatrist and psychologists who testified

---

[12] 406 US 715 (1972)

[13] At the time, Rawley had been at the hospital for nearly 15 years.

couldn't seem to agree on what type of mental disorder Rawley suffered from, other than mental retardation.

Given the circumstances, I was not surprised that the D.A. had not tried to reinstate the Ledbetter murder charge following the insanity verdict in the case involving Anna Carter. There are a couple of reasons why this decision might have seemed to make sense at the time.

First, and perhaps foremost, the finding of "not guilty by reason of insanity" meant that Rawley *could* spend the rest of his life at the mental hospital. He had been tried in court – at least allegedly while competent – and found to have committed the rape while he was insane. This finding gave the authorities jurisdiction to hold him indefinitely at the State Hospital, if necessary. My best guess is that the authorities believed he would never be released, due to his documented history of violence.

Second, the case was by this time more than 17 years old, and even though Rawley had been found "competent enough" in the Carter case, it would be a real issue if the District Attorney re-filed the Ledbetter murder case. So I think the D.A. probably thought it best to let that sleeping dog lie, and, with Rawley's open-ended commitment to the mental hospital, declare victory and go home. Case solved. Case closed. Streets safe.

Still, the takeaway for me was that no court or jury had ever assessed the evidence against Rawley in the murder case, and I wondered how strong a case the prosecution really had against him.

So I decided to try to find out. Over the next few weeks, I reviewed the evidence and interviewed all the witnesses I could locate. One was Jack Peterson, the crime scene technician who had processed the scene. He was now retired, but he walked me through the evidence and the crime scene. I learned that Rawley and Rosaline had known each other, and that Rawley had led police to the burial site and then described how he had killed her. Peterson said that Rawley told the police in his confession that Rosaline had made him angry by rebuffing his advances. Peterson also told me that when Rawley first led police to the area of the crime, he initially had some difficulty pinpointing the gravesite, because Rawley remembered that there were railroad tracks in the ravine, and he couldn't find them. Peterson said that in the two years since the murder had occurred, the tracks had in fact been removed from the ravine.

I also spoke to Captain Charles Blevins, who, as a rookie officer, had apprehended Rawley on the charge of raping Anna Carter. Blevins explained the circumstance of the rape case and said that while confessing to the Carter case, Rawley kept saying that he had tried to bury Anna Carter "just like with Rosaline," but the ground was too hard, so he had to use bushes and branches instead of dirt to cover her up.

As a newly-hired officer not familiar with the Ledbetter case, Blevins didn't attach any significance to the name "Rosaline," but after Rawley mentioned the name several times, Blevins called the station to ask if they had an unsolved case involving a victim named "Rosaline." Blevins' sergeant got on the line and told him in urgent tones to bring Rawley to the station right away.

As part of my investigation, I spoke with Anna Carter, now Anna Epperson, who relayed to me what had happened to her as a four-year-old, and how profoundly it had affected her life. She said that in 1955 she had encountered Rawley in Memory Grove, a park just north of downtown Salt Lake City. She said he had come up to her on a bicycle, grabbed ahold of her, and dragged her into the bushes alongside the creek. He sexually assaulted her, knocked her unconscious, and tried to bury her under a pile of foliage, leaving her for dead.

Finally, I investigated the claim that Rawley might not have had the opportunity to commit the murder, as Dr. Van Gellar had intimated. While it was true that Rawley was a resident at the American Fork Training School at the time – a facility that housed those with mental retardation – he was not continuously locked up, and had opportunities to leave.

In the end, after talking with the witnesses and reviewing the evidence, I came to the conclusion that there was ample evidence that Mont Rawley had killed Rosaline Ledbetter. But I didn't start out with that presumption. Based on the teaser that had been given to me by Dr. Van Gellar, my instincts had gone the other way – to give every consideration to evidence that might point to Rawley's innocence.

Back in court for the review hearing, I was prepared to put on evidence to establish that Rawley had in fact killed Ledbetter, which was relevant to the issue of his future dangerousness, especially since the doctors were of the opinion that his mental condition had remained essentially unchanged over the years.[14]

Rawley's attorney objected to any evidence coming in relating to the murder, since Rawley had never been tried for it. I asked the Court to allow it, stating:

"All the Court has is statements in various psychiatric reports indicating the defendant "confessed" to murdering Rosaline Ledbetter. We request the opportunity to put on evidence to show there is a substantial basis for crediting that confession. The State believes it would aid the Court to know the circumstances of the confession and to what degree it was corroborated by other evidence. The fact that the Defendant was adjudged "insane" in 1957 does not mean he confessed to a crime which he did not commit."

Despite my argument, Judge Lee refused to allow the evidence, and at the end of the hearing, he made statements from the bench lamenting Rawley's situation, characterizing his ongoing commitment to the State Hospital as a "tragedy." He went so far as to suggest that perhaps the only reason Rawley was being confined was that he was mentally retarded and that society didn't know what to do with him.[15] Nevertheless, at the end of the day, Judge Lee refused to release Rawley from the State Hospital,

---

[14] I did not need to put on any evidence of the rape of Anna Carter, because the court finding of "not guilty by reason of insanity" was sufficient to establish that he had committed the act, although he was insane at the time. So the judge could already consider the rape of Anna Carter in determining Rawley's dangerous propensities.

[15] Judge Lee's statements were reported in the press and were particularly galling to Anna Carter Epperson and to Rosaline Ledbetter's family, especially in light of the fact that the judge had refused to allow testimony or evidence relating to the murder.

based on the testimony of the doctors that Rawley, in addition to being mentally retarded, still suffered from some kind of mental illness.

POSTSCRIPT

The following year, in 1985, there was another annual hearing to determine whether Rawley's mental condition had improved. Doctors from the State Hospital suddenly did an about-face, changed their opinions, and certified that Rawley no longer suffered from a mental illness. One doctor even suggested that although Rawley was mentally retarded, perhaps he never really had been mentally ill, notwithstanding the fact that he had been found "not guilty by reason of insanity" of raping Anna Carter, in 1972.

Although the doctors certified that Rawley was no longer mentally ill, they didn't recommend his release into the community. They were concerned because of his 30-year institutionalization at the State Hospital and his inability to live without supervision. They were also concerned that Rawley had made "unprovoked violent threats" to another patient and to staff members at the hospital. So they weren't prepared to endorse the idea that he wasn't dangerous.

At the conclusion of the hearing, Judge Lee, who I believe was also concerned about how Rawley might act out if he were released into the community with no supervision or oversight, refused to order his release.

Rawley's attorney appealed the decision, and in 1988 the Utah Supreme Court ordered Rawley's release, with instructions to Judge Lee to develop a plan to help Rawley gradually transition back into a more normal life.[16]

As I think back on the Rawley case now, I realize that one of the reasons I was concerned he might be an innocent man was because he had never been tried in court for the murder of Rosaline Ledbetter. No

---

[16] Not long after Rawley's release from the State Hospital, Rosaline Ledbetter's sister committed suicide by jumping to her death from the third floor of the State Capitol to the rotunda floor below, near the steps leading to the courtroom of the Utah Supreme Court.

prosecutor had ever presented the evidence against him to a jury, and no jury had ever unanimously found beyond a reasonable doubt that he was the killer.

If Rawley had been convicted of murder, or had been found "not guilty by reason of insanity," I wouldn't have felt the need to dig so deep to try to determine, one way or the other, whether he was innocent or guilty. The jury's verdict would have given me confidence that Rawley was in fact the killer.

But my confidence in jury verdicts was to be shaken to its core in the 1990s when DNA testing started exonerating convicted felons around the country, including some convicted of capital murder. Years after reopening the Mont Rawley case, I came to the realization that a jury trial, with all its procedural safeguards and its high burden of proof on the prosecution to prove a defendant's guilt beyond a reasonable doubt, could still sometimes result in an innocent person being convicted. It was a sobering thought.

CHAPTER 6

Death at the Courthouse

WHEN I FIRST STARTED TRYING CASES in the early 80s, there was no courtroom security to speak of – no magnetometers, no officers screening people entering the courthouse – and most of the time, those of us who worked there didn't think too much about it. After all, there hadn't been any incidents of concern, so things were pretty loose.

The year was 1985, and I had just inherited cases from John Soltis, who was leaving the D.A.'s Office to join the Attorney General's Office. John was an experienced and effective prosecutor whose forte had been prosecuting difficult circumstantial murder cases. John was team leader of the Career Criminal Team, and I was a member of that team. When he left, I took over as team leader and inherited a couple of difficult cases John left behind.

One was a triple capital murder case. A man named Francis Vickers had shot and killed his own two young children and his father-in-law, in a murderous rage to punish his wife. When officers arrived at the house that day, they found Vickers' eight-year-old daughter with a bullet wound in her head, but still conscious. Just before she died, she told the officers, "My Daddy shot me."

Before he left the office, John briefed me on the case, and told me that Vickers was at the State Hospital awaiting trial, having suffered a mental breakdown after realizing what he had done. He told me the doctors said that Vickers was suicidal. How could he not be?

I never tried Francis Vickers. He committed suicide before the justice system could make him account for his crimes. But it was hard to get out of my mind the haunting image of an eight-year-old child with a bullet wound in her head saying, "My Daddy shot me." I can't even imagine what it did to the officers who found her that day.

Another of John's cases was *State v. Lane Heath & James Bynes*. In 1984, Lane Heath was on parole, having served time in prison for the crime of possession of stolen property – thousands of dollars worth of jewelry that had been stolen from the residence of Keith and Audry Wagner in 1981. Now, three years later, the Wagners had suffered an even worse crime.

On October 29, 1984, while Mrs. Wagner was home alone, two young men in their twenties entered her home, wearing ski masks and brandishing handguns. They stole more of her jewelry, and one of the burglars sexually assaulted her. Shortly afterwards, the police got a tip from an informant that Lane Heath was responsible. When officers pulled over a car Heath was driving, they saw Heath's passenger, James Bynes, stuffing something under the back seat of the car. It turned out to be some of the stolen jewelry from the Wagner burglary.

Lane Heath was charged with aggravated robbery, aggravated burglary and theft by receiving, for being in possession of the stolen property. James Bynes was charged with theft by receiving.

John told me it was a tough case because the victim was not able to positively identify Heath during a lineup, and the evidence of his involvement in the robbery and burglary was not as strong as John wished it were. He said Heath would likely claim he wasn't involved in the crime at the Wagners' house, and that he'd just received the jewelry from somebody afterwards. And since Bynes was the one seen stuffing the jewelry under

DEATH AT THE COURTHOUSE

the car seat, Heath might claim he hadn't known anything about it at all.

The judge had already ruled that the prosecution could not put in evidence that Heath was on parole for possessing jewelry stolen in the 1981 burglary of the Wagner residence, so it looked like an uphill battle at trial. The trauma suffered by the Wagners was intensified by realizing that the same person who had victimized them back in 1981 had done it again, only this time it was even worse than before. Finally, John told me that the defendants had moved for separate trials, and Third District Judge Charles Renato had granted the motion. This would make success at trial even more difficult.

Heath's trial went first. Since he had been on parole at the time he was charged with the new crimes, he had been returned to the Utah State Prison pending the outcome of the trial. As was standard procedure, prison transportation officers brought him to court every day, and took him back to the prison after court each afternoon. To avoid any prejudice against Heath that the jury might have if they knew he was in custody, Heath came to court each day dressed in a suit, and during all court proceedings, he was unshackled and uncuffed.

A number of times at recesses during the three-day trial, I noticed that Heath was allowed to have unsupervised contact with his girlfriend, who had come to watch the proceedings. At one point near the end of the trial, I became particularly alarmed, because the prison transportation officer, Arnold Rennie, was not watching the prisoner at all, but rather was chatting with the court clerk. In fact, Rennie's back was turned to Heath, who was talking freely with his girlfriend and his mother.

I approached Rennie and told him that I was concerned about the lack of security, and the ready accessibility Heath would have to a weapon if a bystander tried to slip him one. To my surprise, Rennie appeared quite unconcerned about it.

Feeling the situation was not being taken seriously or controlled in any way, I went to Judge Renato's bailiff, Ben Stiles, who was in the hallway near the judge's chambers, and told him my concerns. Shouldn't someone be watching the defendant more closely? Shouldn't any contact between Heath and trial spectators at least be supervised to prevent someone from slipping him a weapon? He was, after all, a parolee on trial for two first-degree felonies, and was facing the possibility of being sentenced to 5 years to life in prison on each count if convicted, on top of being returned to prison for violation of his parole.

After hearing my concerns, Ben shrugged and told me it was not his job to monitor the prisoner – it was the prison transportation officer's job. I told Ben it might not be his job, but since Rennie wasn't paying attention to security, it would be everyone's problem if Heath got ahold of a weapon.

As the trial progressed, I saw no evidence that either Ben Stiles or Arnold Rennie was taking any steps to tighten courtroom security. Heath's girlfriend continued to be allowed to approach him during recesses at will.

Fortunately, we got through the rest of the trial without any incident, but the lax security made me very uncomfortable. The jury convicted Heath only of the theft charge, which was galling to the Wagners. Still, Heath's parole was revoked and he was sent back to prison, so at least a measure of justice was done.

Now for the rest of the story: The *Heath* trial was far from my mind months later, on April 2, 1985, as I sat in my office interviewing a witness in a domestic violence kidnapping and attempted murder case. But for that interview, I would have been assigned a court calendar that morning. I was completing the interview when I heard a commotion outside the door. I went out into the hallway and saw one of my fellow prosecutors who had just returned from the courthouse, and he was flustered and agitated. He said that a defendant had just gone on a shooting spree at the courthouse, and people had been shot.

As the details trickled in during the next few hours, I learned that Ronnie Lee Gardner, a career criminal charged with the murder of a Salt

Lake bartender, had been transported from the prison for a court hearing that morning, and had gotten access to a gun. A female accomplice had taped the weapon under a drinking fountain in the basement of the Metropolitan Hall of Justice, just inside the doors from the parking lot where the prison van had been parked. Gardner had told the prison transportation officer that he wanted a drink of water.

Once he got access to the gun, Gardner went on a shooting spree for several minutes before himself being wounded by officers, stumbling outside, and sitting down on the courthouse lawn with a bullet wound to his shoulder, blood staining his white prison jump suit. Gardner surrendered and was taken into custody, but not before he had killed a bystander and shot and wounded a court bailiff on the stairway. The bailiff was trying to prevent Gardner from going upstairs to the courtroom of his judge, before whom Gardner's hearing was to be held that day.

I later learned that the bailiff was Ben Stiles, who was shot trying to protect his judge, Charles Renato. The prison transportation officer guarding Gardner that day? Arnold Rennie.

Gardner recovered from his wound and was later tried for capital murder, convicted, and sentenced to death. After decades of appeals and post-conviction proceedings, he was finally executed in 2010.

Not long after Gardner's courthouse shooting spree in Salt Lake, security became routine, with all persons entering the courthouse being subject to searches – complete with armed officers, magnetometers and X-ray machines. The courthouse was no longer seen as a safe place to conduct business, and nobody wanted another Ronnie Lee Gardner.

CHAPTER 7

The Playhouse Bar Murders:
State v. Douglas Kay & Norman Newsted –
Challenging a Judge

IN FEBRUARY OF 1984, two Las Vegas parolees named Douglas Edward Kay and Norman Lee Newsted jumped parole and headed toward Cedar City, a small Southern Utah community that was to be the scene of one of the most heinous murder sprees in Utah history. Kay and Newsted were accompanied by their girlfriends, Janice Fromeyer and Carita Stafford. Fromeyer had lived in Cedar City before, and the group planned to break into the house of her former roommate's family and rob them at gunpoint.

When they reached Cedar City, they checked into a motel and discussed their plan to rob the family. But when they pulled up to the house, they noticed several cars parked outside and lots of people inside, and decided it would be too risky to try to rob the house with so many people around.

They needed another target, and Fromeyer readily supplied it. She had worked as a barmaid at the Playhouse Bar on the north end of town, knew the layout of the place and where the money was kept, and suggested it would be an easy place to rob. They decided to go over and case the place at about 10:00 o'clock that evening. They drank beer, checked out the layout of the bar, and played pool with some of the locals. There were too many people in the bar, so they decided to go back to the motel and return around closing time to commit the armed robbery.

So late at night on February 14, 1984, just before the bar was to close, Kay, Newsted and Fromeyer drove back to the Playhouse. Stafford did not go with them, having had too much to drink and fallen asleep in the motel room. As the trio entered the bar, they saw customers Gary Hall and Richard Black sitting on barstools, and a barmaid, Katherine Ryser, standing behind the bar. They went into the bar and sat at the first table. Newsted told Fromeyer to rack up a game of pool. A few minutes later, they decided the time was right. Fromeyer went to the door and locked it.

At the same time, Newsted and Kay got up and walked to the main section of the bar, pulled their guns, and said, "This is a holdup." Fromeyer turned to the barmaid and said, "Where's the money, bitch?" Ryser and Hall put their hands up, but Black, perhaps both lulled and emboldened by the amount he'd had to drink, threw his hands out to his sides and said, "Shoot me."

Angry at the man's bravado and apparent nonchalance, Newsted leveled his .25-caliber pistol and fired two rounds into Black's arm and shoulder, wounding him and starting the deadly chain of events that would leave all three victims dead. If there had been any doubt when they walked in, now it was clear – they weren't leaving any witnesses behind.

All three victims were ordered to lie face-down on the floor, and Fromeyer proceeded to clean out the register. Kay then took his .357-caliber handgun and went down the line, executing each victim by shooting them in the head. The barmaid was the last to die. She heard the blasts as Kay cold-bloodedly walked down the line executing the men, and must have lain in terror on the floor of the bar, waiting for her time to come, knowing the inevitability of her own death.

Someone else heard shots that night. There was an apartment above the bar, and the man who lived there was watching late-night reruns of

Hawaii Five-O on TV when he heard some unusual noises downstairs. He couldn't be sure what they were, but a few minutes after everything went quiet, he thought it was peculiar enough that he should go down and check. With some apprehension, he opened the door to the bar, and could see bodies on the floor. He ran upstairs and immediately called the police.

Brent Creswell was a young prosecutor and a native of Cedar City. Although he had not had a lot of experience in criminal law, he had been elected Iron County Attorney shortly before. He got a call late that night from the police – three people had been shot dead at the Playhouse Bar, and they needed him to come down to the scene of the crime right away. Creswell quickly got dressed, jumped into his car and drove to the Playhouse. Police officers met him outside and escorted him into the bar.

There he saw the bodies of the three victims lying on the floor, each having been shot execution-style in the head. It was horrific. He vowed that if the murderers were ever found, he would settle for nothing less than the death penalty. At the same time, he felt overwhelmed at the prospect of trying a capital case, never having prosecuted one in the past.

In 1984 I was a prosecutor in the Salt Lake D.A.'s Office, so I generally would have had nothing to do with a Cedar City murder case, nor would I have had authority to prosecute cases outside of Salt Lake County. But some months after the killings, I was called in by Chief Deputy John T. Nielsen of the D.A.'s Office, who asked if I'd be willing to help the Iron County Attorney prosecute a triple murder case.

By then I had participated in prosecuting three capital murder cases in Salt Lake, and since capital cases have a number of unique aspects and issues, Brent had requested help from someone who had actually handled one. I agreed to help, and was appointed as a Special Assistant Attorney General for the purpose of assisting Brent in prosecuting the case.[17]

Soon afterwards, I met with Brent, who briefed me on the case. After the murders, police officers had talked to witnesses who had played pool

---

[17] Unlike local prosecutors, the Attorney General had authority to prosecute cases anywhere in the state.

with some strangers from out of town, and one of the out-of-towners had mentioned that they were staying at a local motel. Officers had checked motels and found that a room had been rented that night in the name of Janice Fromeyer, whom they traced back to Las Vegas.

When the police went to Vegas to interview Fromeyer, she put them off. A short time later, a lawyer contacted the police, and said he had been retained by Fromeyer. He told the officers that Fromeyer was an eyewitness to the Playhouse murders, but that she did not herself shoot any of the victims, and that she could give information about the killers and their whereabouts. The price tag for her cooperation? Complete immunity.

By that time, it was three days after the killings, and two cold-blooded murderers were still at large. Utah law provided no mechanism to get Fromeyer's cooperation without affording her "transactional immunity," meaning that she could never be prosecuted for her participation in any of the crimes that night. Uncomfortable with the choice, but with his hands tied by Utah law, Creswell had authorized immunity for Fromeyer.

After receiving the "immunity bath," Fromeyer provided a detailed description of the crimes she both witnessed and participated in, as well as what she knew of the whereabouts of Kay and Newsted. But the information did not come in time to save a fourth victim, Tommy Logan, a cab driver in Oklahoma, who was shot and killed by Newsted on February 20 with the same gun he had used in Cedar City.

Newsted had hopped a plane back to Oklahoma, where his sister lived. He had hailed a cab at the Tulsa International Airport and asked Logan to take him to his sister's house. After having difficulty finding the address, they stopped for directions. Newsted got out of the cab, and when he returned to the taxi, he shot Logan twice in the back of the head.

In Fromeyer's statement, she didn't sugarcoat her own involvement. She admitted that she was the one who had suggested robbing her old roommate's family, then the Playhouse Bar where she had worked a few years before. She had gone to the bar late that night with Kay and Newsted, knowing that they were going to rob the place, and she herself had barked some of the orders at the victims before they were killed.

Part of Fromeyer's immunity agreement required her to testify against Kay and Newsted, and she had already done so at a preliminary hearing, before I became involved in the case. Brent said the circuit court judge who presided over the preliminary hearing had told him afterwards that Fromeyer was a very credible witness who appeared to be telling the truth, including giving details that showed her own deep complicity in the crimes. The judge also told Brent that, at the same time, she came across as a "black-hearted bitch." Both observations sounded accurate, and Brent and I both wondered how a jury would react, especially since they would be told that Fromeyer had received absolute immunity for her cooperation and testimony.

Fromeyer had relayed other details: After the murders, the trio returned to their motel room, "laughing like it was some big joke." They woke up Stafford and the group went out to get something to eat. They drove down Main Street past the bar, and saw police cars everywhere. As they drove out of town, they ran into a police roadblock. Kay threw his .357 magnum out the car window before they hit the roadblock. The police questioned them at the roadblock, but allowed them through. At the time, they had the victims' belongings in a paper bag in the backseat of the car. The officers asked them about the bag, but never examined it after the group told them it was just trash. Fromeyer said they were surprised they made it through. She also said that Kay made a statement right after the killings that he was sorry he didn't have enough time to "jack off on the bitch," referring to the barmaid.

After getting through the roadblock, the group went to a restaurant and had a big meal. On the way back to the motel, they ran into another roadblock, which they also cleared. Next morning, the police arrived at their motel, and they all went downtown to give statements. They admitted to being at the bar the night before, but said they had left early and knew nothing about the killings.

Later, when they returned to Las Vegas, the group holed up at the Westward Ho Motel, where they took pictures of themselves holding guns and money from the robbery. Police found out that they had stayed there after Kay's girlfriend threw a table through a window, and a security guard was called to the room. From that room, police recovered an undeveloped canister of film. When they developed it, there was a picture of Kay proudly holding a gun and a wad of bills. There were also photos of the women, scantily clad, with guns and cash, striking poses and playing to the camera.

The commotion at the Westward Ho had led to the apprehension of Douglas Kay, and his eventual extradition to Utah. Meanwhile, Newsted was in custody in Oklahoma, where he was facing capital murder charges for the murder of Tommy Logan.

In Utah, the trial judge had already ruled that there would be separate trials for the defendants, to guard against any legal prejudice that might result from trying them jointly. Kay's case was to go first. Brent reiterated his view that the case should go to trial rather than be plea-bargained, and that he should ask for the death penalty. I told him the circumstances of the case certainly justified that, as it involved cold-blooded executions by parolees who had a long history of violence. I told him that some murder cases technically qualify under the statute for capital consideration, but are unlikely to result in the jury returning a verdict of death, because of mitigating circumstances. Others not only qualify, they're compelling – and this was such a case.

Over the next few months, Brent told me he was receiving pressure to resolve the case through a plea bargain that would spare Kay the death penalty. This I took initially as nothing unusual – just defense attorneys trying to get the best deal for their client, who otherwise stood a good chance of getting the death penalty. But Brent went on to explain that the pressure was coming not just from Kay's attorneys, but also from the judge assigned to try the case, Judge Callister Vaughn. He said that for some time, Judge Vaughn had been making statements to the effect that the finality of a conviction could only be assured through a plea, because death penalty cases are scrutinized forever on appeal. Vaughn had even told Brent in passing that "Neither one of us is good enough to try this case."

Because of the judge's insistence that the case should be negotiated, Brent asked me on several occasions whether I thought it should be tried or plea-bargained. I told him that as much as any case I had ever seen, this was one where the death penalty should be considered by a jury.

And so it would have gone, but for a most unusual series of events.

On August 22, 1984, I had just returned to my office in Salt Lake from a court appearance when my secretary told me I had an urgent call coming in from Brent Creswell. I picked up the line and Brent told me that a court hearing had been scheduled that morning by the defense, who had given him no idea what it was about. When he had gotten there, Kay's attorneys had said they all needed to convene in the judge's chambers to discuss an issue. Brent had then learned that the hearing was to solidify a "deal" in which Kay would plead guilty as charged in exchange for taking the death penalty off the table. This option had been discussed before with the defense attorneys, and Brent had said no – but now it was also the judge who was pushing the deal.

In chambers with the defense attorneys, Judge Vaughn told Brent he could either agree to the deal, stand mute and say nothing, or oppose the deal. Vaughn went on to say that if Brent opposed the deal, he, the judge, had ways of protecting his own position. Brent said the judge had sent him an unmistakable message that, at most, he should stand mute and not oppose the plea deal – in essence, get out of the way and let it happen.

Brent also told me that Judge Vaughn had then given him 15 minutes to "go call your Salt Lake advisors" and come back with an answer. That was why he was calling me. Brent reiterated once again how he had felt that terrible night in February when he saw the victims' bloody bodies lying on the barroom floor – how he had resolved not to plea bargain with the killers. But he said he was now feeling tremendous pressure to go along with what the judge wanted. I told him that standing mute during the proceedings would be the same as agreeing to the plea bargain, and that as difficult as it was, he had to oppose it, even if it meant angering the judge. He agreed, but was afraid of what price Judge Vaughn might exact for his refusal to go along with the plea deal.

And Judge Vaughn was not just any judge. He was the main felony judge in the Fifth Judicial District at the time, which encompassed Cedar City and St. George. He was known as a tough and crusty old judge who always had complete control of his courtroom, and everybody knew it and respected his authority. To go against Judge Vaughn's express wishes in a case of this magnitude was going to take a lot of courage, and would probably come at a great price for a lawyer who wanted to keep practicing in Cedar City. As I hung up the phone with Brent, I felt for him.

Within the hour, I got another call from Brent, who said, "I feel like I've just been run over by a train." He said that when they went back into the judge's chambers after our phone call, Vaughn asked him what he had decided, and Brent told him that he had to oppose the deal. Brent said that Judge Vaughn was visibly annoyed at his intransigence, and announced that he was going to go out in open court and take Kay's plea, once again stating that he was going to do what he needed to do to "protect his position."

What happened next took Brent by surprise. He said that in every plea he'd ever been involved with, Judge Vaughn had always turned to the prosecutor at some point during the hearing and asked for the prosecutor's position as to the plea. He said he waited in dread for the moment he'd have to stand up and openly oppose Vaughn, but instead, Vaughn never asked him whether the prosecution agreed to the deal. Instead, Vaughn repeatedly asked Brent to ratify routine things such as, "First degree murder is punishable by life imprisonment or death, isn't that right, Mr. Creswell?" In the 63 pages of the plea transcript, Judge Vaughn asked Brent those types of leading questions – "Isn't that right, Mr. Creswell?" "Isn't that so,

Mr. Creswell?" – but never asked for the prosecutor's position as to the plea, because he knew what it would be.

So now we had a silent record, as Brent had not voiced his objection to the deal. In retrospect, he said he wished he had stood up at some point and interrupted Judge Vaughn, but he thought he would surely get the chance to give the State's position. Judge Vaughn, as always, had tightly controlled the proceedings and had done "what he needed to do" to get the desired result – a conviction on three counts of first degree murder and three counts of aggravated robbery, in exchange for a guarantee that Kay would not face the death penalty.

Brent was demoralized and drained by the events, and wondered if anything could even be done at this point to unravel the unilateral plea bargain between the judge and the defendant. I didn't know either, but I knew who would – Earl Dorius, the Assistant Attorney General who handled the appeals on all capital cases in Utah. We needed a quick consult with Earl, for if we were to do anything to challenge the plea, we had to act quickly.

When we reached Earl, his reaction was immediate – we couldn't let Kay's pleas stand, and the judge had no authority to take the pleas without the prosecutor's agreement. If left standing, this anomalous plea bargain could convolute the landscape of capital case law in Utah. To bargain away the death penalty in a case this egregious, one involving the cold-blooded execution of three people, could result in defense attorneys in other capital cases arguing that the death penalty was inconsistently sought by Utah prosecutors.

We knew time was critical, so we called and arranged to have a state plane fly us down to Southern Utah that night for an emergency hearing the next morning. I hurried home and grabbed a few things for an overnight stay. Just before I was about to leave for the airfield, Earl called and said the pilot had decided it would be too risky to fly, because a major storm was closing in. So we decided to take the 5-hour trip in Earl's large family van, and an hour into it we hit terrible weather, with torrential rains and thunder and lightning. I was happy to be on the ground at the time, rather than "up there" bouncing around in some small plane. We arrived late at a condominium Earl had access to in St. George, where the hearing was to be held before Judge Vaughn the following day.

When we arrived in court the next morning, the courthouse was abuzz. Lawyers from the Attorney General's Office were in town to challenge Judge Vaughn, who was by now getting heat from Cedar City residents who were outraged at the plea bargain. A local reporter, Cliff Binkerd of the St. George newspaper, the *Daily Spectrum*, was there for the story. We learned that some people in Cedar City had driven a pickup truck around town, carrying an effigy of Douglas Kay crowned with the head of a dead pig and a sign that read, "Fry Kay! Impeach Vaughn!"

Judge Vaughn's bailiff came out and said the judge wanted to see counsel in chambers before the hearing started. As I was to be trial counsel and Earl was the capital appeals ace, Earl was to make the arguments in open court challenging the judge's actions. I was to call witnesses if we needed to have an evidentiary hearing on the facts of the plea bargain.

Earl was aware of Vaughn's reputation, and wary of doing anything off the record. Judge Vaughn was all smiles as he welcomed us in chambers. He was particularly solicitous of Earl, almost obsequious, saying how much he appreciated having the Attorney General's Office come down to appear on the case. He tried to get Earl to give a preview of his legal argument, but Earl deftly and politely insisted that he would make his arguments on the record, in open court.

As we started to leave his chambers, Judge Vaughn asked Brent Creswell to stay behind a moment, and after we left, asked him to close the door. A few minutes later, a shaken Brent emerged from the judge's chambers with tears in his eyes. He told us the judge had said to him, "What are you trying to do, crucify me?" and had told him that he would never rule in Brent's favor again. Brent felt that his career was ending, and it wasn't lost on me how easy it was for Earl and me to come down from Salt Lake and stand up to the judge, knowing he'd probably rule against us and we'd appeal his ruling to the Utah Supreme Court. We didn't have to practice before Judge Vaughn in the future, so it was easy for us to challenge him and then go on home. The stakes were much higher for Brent.

What happened next astonished me. After Earl made a strong argument in open court that the unilateral plea bargain with Kay was illegal and must be set aside, the judge started to engage in re-writing history about whether Brent had ever communicated his opposition to the deal. When Earl said that Brent had done so in the second meeting in chambers, after calling me in Salt Lake, the judge said, "Second meeting? What second meeting? I don't remember any second meeting in chambers."

Turning to lead defense counsel, Samuel Becker, Vaughn asked, "Do you remember any second meeting in chambers, Mr. Becker?" Becker allowed as how he didn't recall any such meeting either, although I was aware that immediately after Kay entered his guilty pleas, Becker had walked out of the courtroom and told the press that Brent was opposed to the plea bargain. Since there was nothing on the record during the plea hearing, Becker could only have known that Brent was against it because Brent objected to the deal during that second meeting in chambers.

Vaughn then asked the same question to Kay's other lawyer, Clifton Carstairs. "Do you remember any second meeting in chambers?" Carstairs just made a vague gesture, mumbled something and didn't really respond to the question.

By now I was livid. It was one thing to strong-arm Brent into remaining silent during the plea hearing, but quite another to claim Brent had never communicated his opposition to the deal. I turned to Brent as we sat at counsel table and quietly asked him if there were any witnesses to the second meeting other than the judge and defense counsel. He said that Cliff Binkerd had been there. I couldn't believe the judge had allowed a newspaper reporter to sit in on crucial pre-plea discussions in chambers, particularly in a capital case that involved the possibility of the death penalty.

As soon as the judge took a recess, I bolted for the door, and found Binkerd standing in the hallway. I tried to affect an air of nonchalance and a conversational tone, although I was seething at the time. Had he been present in chambers during the meeting when Brent was told he could take a few minutes and consult his Salt Lake advisors? "Yes." Did he recall a second meeting in chambers? "Yes." What had Brent said? "That he wouldn't agree to the deal." I told Binkerd I was calling him as a witness, and he immediately became very anxious, saying he had to consult with someone at the newspaper, and thought he had some kind of news reporter's privilege not to testify.

As Binkerd ran to make a phone call, I confronted Samuel Becker in the hallway and challenged his endorsement of Vaughn's version of events – that there had never been a second meeting in chambers in which Brent had announced his opposition to the plea bargain. Why then had Becker walked directly out of the courtroom after that hearing and told a reporter that Brent was against it? How would he have known? Without responding to my question, Becker turned and walked back into the courtroom.

By the time he took the bench again, Judge Vaughn, now confronted with the possibility of an evidentiary hearing, backed off and said that there "might have been" a second meeting in chambers after all – he wasn't sure. But in any event, Brent hadn't objected on the record, and all we had to do to verify that was consult the 63-page transcript of the plea hearing.

Earl, who was brilliant – a very polished advocate – made a strong argument that the plea bargain was illegal and could not stand. The defense attorneys, of course, argued that it was too late now, and that Vaughn had to honor the "no death penalty" provision of the plea bargain. The stakes were high and it was clear that either side would appeal an adverse ruling. A higher court would ultimately decide the legal issue presented by this bizarre plea bargain, and now it was up to the judge to decide which way to go.

At the end of the arguments, Judge Vaughn announced that he would give Kay the choice of: 1) letting his guilty pleas stand and proceeding to sentencing without a guarantee that he would not receive the death penalty, 2) withdrawing his pleas and proceeding to trial, or 3) appealing the court's decision. Earl and I were content to have the ruling, which we knew Kay's attorneys would appeal. We would get the issue before the Utah Supreme Court, which is where we wanted it to be.

So what might have motivated Judge Vaughn to take such an extreme and unusual action as to plea-bargain a case over the objection of the prosecutor? I don't know for sure, but I suspect he probably told it straight when he said to Brent that he was concerned that neither of them could try the case without error. This was the first triple murder in Southern Utah that anyone could recall, and I think Judge Vaughn was concerned that even if Kay were convicted of capital murder at trial, his case might be reversed on appeal, since every aspect of capital cases are scrutinized on appeal with a fine-toothed comb by the Utah Supreme Court. I think he felt the only way to guarantee a conviction that would stick was through a plea agreement – and given the terrible crimes Kay had committed, that was of paramount concern to the judge.

Whatever Judge Vaughn's motivation, now it would be up to the Utah Supreme Court to try to make sense out of this strange record, and we would have to wait months, maybe years, before learning what the effect of the legal maneuvering would be, and what it would mean for Douglas Kay. In the meantime, we would turn our attention to trying Kay's co-defendant, Norman Newsted, who had now been extradited from Oklahoma, and whose case would also take some strange turns.

CHAPTER 8

Trying the *Newsted* Case, Resolving the *Kay* Case

DURING THE NEXT SEVERAL MONTHS, while Earl Dorius was handling the *Kay* case on appeal before the Utah Supreme Court, Brent Creswell and I were gearing up to try Norman Newsted, who had been extradited from Oklahoma after being convicted of murdering the cab driver he'd hailed at the airport. Newsted was represented by MacArthur Wright and John Miles, two able attorneys from St. George. Because of what had happened in the *Kay* case, including the inflammatory pretrial publicity, the venue for Newsted's trial was changed to Salt Lake County, and we learned it would take place before Judge William Ballinger, who had recently been voted out of office as a judge, but had somehow managed to maintain his senior judge status.[18]

During the early days of the *Kay* case, before the unilateral pleas, when Brent used to tell me how tough it was to practice before Judge Vaughn, I would respond that Vaughn might be difficult, but was nothing compared to this judge we used to have to deal with in Salt Lake named Ballinger,

---

[18] Ballinger was likely voted out of office because his courtroom behavior had alienated so many of the lawyers and litigants who appeared before him.

who was prone to tantrums and outbursts in court. Ballinger had been merciless in his treatment of me when I was a young prosecutor, which was apparently typical of how he treated most attorneys, except for a handful of his designated "favorites." I had been dressed down often enough for no particular reason that I'd developed a fairly thick skin.

One recurrent point of outrage with Ballinger was that when "the goddamn County Attorney" moved out of the basement of the Metropolitan Hall of Justice, they closed the coffee shop. I could never quite see the connection between my courtroom role and his coffee shop blues, but, although I found it obnoxious at the time, Ballinger's tirades against me, often before juries, stood me in good stead when I had to appear later before other imperious judges. I got to the point where, during Ballinger's tongue-lashings, I would look down at my notes and just let the storm rage, and when it passed and the judge stopped talking, I would look up and then go on with my case as if nothing had happened.

Still, having Ballinger brought back out of his forced retirement and assigned to the *Newsted* case felt a bit like being stung by a dead bee, and I had to do damage control with Brent, saying that Ballinger wasn't really all that bad. Besides, once Ballinger had skewered me enough times, he had let up on me, even seemed to like me, as if I'd passed some kind of test. So we'd probably be OK. And maybe Ballinger would be different now that he'd been voted off the bench.

We tried Norman Newsted in the fall of 1985, and during jury selection, bombs started going off around Salt Lake City. Steven Christensen and Kathleen Sheets were killed in successive bombings, and the city was gripped with fear. Nothing like this had ever happened before in Utah.

About the third day of trial, we got the word that another bomb had gone off in a car downtown. The injured driver turned out to be Mark Hofmann, a dealer in antiquities who was later proven to be a master forger of historical Mormon documents, and who had murdered Christensen and Sheets in an effort to keep his fraud from being discovered.

It was a busy time for the courts, since at the same time we were trying Newsted, Bob Stott was also trying Ronnie Lee Gardner for capital murder for his shooting spree at the courthouse. The *Salt Lake Tribune* noted in its story of November 1, 1985, that the Newsted trial had "been over-shadowed by the Ronnie Lee Gardner murder trial and the Salt Lake City bombings, but involves a crime that left more people dead than either of those events."

At the beginning of the trial, another news article had mentioned that this was Brent Creswell's first capital homicide trial, and so he had sought help from "more experienced quarters." It went on to say, "He will be assisted at trial by Deputy [Salt Lake District] Attorney Creighton Horton II, an unimposing and meticulous prosecutor whose experience includes co-counsel in the trial of convicted serial killer Arthur Gary Bishop."[19]

"Unimposing and meticulous." I kind of liked the sound of it. After all, it beat "flashy and sloppy." The article went on to say that I had extensive experience in dealing with psychiatric testimony, and that Newsted's attorneys were going to be running a defense based on "drug-induced diminished mental capacity."

During the *Newsted* trial, we called Janice Fromeyer as our primary witness, and she testified about the events of February 14, 1984, including her involvement in the crimes. It came out, of course, that in exchange for her testimony she had been granted immunity and was walking away scot-free. Her immunity deal deeply offended the jury, as some members of the jury reported to us later.

I knew that Utah's immunity laws were not required under the U.S. Constitution, and that other states and the federal government had a more limited form of immunity. I also remembered that Judge Vaughan had publicly lamented the fact that both Janice Fromeyer and Carita Stafford were not going to be held accountable for their part in these crimes. At

---

[19] *Salt Lake Tribune,* October 15, 1985.

the time that Stafford could no longer be held as a material witness, Judge Vaughan had told her that it grieved him to release her with no culpability at all, and that he personally felt that both Stafford and Fromeyer should be prosecuted.

On that point, I agreed with Judge Vaughn, and vowed one day to take the issue to the Utah State Legislature. This was not the only case where I had witnessed people literally get away with murder because of Utah's antiquated immunity laws. It was to become the first bill I would work on when I joined the Attorney General's Office two years later.

For the most part, during Newsted's trial, Judge Ballinger treated us well, only becoming exasperated when we didn't object to some cross-examination questions from Newsted's attorneys – questions we thought were appropriate. We didn't want to cut off cross-examination by the defense, for fear of giving them an issue on appeal. Besides, the defense attorneys' questions seemed legitimate to us, and we felt that they conducted themselves ethically throughout the trial. They tried to run an intoxication defense, based on a combination of drugs and alcohol that Newsted had allegedly consumed before the murders, but the jury didn't buy it and convicted Newsted on all counts.

At the time, a convicted murderer had the right under Utah law to choose whether to be sentenced by the jury or judge. Newsted waived the jury and decided to go with Judge Ballinger.

During the penalty phase, we presented evidence of Newsted's long history of violent crime. The defense put on its case, and then it was time to argue whether Newsted should receive the death penalty. We were past the trickiest aspects of the trial, when a wrong word before a jury could result in reversible error,[20] and it seemed like we would have relatively smooth sailing from this point on. What we didn't count on was the "Ballinger Factor."

---

[20] Reversible errors refer to mistakes at trial that are serious enough to cause appellate courts to overturn a conviction.

When the time came, Brent stood up and started to make his penalty phase closing argument. For reasons we could not understand, Ballinger cut him off at almost every turn, refusing to let him make any of his arguments. Brent became flustered and sat down, at which time Ballinger ordered him to stand up and finish his argument. Brent just looked down and said, "No, sir. We'll try to do better on rebuttal." At this, Ballinger went into a rage, called a recess, and ordered us all into chambers.

When we walked into his chambers, Judge Ballinger was pacing up and down, gesturing and yelling at Brent, saying that the trial was all over, that Brent had messed up, that Brent's career was over, and that he was going to report Brent to the Bar. He asked the defense attorneys, who I think were as confused as we were at the judge's outburst, if they felt they needed to make any argument, and they took the judge's drift, saying they didn't think it would be necessary. Ballinger kept repeating, "It's all over. It's all over." He then told us all to come back at 9:00 the next morning to finish the case.

As we walked back to the office, Brent was devastated. Neither of us could understand why Ballinger had so vehemently cut him off from every argument, as if he had been about to commit reversible error before a jury. The points Brent was trying to make were valid – the circumstances of the crimes; Newsted's deep involvement, including firing the first shots and starting the chain of violence that resulted in three deaths; and his long record of violence. There was no understanding Ballinger's apparent belief that Brent had done something so bad as to automatically derail the case from death penalty consideration, or his repeated chanting of "It's all over!"

Before Brent left to go back to his hotel that afternoon, I tried to tell him that this was Ballinger's pattern – that he often exploded and then got over things just as quickly. I told him I wouldn't be surprised if everything blew over by the next morning. Brent just walked out, shaking his head. He seemed sure his career was over. First Vaughn, now Ballinger.

Next morning, I called Ballinger's clerk to find out what we should expect at the hearing – what did the judge want to do? She told me there was good news: Ballinger had spoken to another senior judge about the penalty phase argument Brent had tried to make, and had changed his mind. I was to relay to Brent that all was forgiven, that Ballinger was going to start the arguments over again, and that this time, Brent would be allowed to make the points he had tried to make the day before, when Ballinger had gone ballistic.

While I was pleased with this news, I had another concern: Where was Brent? It was past 8:00, then past 8:30. No Brent, no phone call. I wondered if he was going to make it to court. At the last minute he showed up at the office, saying he'd had some difficulty with transportation. I told him the good news about the judge's change of heart – no automatic "you lose," no reporting to the Bar, just a second chance to do what he had tried to do the day before.

When we got to the courtroom, the clerk told us the judge wanted to see us all in chambers. There we found a jolly Judge Ballinger, who appeared to be in a right good mood, and who told us all that he was going to start over and allow both sides to argue, and that this time, things would go smoothly. He didn't explain either his outburst of the day before or what had caused his change of heart. What had been a threatened Bar complaint the day before became a joke that Brent should be required to buy "these fellas" (defense counsel) milk shakes.

Ballinger did exactly as he promised. He heard Brent's arguments with no further outbursts, then heard the arguments from defense counsel. At the end of it all, he announced that he was imposing three life sentences on Newsted.

It was not an illogical decision. Newsted had already been convicted of the murder of Tommy Logan in Oklahoma, and the prosecution there had presented evidence at his penalty hearing of the Utah murders to show the probability that Newsted would commit acts of violence in the future, and that he would be a continuing threat to society. Newsted had been sentenced to death for his Oklahoma murder, and I think in the end, Judge Ballinger figured that Newsted was from Oklahoma, and Oklahoma could take care of him.[21]

RESOLVING THE KAY CASE

One of the reasons Brent and I had not been willing to plea bargain with Newsted was that Kay's case was still under appeal by the Utah Supreme Court, and, if the Court ruled our way, we planned to take Kay to trial and ask for the death penalty. We did not want to do anything that might jeopardize our case against Kay, and allowing a plea bargain for Newsted could have fed the defense argument that the prosecution was treating the two killers differently, one of the things Earl Dorius was concerned about.

In those days, it was fairly common in capital cases for defense attorneys, over the objection of the prosecution, to be allowed to introduce evidence of other Utah capital killers who had not been sentenced to the death penalty, in an attempt to bolster their arguments that their clients too should be spared. Since the Cedar City killings were so aggravated – multiple victims, execution-style killings, defendants with long violent criminal histories – we thought both cases should go to trial, rather than being bargained away.

But at the end of the day, Douglas Kay was never tried. After Newsted's conviction, the Utah Supreme Court ruled that Kay's plea could be characterized as a "misplea" – similar to a "mistrial," when an error occurs during trial that requires starting over.[22] The concept was novel in Utah law. While the Court did find that Judge Vaughn had acted improperly by becoming involved in the plea bargaining process and accepting Kay's unilateral pleas, it went on to reinforce the erroneous idea that Brent

---

[21] In that, the judge was right. Newsted was extradited back to Oklahoma, where, in 1999, after exhausting all his appeals, he was executed by lethal injection for murdering Tommy Logan.

[22] State v. Kay, 717 P.2d 1294 (Utah 1986)

Creswell had never made his objection known before the plea was taken, and had only done so two weeks afterwards.

The Court viewed all those questions Judge Vaughan had asked Brent during the plea hearing, most of which ended forcefully with, "Isn't that so, Mr. Creswell?" as opportunities to object. Of course, the Court had no way of knowing the dynamics of how Judge Vaughn ran his courtroom, so from the Court's perspective, why wouldn't a prosecutor jump up and object during a plea hearing?

Still, the bottom line for the Court was that the prosecutor had not in fact agreed to the plea bargain, so although it found fault in Brent's not speaking up at the hearing, it also found that there was no meeting of the minds between the real parties in interest – the State and the Defendant. Hence, the concept of a "misplea" was introduced into Utah law, which meant that Kay could either withdraw his guilty pleas or proceed to a penalty hearing without any guarantees.

Technically, the Court's decision did not prevent Kay from being tried. But after consulting with Earl Dorius, Brent and I felt that due to the legal problems presented through the unilateral plea bargain and the subsequent lengthy battle in the courts, we should settle the case. A rock-solid plea was preferable to the uncertainty of endless capital litigation, which is common even without such complications.

I say "rock-solid" because one of the reasons we felt we needed to challenge Judge Vaughn's unilateral plea bargain with Kay was that it could have been subject to challenge, as there was case law indicating that if a judge gets too involved in advocating for a plea bargain, the defendant's plea may later be withdrawn as involuntary. Here, Vaughn had not only advocated for the plea bargain – he had all but insisted on it, even over the objection of the prosecution.

Another factor in our decision to settle the case was the fact that it was getting near the end of Brent's term as Iron County Attorney, and he was not running for re-election. The case was not going to be tried until after he left office, and it was almost a certainty that his successor would be Judge Vaughn's son. It was an unusual situation, and Brent wanted to resolve the case before he left office.

So in August of 1986, Kay pled guilty to all charges, agreed to consecutive sentences, and was sentenced to the Utah State Prison for what in effect would likely be the rest of his natural life. In case the multiple life sentences themselves were not enough, Brent Creswell and I sent our strongest recommendation to the Board of Pardons that Kay spend the rest of his life in prison.

On August 2, 1986, the *Salt Lake Tribune* ran an article about the *Kay* case, which included the following paragraph:

> "*Kay initially had pled guilty to the charges in 1984 in exchange for an agreement from the Iron County Attorney's Office that prosecutors would not seek the death penalty. But {the judge} overturned the plea bargain, and the case was appealed to the Utah Supreme Court.*"

Huh? Not even close. It annoyed me to see the myth perpetuated that it was Brent Creswell rather than Judge Vaughn who had agreed to the defense's plea deal. I quickly penned a letter to the editor to try to set the record straight. It was published on August 23, 1986, under the title, "Didn't Plea Bargain."

My letter read, in part:

> " ... *In fact, there never was such a plea bargain entered into by Iron County Attorney [Brent Creswell]. Rather, Kay and his attorneys made the agreement directly with Judge [Vaughn]. . . During the past two years, the Southern Utah press has erroneously perpetuated the misconception that [Brent Creswell] agreed to the 1984 plea bargain and changed his position only after public pressure and the Attorney General's Office forced him to do so. That simply is not true.*"

While I believe that Kay would have been a worthy candidate for death row, I also believe that spending the rest of his life in prison, knowing he will never be released, provides a measure of justice. More importantly, it provides finality for the victims' families – finality that they probably still would not have achieved had Kay been sentenced to death. Several of the inmates currently on death row committed their crimes during the same time period as Kay, and still have not been executed.[23]

Once Kay's case ended, there were no appeals, no news stories about him, no upheaval for the victims' families or fear that his convictions might be further challenged or his case might need to be retried. There was also no ongoing notoriety that inmates often receive by being on death row – only an endless sentence and well-deserved anonymity.

The justice system often provides rough justice at best, but as the cases ended, it continued to gnaw at me that two of the players in this crime never had to face any consequences for what they did: Janice Fromeyer and Carita Stafford. Both had accompanied Kay and Newsted from Las Vegas to Cedar City with the express plan of committing armed robbery. Fromeyer had even provided the targets, having lived and worked there some years before. If it's true that Stafford didn't go back to the bar as Fromeyer claimed, it was only because she got too drunk and fell asleep in the motel. Her actions before and after the crimes, including posing with a gun and money shortly after the robbery, showed her deep involvement in the criminal episode.

But under Utah Law at the time, there was no way to get their information or testimony against Kay and Newsted without providing them with complete immunity for everything they did during the crime spree – the armed robbery as well as the murders. I resolved to someday go to the Utah State Legislature to try to change the law. While it was to take

---

[23] For a detailed discussion on the death penalty, see Chapter 22.

three attempts and ten years to get it through the Legislature, the bill finally passed and became law in 1997.[24]

The *Kay* and *Newsted* cases were over. Both had played out in bizarre ways, but Newsted was now on death row in Oklahoma and Kay was locked up at the Utah State Prison serving multiple life sentences, and likely to die in prison before ever being paroled. I was still working at the Salt Lake D.A.'s Office, but my experience in the *Kay* and *Newsted* cases foreshadowed what I would do many times in the years to come – assist prosecutors all over the state with murder cases.

Still, I had no clue what was just beyond the horizon when, in October of 1987, I packed up my desk at the D.A.'s Office, said goodbye to my friends there, and moved my stuff into my new office at the State Capitol, having been recruited and hired by the Utah Attorney General's Office. A few days before I left, the D.A. had called me into his office to try to talk me into staying. He told me that if I transferred to the Attorney General's Office, I would never work on another high-profile case, and my name would never be in the press again.

I told him that I didn't mind, and figured he was probably right. As things turned out, nothing could have been further from the truth. In fact, I was just getting started.

---

[24] The change in the immunity laws did come in time, fortunately, to assure the conviction of another notorious Utah killer, as well as his girlfriend, who was an accomplice and had obstructed justice. See Chapter 20.

CHAPTER 9

Unlikely Prosecutor

I GREW UP FEELING NEITHER INCLINED nor qualified to judge other people. My grandfather, Mead Horton, a self-made man who rose from a tiny rural town in Utah to the top ranks of the New York Life Insurance Company in Los Angeles, used to put it this way, quoting an unnamed oracle:[25]

"There is more good in the worst of us, and bad in the best of us, so let's not talk about the rest of us."

Yet I stood in courtrooms and pointed fingers at murderers, robbers, and rapists, and asked juries to find them guilty and judges to send them to prison. And in cases of capital murder, I even asked jurors to vote for the death penalty.

By nature, I was better suited to the helping professions – jobs where I could be a peacemaker and consensus-builder. Yet I went into a profession where contention was the order of the day, where battle lines were drawn, where the public spectacle of a high-profile trial, whipped up by

---

[25] It appears the oracle may have been French author Alain-Fournier (1881-1914), and my grandfather may have recited a modified version of the original quote: *"There is so much good in the worst of us and so much bad in the best of us, that it's rather hard to tell which of us ought to reform the rest of us."*

intense press reporting, had almost a circus combat flavor at times. Who was winning? Who was losing? Who got hurt in court today? Who would be the victor at the end of the day?

So how did I become a prosecutor who was passionate about my job?

I think to a large extent, it was personal identification with victims, or, in homicide cases, victims' families. This was before the advent of victims' rights legislation, so victims had very little say in the way cases were handled. I knew that a prosecutor's job was to represent the State rather than any specific victim, but I tended to identify with victims, and I saw too many cases where I felt that their legitimate concerns were ignored. These people had already been victimized once, and I could relate to the feeling of being marginalized by an impersonal system. I didn't want to be a cog in that impersonal system. Instead, I wanted to handle cases the way I would like them handled if I were a victim.

Another thing that motivated me to aggressively pursue cases was when I saw what appeared to be deliberate cruelty. Many defendants hurt others because they themselves had been hurt, or because they had temporarily lost control of their emotions. But some just seemed to enjoy hurting or taking advantage of other people, and I was motivated to stop them from doing it anymore.

Still, even as I rose through the ranks of the District Attorney's Office and was assigned more and more major cases, there were times when I felt that being a prosecutor wasn't a very good "fit" with my personality, since the work involved a good deal of potential conflict and contention. My first passion was never the law, and I was by nature drawn to more creative pursuits. I loved music and was a self-taught musician, and I enjoyed creative writing and amateur filmmaking, which I pursued when I was in college.

But now I was a lawyer and had found my niche. I was, after all, working for the public good – the only aspect of law that really interested me.

IDENTIFICATION WITH THE UNDERDOG

I grew up with a strong identification with the underdog. I'm not sure where that identification came from, but I suspect it was my own insecurities. I'm one of those people who spent my high school years trying to be invisible. I lacked self-confidence, partly because I wasn't particularly athletic, and partly because in 1963, at the pivotal age of 14, I wasn't able to see the blackboard at school and got fitted with a pair of horn-rimmed glasses, which seemed like the only type available at the optical shop. I kind of looked like Buddy Holly, which didn't seem the least bit cool to me at the time – it was so 1950s. I was extremely self-conscious and didn't have the confidence to ask any girl out on a date, including a couple I secretly pined for. I felt kind of like the male counterpart of Janis Ian's song, "At Seventeen." Being a teenager wasn't all that great, and while I got some strokes for doing well academically, it didn't mean much to me.

Bad eyes also put me out of the running for most of the cool things I wanted to do – like surfing, the ultimate sport for kids growing up in Southern California in the 60s. Most of my friends had boards, and I desperately wanted to be part of the surfing scene. I remember asking for a subscription to "Surfer Magazine" for my birthday one year, and taping up surfing pictures up all over my room, along with my Beatles posters.[26] But while I fantasized about surfing, when I actually tried to do it, it was a disaster. I couldn't wear my glasses when I was surfing, and since I was quite nearsighted, I couldn't see the waves forming soon enough to line up my board to catch one. Instead, I pretty much got creamed by all the big waves, and soon realized it wasn't going to happen. I wasn't going to be a surfer.

Wearing horn-rimmed glasses also tended to draw the attention of some of the class bullies in high school. One in particular seemed to enjoy

---

[26] *I was a huge Beatles fan. If there was a bright spot in my life during high school, it was the "Lads from Liverpool." They inspired me to learn how to play guitar, and from there I branched out to other instruments – piano, banjo, bass, mandolin and harmonica. It sparked a love affair with music and performing music that continues to this day.*

intimidating me, often in gym class. Although he never actually did anything to me, he kept me on edge, and I tried to avoid him whenever I could. Being in high school felt to me kind of like being in jail. I had no choice but to be there, and I couldn't get away from some of the other "inmates." I couldn't wait to complete my sentence and move on to college.

The upshot of all these experiences was that I felt pretty much like an outsider and an underdog throughout my high school years.

Once I got out of high school, my life immediately got better. I thoroughly enjoyed college – living away from home, taking interesting classes, getting to know new friends, dating – it was all good. Most of the courses I took had so many students that there wasn't much danger of being called on by the professors, which was good because I was naturally timid and afraid of being put on the spot.

But once I started law school, I was in for a bumpy ride.

MY LAW SCHOOL GAUNTLETT

The intimidation factor was huge during my first year of law school. Students who were used to excelling as undergraduates struggled to navigate the uncertain path of responding to professors' questions in what was known as the "Socratic method," during which professors could put students on the spot for an entire class period by peppering them with questions. The idea was to probe the students' reasoning process and analytical abilities. You had to be able to think on your feet and overcome your fear of failing spectacularly before your peers, and it wasn't a method any of us had experienced before.

A couple of months after I started law school, I saw a flyer at the law library advertising a new movie called *The Paper Chase*.[27] The movie depicted the experience of James Hart, a first-year law student at Harvard, who was struggling to succeed in a system that seemed designed to keep students off-balance and uncertain of their own abilities, let alone their

---

[27] Based on the book by the same name by John Jay Osborn, Jr. (Houghton Mifflin, 1971).

grades. When I saw the movie, I identified with Hart, who was shown running the same gauntlet I was. That identification was probably strengthened by the fact that the actor who played Hart looked somewhat like me, with rimless glasses and bushy, unkempt hair. He even wore a brown corduroy coat like the one I had.

In the film, Hart's biggest challenge was distinguishing himself in Professor Kingsfield's contracts class. Kingsfield, a stern and intimidating figure, described the Socratic method this way: "You teach yourself the law, but I train your minds. You come in here with a skull full of mush and you leave thinking like a lawyer."

My "Kingsfield" was a very bright and distinguished professor named Melville Nimmer. He had quite literally written the book on copyright and entertainment law, and he was my contracts teacher. He was an imposing figure, and like Hart in "The Paper Chase," I wanted to do well in his class. Unlike some professors who were less formal, Professor Nimmer, while in no sense a curmudgeon like Kingsfield, followed the strict Socratic method in the classroom, and if you weren't well-prepared or able to think on your feet, you were likely to end up looking stupid, not just to the professor, but also to the other students in the room.

On the first day of class, Professor Nimmer looked down at his seating chart to select a student to present the first case. My heart was racing and I was something close to terrified of being called on. After looking at the chart, which had all the students' names below their pictures, he called on the student sitting right next to me. I took a deep breath and let myself calm down, amazed at my close call. I felt like the guy in the foxhole next to the guy who gets hit.

Professor Nimmer asked the student to describe the facts of the case, then asked him a series of questions, and while the student stumbled at times, it wasn't lost on me that he did a much better job than I would have. I didn't see how I was going to survive when it was my turn to run the gauntlet. If this was the method required to get me to "think like a lawyer," I wasn't at all sure I was up to it. While I was relieved that another student had taken the hit and had spared me the humiliation, the next day I noticed that the student's seat was empty. He had dropped out of law school.

As the first year was coming to an end, it hit me that Professor Nimmer had only called on me once to present a case, and in my estimation, I had not done that well during the lengthy and embarrassing exchange. Now that the course was coming to an end, I felt that I needed to do something more to prove myself, not just to Professor Nimmer, but to the other students as well. The last day of class was the only day the Professor asked for a volunteer to brief a case, and for some reason, I had an inkling he might do that, so I had time to think about it and work up my nerve. This was, after all, the last day I was going to be in his class, so it was now or never.

When the class began, Professor Nimmer asked if anyone wanted to volunteer to present the last case. I raised my hand, opening myself up for either vindication or humiliation – I wasn't sure which. He seemed quite surprised, looked down at the seating chart and, figuring out who I was, called me by name. Luckily for me, the case was not complex, and I did OK with it – well enough that when Professor Nimmer told us at the end of the class that we were the brightest group of students he had taught, I felt for the first time like I could be included in that group, if only peripherally. Still, what I had done by volunteering was more of a psychological than an intellectual achievement.

After surviving that first year of law school, I decided I wasn't going to be intimidated anymore by the Socratic method. I started raising my hand in class just to face down my fear, and it worked out reasonably well. It got to the point where I was raising my hand recklessly, like the time I arrived late to class, heard only half the case presentation, and raised my hand anyway. It felt empowering.

During my third year, a professor called on me in my Constitutional Law class, and although I generally read all the assigned cases before class, for some reason I hadn't read this one. I considered just admitting that I hadn't read the case, but since this was the new era of not being intimidated by law school professors, I decided on another approach. While I knew absolutely nothing about the case, I quickly glanced down at the text book and noticed the phrase "rifling through people's belongings" in a dissenting opinion by Justice Stevens.

So when the professor asked me a second time to present the case, I said, "Well, I really think Justice Stevens has a good point about rifling through people's belongings." It started just enough discussion among the class that I was able to quickly read the rest of the case and make my way through the questioning more or less unscathed. I considered it one of the best days of my law school career.

PLAYING AGAINST STEREOTYPE

I never really wanted to look like a lawyer, let alone a prosecutor, so I ignored the norm and pretty much kept the same look I had had in college. My hair was long and bushy, and I had more than one judge suggest that it was too long and that I should get a haircut. I didn't take the hint because there was something about having it long, playing against stereotype, that I liked. Maybe I thought it signaled that although I was playing a traditional role in a government system, I didn't identify myself too closely with the establishment. I wasn't a "company man."

I think at times my appearance did throw people. There's a lot of emphasis placed on first impressions in the courtroom, and I suspect some judges, juries, and even defendants had some difficulty, at least initially, picturing me as a prosecutor.

Once after a court hearing, when I was walking back to the District Attorney's Office, a defendant who had been in the courtroom came up to me on the street while I was waiting for the light to change. He looked at me with a rather distressed look on his face, and in a voice that rang with profound disappointment, even a sense of betrayal, said, "Hey man,

I'd buy dope from you." I guess I'd let him down. Guys who looked like me weren't supposed to be prosecutors. And it was true that I looked more like I was from the counterculture than the establishment. This guy undoubtedly knew about undercover cops, but undercover prosecutors?

But there were other ways besides my appearance in which I didn't particularly fit the profile of a government prosecutor. I was by nature a nonconformist, having internalized Emerson's *Self-Reliance* and Thoreau's "different drummer." Suspicious of authority and likely to question what "everybody knows," I was generally leery of government and those in positions of power, probably at least partially because of an experience I'd had when I was in college.

MY EXPERIENCE WITH THE DRAFT BOARD

When I was 20, Nixon was in the White House, the draft was in full swing, and the Vietnam War was raging. I was becoming more and more opposed to the war and concerned about the prospect of being drafted. The government had just instituted a lottery system in which young men would be assigned numbers on a random basis that correlated with their birthdays. It was supposed to foster fairness in the selection process. If you got a high number, you were safe. If you got a low number, you were probably toast.

Those of us who were draft-age awaited the lottery day with great anticipation. Would we get a low or high number? Was it going to be life at home, with all its possibilities – college, girls, drives to the beach – or would we be drafted and sent to fight in the jungles of Vietnam? *Time Magazine* had recently featured a cover story showing the pictures of all the soldiers who had died there in just one week of fighting, and there were an awful lot of guys' pictures in there.

A friend and I found out about our draft lottery numbers at the same time. His birthday drew number 366, the highest number you could get (366 instead of 365 because of leap year), and he was hopping and dancing around. Then came mine – number 72, close enough to the front of the line that it might as well have been number 1. Hello, Vietnam.

Some time went by before I heard from the draft board. Then I got a letter ordering me to appear for a physical exam, since I had been classified "1-A," which meant "draft-ready." It was the first I had learned about the classification, so I called the draft board and found out that they had sent the classification notice to the wrong address, and that the time to appeal had expired. I assumed that once they recognized their mistake, they would reinstate my right to appeal – which was important because even after the lottery, there still were some deferments possible, including deferments for medical reasons.

While the person I talked to at the draft board confirmed that they had received the change of address form I'd sent in and that the board had mistakenly sent the notice to the wrong address, he said there was nothing I could do about it. He essentially said, "It's too late. You're in the army now." I was stunned. Could they really do that?

That year, I marched against the war and seriously considered going to Canada if I got drafted. No matter how many times I tried, I couldn't get the draft board to re-consider my case. Finally, I talked to a lawyer who sent a letter to the board making the same points and arguments I had made. This time, they agreed to give me a hearing. It left a bad taste in my mouth about institutions that won't treat individuals fairly. Why did I need to hire a lawyer to make the same points I had been making all along? Why weren't they willing to give me a fair shot *before* I got a lawyer?

The draft board scheduled a quick hearing, and I flew home from college the day I got notice that they were reconsidering my case. At the hearing, they seemed skeptical of my medical claim. I had developed a medical condition called spondylitis which caused me a fair amount of back pain. But the disease was in the early stages, I had not been diagnosed, and no confirming genetic tests were available in those days. Since the disease involves a slow process in which inflammation may fuse the spine, my x-rays at that time looked normal. All the board had to go on was my say-so and a supporting letter from a doctor reporting that I had been seeing him for about a year complaining of back pain.

Back when so many guys were trying to avoid the draft, such claims were, not surprisingly, viewed with suspicion. I could tell they weren't too impressed with my medical case, and I wondered if they picked up on my unstated opposition to the entire process of being drafted to fight in the Vietnam War. I felt that if they sensed my opposition to the war, it could hurt my chances.

After the hearing, I waited anxiously for the decision to come down. Was it the lady or the tiger? I got the word a few days later – they would give me a temporary medical deferment, but they would re-evaluate my status in a year. I was glad to have the deferment, but wondered how long it would hold, and what I would do if they revoked it the following year.

Sometimes you get lucky and you don't know why, and you don't ask why. I never heard from the draft board again – no review hearing, no re-classification back to 1-A status, no draft. A few years passed, and the U.S. pulled out of Vietnam and abolished the draft. It became clear that I wasn't going to be faced with the Hobson's choice of forced military conscription or illegal flight to Canada. I had dodged a bullet, perhaps quite literally, but the experience had left me leery of my own government – a mistrust that only intensified as the Watergate scandal unfolded in the early 70s.

It would still be years before I would think about going to law school. But I came away from the experience recognizing that, had things played out differently, I could have ended up on the wrong side of the law. I don't know how many people who become prosecutors have the sense that they could, under certain circumstances, find themselves on the other side of the courtroom, but I believe my experience with the draft and the draft board did influence my approach to being a prosecutor.

TAKING A NON-INSTITUTIONAL APPROACH

To a certain degree, I found myself a non-institutional person in an institutional job, and from time to time, I even felt a sense of identification with some of the suspects and defendants whose cases crossed my desk. I also was determined not to be like the government bureaucrats I had dealt with at the draft board who had refused to consider my claim because I was "just" an ordinary citizen. Baloney to that.

I remember one case I handled as a young prosecutor where I think I bent the rules a bit. I was assigned to court one day when the judge called up a case involving a man who had been mistakenly picked up by the police on a warrant and had spent some time in jail while the mistake was being sorted out. They had brought him up from the jail for the hearing, and I listened as the man's attorney explained the convoluted situation that had resulted in his client's arrest and continued detention. The guy had been in trouble with the law before, and the reason he was still in jail was because of some kind of glitch in the paperwork, whether intentional or inadvertent. In any case, not all the "I"s had been dotted and "T"s crossed for him to be released.

It was apparent to me that this guy shouldn't be in jail. Still, the judge was inclined to hold him until the paperwork got sorted out. At that point, the defense attorney turned and asked me if I would stipulate to his client's immediate release. It was pretty early in my career, and I assumed that, as a prosecutor and representative of the State, I was expected to insist that all necessary procedures be followed. But in looking at the circumstances of the case, it seemed obviously unfair.

I thought about it for a moment and then told the judge that the State's position was that the guy should be released immediately. I think this decision surprised both the defense attorney and the judge, who then ordered the man's release. As we left the courtroom, I wasn't sure if someone in the jail administration or police department was going to complain to my boss about what I did, but I never heard anything more about it.

Perhaps my experience with the draft board was also playing somewhere in the back of my mind when, years later, I was sitting in my office at the D.A.'s Office preparing for a court hearing, when I got a call from the office receptionist, saying she had an irate caller on the line. It was a witness who had been subpoenaed to appear later that week at a preliminary hearing in a robbery case, a hearing to determine if there was sufficient evidence to require the defendant to stand trial. The witness had called to say he couldn't come – he had an important personal matter to attend to.

The receptionist told me she had informed the witness that he was under a legal obligation to appear, and that if he didn't show up for the hearing, a warrant could be issued for his arrest. He had become more and more agitated, and finally the receptionist had told him she would put the call through to the attorney handling the case.

By the time I took the call, the witness was extremely upset. How dare our office treat him this way, as if he were a criminal? He told me it would be virtually impossible for him to appear on such short notice, and that he had a long-standing appointment to take his elderly father to see a doctor for a serious medical condition. He said he would rather go to jail than break that appointment.

I knew from studying the case file that the man was a key witness – perhaps the only eyewitness who could definitely identify the defendant as the robber – and I also knew that the judge was unlikely to postpone the hearing any longer, since it had already been continued twice, and the defendant was in jail. Still, I thought about how I would feel if I were in this man's position, and so my first statement to him was that I understood how he felt and that it sounded to me like he was in a really tough spot.

I also told him that we would only have one shot at binding the defendant over for trial, that he was a key witness, and that if the judge didn't find enough evidence at the hearing, the defendant's case would be dismissed and he would be released from jail.

I thought about it for a moment and then said, "I wonder if there's a chance we might be able to bind the defendant over without your testimony, so you can make that appointment."

There was a pause on the other end of the phone. Then, in a different tone of voice, the man asked me what the odds were that the defendant would be bound over for trial if he didn't testify at the hearing. I told him it would be more difficult, but I thought there was an 80% probability we could do it. He then asked, "What about if I do testify?" I told him I was very confident we could get a bind-over if he testified.

At this point, I told him, "You know, I think we'll be all right. Why don't you keep your appointment? Of course you'll be a key witness at trial. I couldn't try the case without you. But I think I'll manage OK without your testimony through the preliminary hearing."

Then something curious – but perhaps not so curious – happened. I expected him to say something like, "OK, thanks for understanding the situation. I'll be happy to come to the trial." Instead, there was another pause, and then he said, "But you said you might not be able to bind the defendant over for trial without my testimony."

I replied, "Yeah, but I'm pretty sure I can do it."

He then said, "Listen, maybe I can arrange to have my brother take my dad to the doctor's, and I can come to the hearing." I told him I appreciated it, but it wasn't necessary. At that point, the witness emphatically declared, "No, I'm coming. I'll be there," and my impression was that from that point on, I couldn't have talked him out of coming to the hearing even if I had tried.

As I hung up the phone, it struck me how differently people react when they think their concerns are being taken seriously and they feel they're being treated with respect. The receptionist had told the man the truth about the potential consequences of ignoring a court subpoena. But there was no human understanding in it. And that made all the difference. I didn't tell the witness anything I didn't think was true, including my willingness to take on the challenge of putting on the hearing without him, but when I empathized with his situation, it changed his attitude. He no longer viewed me as an adversary, but as someone with whom he shared a common goal. And from that new perspective, he wanted to find, and did find, a solution that would meet both our needs.

And so, while I don't think I consciously thought very much about the experiences I had before becoming a prosecutor, I do think they influenced me – everything from my identification with the underdog to my leeriness of government and bureaucratic red tape to my view that my job was just as much about not prosecuting the "wrong" people as it was about prosecuting the "right" people.

Perhaps those experiences also made me more likely to ask questions and consider that the system could make a mistake, more likely to want to help suspects or defendants if I thought the system might be treating them unfairly, and more likely to come into conflict with some of the players in the criminal justice system. Particularly early in my career, I had more than my share of that.

CHAPTER 10

The *Singer-Swapp* Case:
A Bombing, a 13-Day Standoff,
a Shootout, and the Death of an Officer

BY THE TIME I WAS HIRED by the Utah Attorney General's Office in October of 1987, I had spent nine years in the Salt Lake D.A.'s Office specializing in violent crime, and was the team leader of the Career Criminal Team. I had handled about a dozen homicide cases and many robberies, rapes, and assaults, and was ready to take on a less violent caseload. I was recruited by the Attorney General's Office to prosecute white-collar crime cases, but circumstances were to conspire against it.

In the early morning hours of January 16, 1988, about three months after I became an Assistant Attorney General, a family of religious extremists, the Singers and Swapps, bombed an LDS[28] Stake Center church building in the rural mountain valley community of Marion, Utah, about 45 miles east of Salt Lake City. The blast occurred in the middle of the night when no one was inside, and it devastated the chapel.

The leader of the group, Addam Swapp, stuck a red pole in the snow near the location of the bombing. Written on the pole was a message that

---

[28] LDS refers to "Latter-Day Saint,", which is an abbreviation of the formal name of the Mormon Church, which is "The Church of Jesus Christ of Latter-Day Saints." Throughout the book, I will use the terms "Mormon" and "LDS" interchangeably.

left little doubt who was responsible for the blast. It said: "Jan. 18, 1979, J.S., Church, State and Nation will now be destroyed."

Officers recognized the date. Nine years earlier, on January 18, 1979, John Singer, Addam Swapp's father-in-law, had been shot and killed by state law enforcement officers as they were trying to serve an arrest warrant. Singer was a religious extremist prone to fiery rhetoric – not willing to compromise on anything – and he had previously threatened what he would do if any officers dared come onto his property. While he was prominently known as a polygamist in conflict with authorities because of the home-schooling of his children,[29] that wasn't what caused John Singer's demise. In 1978, Singer had taken a second wife, by marrying a woman who was still married to another man. The man sued for custody of his children and won, but Singer refused to return the children to their father despite a court order. As a result, a warrant was issued for his arrest.

The Summit County Sheriff's Office was not eager to serve the warrant, given Singer's threats of violence, but the judge ordered Sheriff Fred Eley to act. Sheriff Eley then enlisted help from state officers, hoping to have sufficient manpower to persuade Singer not to resist. On that snowy day in January, armed officers surrounded Singer on snowmobiles when he left his house and went out to the road to retrieve mail from his mailbox. Despite being surrounded, John Singer pulled his gun on the officers and was then shot and killed. It happened on the same property where the Singer-Swapp family still resided nine years later, in 1988.

After Singer's death, Vickie Singer, John's widow, raised her children, including young John Timothy, on the constant battle cry that her husband had been murdered and that the outside world was wicked and corrupt. Addam Swapp, who had never met John Singer, watched TV news reports about the family and became enamored of the Singer daughters, partic-

---

[29] One of Singer's reasons for taking his children out of public school was that he objected to pictures of black and white children together. Ultimately, school authorities did allow the Singers to home-school their children, under some supervision.

ularly Heidi. Not long after Singer's death, Addam drove to Marion and introduced himself to Vickie Singer. He sympathized with the family for the "great injustices" they had suffered, thereby ingratiating himself with Vickie. Addam and Vickie had something else in common – they both embraced fundamentalist Mormon beliefs, which included polygamy.

Addam eventually "married" two of Vickie's daughters, Heidi and Charlotte, moved to the compound, and fathered several children. Addam's brother Jonathan, who shared his religious views, also moved onto the property.

In the years leading up to the bombing, the family was often in conflict with their neighbors over disputes about water rights, and Addam became more and more provocative as time went on. Shortly before the bombings, he went around to neighbors' homes and cars and spray-painted on them that the people there had "murdered John Singer." When Sheriff Eley went up to the property to talk to Addam about the vandalism, Addam pulled a pistol and fired it in the air over Eley's head, ordering him off the property with threats of bloodshed. Things were becoming more and more volatile, and law enforcement officers and the community at large were becoming increasingly anxious about what the group might do next.

And now it had come to this – a bombing and a standoff. Like everyone else, I watched the evening news to see what was going on, never thinking I would become personally involved in the case. After all, it was all taking place up in Summit County, where there was an able county attorney, Bob Adkins, with an experienced deputy prosecutor, Terry Christiansen. I assumed they would handle any state criminal charges stemming from the incident. And besides, it was shaping up primarily as a federal case, with FBI and ATF agents from around the country playing the primary roles in the operation.

Over the course of 13 days, Swapp and his group of polygamists holed up in the 2-acre family compound and defied all efforts to negotiate with the police or end the standoff peacefully. The story was constantly in the news, and the public interest was intensified by the fact that six young children of the Singer-Swapp clan were inside the compound with the family, potentially in harm's way. How was it going to end? Was the group really intent on a bloody confrontation with police, even if it meant exposing their own children to the risk of injury or death? Would officers storm the house, knowing six young children were inside, or would they continue to try to wait them out?

Before it was over, there were more than 100 officers, mostly FBI and ATF, surrounding the property, attempting to resolve the standoff and take Addam and his co-conspirators into custody. During the many attempts by the officers to negotiate with Addam, he made it clear that he had no intention of surrendering, that the family had plenty of provisions to last through the winter, and that he believed the bombing was a God-sanctioned response to the mistreatment he and his family had suffered at the hands of their neighbors, the LDS church, and law enforcement officers.

It seemed from his posturing that Addam relished his role in the spotlight. Shortly before the standoff, he had posed for a reporter and appeared on the cover of a Utah magazine dressed in buckskin and a double holster, with a six-gun on each hip.

During the early days of the confrontation, officers received intelligence from associates of the family who were allowed to go onto the property that Addam was seeking a violent confrontation with law enforcement officers because he believed it would bring about the resurrection and second coming of John Singer. It didn't bode well for a peaceful settlement.

Several days into the standoff, officers dropped from a helicopter a letter from Utah Governor Norm Bangerter, who entreated Addam to end the standoff peaceably for the sake of the children inside the compound, and assured him that all his grievances would be addressed.

Addam was unmoved. He responded by writing a letter back challenging the Governor's authority over him and his family, declaring the Singer property a sovereign nation, ordering authorities out of the valley, and warning that any officer who set foot on the property would be treated as an aggressor. He said they would defend themselves in any manner they saw fit.

The first day of the standoff, Addam cut off communications with an FBI negotiator by disconnecting the phone from the wall. Given the fact that the family had provisions sufficient to get them through the entire winter quite comfortably, the FBI was looking for another technique to give Addam an incentive to talk with them. A week into the standoff, Addam was showing no signs of being willing to negotiate or even talk with state or federal authorities at the scene.

Public interest intensified with news reports that federal officers had cut the family's power and were erecting lights around the perimeter of the Singer-Swapp compound. Officers were also putting up speakers to blast loud noises at the group to keep them from sleeping at night. Addam and his brother Jonathan responded by shooting at the lights and speakers. Some of the shots came very near to federal officers, who had to duck for cover.

While the tactic of blaring noise and shining lights in their windows at night may have worked with most "ordinary criminals," it backfired by feeding into the group's paranoid Armageddon-type religious ideology, and causing Addam and the others inside to dig in deeper. Additionally, it spawned news reports that the family was being "tortured" by officers. One Salt Lake academic, Elliot Landau, went on the news shortly after the loudspeakers were deployed and announced that, in his opinion, the officers' actions were tantamount to child abuse.

Day after day in sub-zero temperatures, officers waited in frustration while Addam and Jonathan Swapp were permitted to walk around the property with their firearms. Because of the presence of the children inside, stringent rules of engagement had been established. Officers were not to fire in the direction of the house even if they were fired upon, for fear of harming the children. It was clear from the lengths the officers went to in exposing themselves to danger that nobody wanted another John Singer. And Addam was using that to his advantage.

On the 13th day, officials at the scene devised a plan to try to capture Addam and his brother Jonathan as they returned to the main house after milking the family goat – a daily routine. The goat pen was partway between the main Singer house and the house of Roger Bates, where officers had taken up positions during the standoff. The Swapp brothers took their rifles with them, as they did whenever they walked about the compound.

When the Swapp brothers finished milking the goat that morning and started back towards the main house, officers in the Bates house opened the door to send police dogs to take down Addam and Jonathan without having to resort to deadly force. There were two police dog handlers in the Bates house, Fred House and Jerry Pope, both from the Utah Department of Corrections. As the officers opened the door to send the dogs, a volley of shots erupted from the Singer-Swapp group. Bullets started striking the front of the Bates house where Fred, Jerry, and several FBI Hostage Rescue Team (HRT) sharpshooters were located. Fred was hit by one of the bullets as he stood sideways in the doorway, urging forward his dog, Mike. The bullet struck him just past the edge of his bullet-proof vest.

Richard Intellini, one of the FBI HRT members in the Bates house with Fred, saw that he had been hit and called out to him, "Hang on, Fred. We'll get you out of there." But bullets kept slamming into the front door, and by the time anyone could reach Fred, he was unconscious.

Officers rushed to administer first aid at the scene. Fred was airlifted to the University of Utah Medical Center, but he was pronounced dead on arrival.

During the fatal shootout that morning, Addam Swapp was wounded in the wrist and the chest by a single shot fired by one of the officers at the scene. Addam ran back into the Singer house for a brief time, then came out of the house waving a white cloth. He was losing blood, and he staggered down and surrendered to officers around the Bates house, seeking medical help. FBI agents knelt down in the snow, applied pressure to Addam's wrist and a battle dressing to his chest, and saved his life. Addam was then evacuated to a waiting ambulance and taken to the University of Utah Medical Center.

Shortly after Addam's surrender, the other members of the family came out of the house and surrendered to authorities. The standoff was finally over, but a terrible price had been paid.

I was in my office at the State Capitol that morning when I heard the news that the standoff had ended, and that a state officer had been killed. I had a vague feeling that I should be doing something, but I wasn't sure what, since no one had asked for our office's help, and, as I said, it was a matter for the Summit County Attorney's Office and the U.S. Attorney's Office, given all the federal officers involved in the incident. My involvement with the case at that point had been limited to assisting Assistant U.S. Attorney Dave Schwendiman in obtaining a state wiretap order, so that officers could place a listening device in a cooler that a family friend, Ogden Kraut, delivered to the family mid-way through the standoff. Kraut was not a police operative, nor did he have any knowledge of the listening device. When he walked up to visit the family, he left the cooler outside on the porch, so it ended up yielding no helpful information about the group's intentions.

About noon the day the standoff ended, I got a call from Dave, whose position I had taken when he was hired by the U.S. Attorney's Office the previous fall. He had been close to the ongoing investigation in Marion, and relayed to me what he had been told by officers at the scene – that when officers tried to send police dogs to bring down Addam and Jonathan Swapp, Addam heard the commotion, turned around, saw Fred House in the doorway, shouldered his weapon, and shot Fred down in cold blood. If that was true, it was unquestionably capital murder, the intentional killing of a police officer.[30]

---

[30] Like other rumors we were to hear in the course of the investigation, this one turned out to be far from accurate.

Dave then asked if I had called Bob Adkins, the Summit County Attorney, to see if his office wanted any help in the matter. He noted that the Attorney General's Office was often asked to step in to handle cases late in the game, without an opportunity to help direct the investigation, which could be critical to a successful prosecution. I told him I hadn't called Bob, but agreed that it made sense to find out sooner rather than later if he wanted our office's help.

I then called Bob Adkins and asked him if he anticipated needing help from our office. He said no, he thought they could handle it locally. I hung up the phone, somewhat relieved that we weren't going to be asked to step into the case. I had had more than my share of high-profile cases at the D.A.'s Office, and wasn't looking for another. Besides, I was supposed to be doing white-collar crime cases now.

About twenty minutes later, I got a call back from Bob. He had reconsidered, and said that, due to a potential conflict of interest his office had because they were handling a civil lawsuit involving the Singer-Swapp family, it would be best if our office would prosecute the case. For me, it wasn't good news. I could see the writing on the wall – I was going to get stuck with this case. Still, Dave was right. It was better for us to get involved right away, if the case was coming our way anyway.

That afternoon, Bob Adkins came up to the Capitol and met with me and Utah Attorney General David Wilkinson, and formally requested that our office take over the prosecution of the Singer-Swapp clan, as they were referred to in the press. I remember Dave Wilkinson telling Bob that "Creight Horton is just crazy enough to take on the case." I guessed it was a compliment, but I wondered just how crazy things might get. And so began the case that was to take most of my time over the next year, involving trials in both state and federal court.

It wasn't long after the shootout that we learned who had actually fired the fatal shot. Agent Ron Miller of our office participated in an interview of 21-year-old John Timothy "Tim" Singer shortly after the shootout ended and the group surrendered. Ron reported that Tim, who had been partially paralyzed some years before in a logging accident, had admitted to sitting in his wheelchair and firing his rifle from the Singer house window, but claimed that he was only shooting at dogs, not people.[31] Tim said he saw the dogs running toward Addam and Jonathan as they walked back from milking the goat, but didn't see or aim at any officers. It became clear that the case was going to be much more complicated than initial reports had indicated.

One of the first things I had to do was slow down the train. We were all preparing to go process the scene the morning after the fatal shootout when I realized that the federal search warrants that had been issued during the standoff only authorized federal officers to search for evidence of the bombing and armed resistance, not for evidence relating to the killing of Fred House. Even though the federal agents were on the scene that first day, processing it for evidence, it wasn't enough for us to piggy-back off their federal search warrants. Under the United States Constitution, there is no "homicide scene" exception to the search warrant requirement, and I didn't want the Singer-Swapp clan to have any colorable claim later on that evidence had been illegally obtained, and hence should be suppressed at trial.

Since state and federal agents were going to be processing the scene at the same time on that day, I called the U.S. Attorney's Office and asked them to have the federal officers hold off a couple of hours so we could obtain a state search warrant to search for evidence pertaining to the killing of Fred House. They agreed, and by the time we all arrived at the scene, there was no question that we were authorized to search for the evidence we needed.

Although we were authorized to search, we weren't enabled, because almost all of the more than 100 officers who had taken part in the operation

---

[31] Although Tim said he had fired at the dogs and not at people, neither dog was struck during the shooting.

were gone. Most were federal officers from across the country, and they had returned to their home offices immediately following the shootout. On top of that, many had been granted trauma leave and weren't in their offices.

After the federal agents completed processing the compound for evidence relating to the bombings and standoff, they too left the scene. It was now up to us to find evidence pertaining to the death of Officer House. We spent two weeks combing the Singer compound for evidence – looking for bullets, bullet holes, casings, weapons, ammunition and the like. Fortunately for me, I was there with Agent Ron Miller of our office. Ron was a first-rate homicide investigator, and he became the principal case agent throughout both the state and federal trials. The other agents assisting us at the scene were primarily white-collar investigators from our office. The witnesses had spread to the four winds, and we felt like we were chasing shadows.

One rumor we heard was that when federal officers rolled onto the Singer property in their Armored Personnel Carriers (APCs) the morning of the shootout, more than 100 rounds were fired at them by the Singer-Swapp clan. Our metal detector expert, Retired FBI Agent Richard Graham, spent days trying to find that evidence, but as with so many rumors we heard, that evidence didn't exist. In reality, only ten shots were fired during the shootout, but it took us weeks to reconstruct what had happened, and some of the ballistics evidence was already gone before we entered the property.[32]

The first couple of days were the worst. Sub-zero temperatures had set in and a blizzard was approaching, which was likely to deposit more snow on top of the snow that had already fallen. I was a born-and-bred California boy, the only prosecutor at the scene, and I wasn't prepared

---

[32] One bullet had struck a car in the driveway of a nearby house. We eventually recovered it at the Kamas Body Shop, where the car had been towed. Another wasn't discovered until the federal trial, when an FBI agent's jacket was X-rayed, and a bullet was found inside his jacket lining. He had been in a house that took rounds during the shootout, and had fallen backward from a bullet's impact on the wall of the living room, but never realized the bullet had penetrated the wall and actually lodged inside his jacket.

for the unrelenting frigid temperatures. I borrowed a pair of boots with liners from one of our agents, and when I got home that night, I took out the liners of the boots to dry them out. A good idea, except that I forgot to bring the liners with me the following day. Big mistake. I about froze my toes off, and even with gloves, my hands were in a perpetual deep freeze.

About the second day we were on the scene, several defense attorneys assigned to represent the Singer-Swapp group on their federal charges showed up, saying that a federal judge had issued an order permitting them access to the property. We initially refused: "This is a crime scene – over 2 acres, in the snow. There is hidden evidence. We can't have people walking around. You could be stepping on evidence, contaminating the crime scene." The defense attorneys were unhappy to be turned away, but came back later with a court order. We had to escort them around the property and try to explain as best we could what we thought had happened during the shootout. It was an uncomfortable situation, as we ourselves were still struggling to understand it.

And then we had the press nipping at our heels. Shortly after the shootout, the Utah Commissioner of Public Safety said that the scene would be released and available in a few days for the press to inspect. I'm not sure why he made the statement, but we had to deliver to the press the bad news that we were likely going to be processing the scene for some time, and that once we were done, we had no authority to authorize the press to enter the property.

Because of the unusual circumstance of needing to process the scene for an extended period of time, I drafted a second search warrant asking for authorization to hold the scene for weeks, if necessary. The judge said he'd never seen this kind of authorization in a search warrant before and wasn't sure it was necessary, since we had already obtained a search warrant. I said I hadn't ever seen one either, but asked the judge to humor me because the situation was unique, and I would rather have an express authorization than have to fight in court with defense attorneys over the issue. The judge eventually issued the second warrant.

At times, as we were wandering around the property trying to figure out what we should be looking for, with nothing but rumors to guide us, the whole experience had an "Alice in Wonderland" feel of absurdity about it.

In the "believe it or not" category, there were videotapes of the scene that we didn't know anything about for several days. One was taken by a Summit County Sheriff's deputy, who was stationed quite a distance away from the Singer property to prevent people from driving up a street called Upper Loop Road. He had his video camera trained up towards the Singer compound and had actually captured the sounds of the gunshots during the shootout. Afterward, he watched the tape, but since he couldn't see any movement up at the compound from that distance, the deputy didn't think it had any evidentiary value. It ended up being a crucial piece of evidence, as it gave us both the number of shots fired – ten – and the timing of the shots.

More problematic was the fact that the FBI had an agent assigned to record video footage of the scene during the standoff, and hours and hours of tapes had been created. When we finally learned about the tapes, we were told the bad news: The agent had not replaced the videotape with a fresh tape the morning of the final shootout, and the old tape had run out just before the shootout occurred. The crucial footage was therefore not captured. This not only created a problem in failing to record and preserve evidence that could have helped us reconstruct exactly what happened, but it also later fed into the defense's conspiracy theory at trial that the FBI had intentionally turned off the camera in order to hide the truth about what had happened during the shootout. It meant we had to call the FBI agent who was responsible for the mistake to testify how he had screwed up the crucial videotape. One more problem we didn't need.

During the standoff, the commanders at the scene had focused on the tactical issues of how to resolve the crisis. Little or no thought appeared to have been given to the fact that evidence was being generated every day during that period, evidence that might one day have to be reconstructed in a courtroom for a jury to understand. And as we continued to try to process the scene, we knew that these evidentiary failures could play out badly at trial, depending on just how many and how great the "gaps" in the evidence might be.[33]

A typical example of our frustration happened the second day we were on the scene. As we were trying to understand what had happened in the Bates house where Lt. House had been killed, we saw someone talking to a man nearby who was gesturing like he was explaining something, and we walked over and asked what was going on. It turned out that the FBI was conducting an administrative shooting review with John Butler, one of the Hostage Rescue Team (HRT) officers who had been in the Bates house with Fred during the fatal shootout. We were relieved to finally have an eyewitness we could talk to. It seemed like we had finally gotten a break.

We were astonished to be told by the federal agents that they were only authorized to conduct a shooting review, and that Special Agent Butler was about to fly back to Quantico, Virginia, where he was based. Perhaps if we made a request to the Justice Department, they might fly him back in a day or two. We were dumbfounded: "This is a murder investigation. Fred House is dead. We don't have a clue what happened, or what evidence to look for. We're tromping around a 2-acre compound in a blizzard and a blanket of freshly fallen snow, and we don't even know

---

[33] At night, when I got back home from the scene and warmed up, I would write down things I thought should have been done differently during the standoff – things that would have made it much easier for us to reconstruct in court what had happened during the 13-day siege and shootout. After the trials were over, Dave Schwendiman and I developed an "Extraordinary Criminal Events" (or "ECE") protocol and manual to better handle these on-going criminal incidents in the future. One of its principal features was having an on-site attorney assigned to focus on evidence gathering and preservation during such events. The protocol was eventually adopted by the state of Utah, the U. S. Department of Justice, and some other states.

what the hell happened up here. How many shots were fired? Where did the shooting come from? Did anyone actually see any of the Singer-Swapp clan fire a weapon? Just give us five minutes. You owe it to Fred."

Our frustration was so high that our plea was probably somewhere between an urgent request and a threat to bodily drag Agent Butler over to the house where Fred was killed. The federal officers talked briefly among themselves and then gave us five minutes with Butler.

The initial report we had received claimed that Addam had shot Fred House in cold blood. Yet Butler gave us a very different account. Although Addam had shouldered his weapon after the shooting started, he never fired a shot that morning. Before he could pull the trigger, he was wounded by Butler, who was in the Bates house with Fred and who saw Addam spin around and shoulder his rifle as rounds were striking the front door of the Bates house.

It was helpful to be able to speak with at least one of the hundred eyewitnesses who had been on the scene during the shootout, particularly a key witness like Butler. But for the most part, we had to do the investigation "backwards." We had to reconstruct circumstantially what had happened as best we could, and then wait for the FBI reports of the incident to trickle in after the fact. There were more than a hundred reports to wade through, and many weren't available until after we had finished processing the scene and released the Singer property back to the members of the family who had not been charged.

Several times during the period when we were processing the scene, I returned to my office at the State Capitol and reported to the Chief Deputy Attorney General about the progress of the investigation. From the beginning, he emphasized that he wanted the case charged at the highest possible level. After all, this was an outrageous, protracted crime, and a police officer had been killed in the line of duty while trying to apprehend the Swapps without using deadly force. Legally, the officers could have used that force, but they had chosen not to do so, and Fred

House had paid with his life. The community was outraged. Law enforcement was outraged. Justice demanded we charge at the highest possible level – capital murder.

I told the Chief Deputy that I understood how he felt, but that we'd just have to see how the evidence played out. Despite the impulse to throw the book at these people, the process had to be "The evidence first, then the charges" – not the other way around. He agreed, but said that if at all possible, he wanted it charged as capital. From what I was seeing on the ground, I wanted him to be aware that there was a real possibility we wouldn't have enough evidence to file capital murder charges, and might have to consider lesser degrees of homicide. While Fred's death was devastating, and entirely preventable if Addam Swapp had not insisted on his bloody confrontation, we could only justify charging it as a capital case if we could prove an actual intent to kill, and that was proving to be elusive – even against Tim, who admitted to firing the fatal shot.

At this point in the investigation – about three days in – here's what we knew: The fatal shot had been fired by Tim Singer, who claimed he was just shooting at dogs. In his taped interview, Tim seemed genuinely surprised to hear he had struck an officer. Addam was clearly the leader of the group, but he hadn't fired his rifle that morning, nor had he tried to until after Tim had already shot Fred. While we were still uncertain about Jonathan Swapp's role during the shooting, we knew from the ballistics evidence as well as from Tim's statement that Jonathan had not fired the fatal shot, and as far as we knew, probably hadn't fired at all.

Since the defendants were all in federal custody awaiting trial on the federal charges – bombing the church, assaulting some federal officers with deadly weapons, and attempting to kill others – we were not under a time deadline to bring immediate state charges against them. They weren't going anywhere. We had time to complete our investigation before deciding whom to charge, and with what offenses.

Several days into the investigation, the FBI flew in a ballistics and trajectory expert named Rick Crum. He was sent to try to help reconstruct what happened during the shootout. When he got to the scene and saw its scope, Rick almost turned on his heels and jumped on a plane back to Washington. What was he doing there? How could he do anything with such a vast and chaotic crime scene? What was he expected to do? Adding to his discomfort, there weren't even any federal officials at the scene – just Utah state people. Fortunately, we called and put him on the phone with officials from the U.S. Attorney's Office in Salt Lake, who convinced him to stay. They told him they understood he might not be able to help at all, but to just do the best he could.

A couple of hours later Rick called us over, and there was excitement in his voice. He had made a startling discovery. The location and trajectory of three bullet strikes on the garage of the Jeppesen house, just west of the Bates house where Fred had been shot, showed that those bullets must have been fired by someone other than the shooter located in the main Singer house.

Up until then, we had assumed that all the shots fired by the suspects had come from the main residence, from Tim Singer. Rick was able to almost pinpoint the location – up at the north end of the house, by the trees – where a second shooter must have been firing. He told us to have our metal detection expert, Richard Graham, look there for casings, and sure enough, Richard was able to find them under the snow. We were then able to piece together that the second shooter had to be Jonathan Swapp, although at this point, we had no report of anyone actually seeing him shooting during the incident.

Weeks after we had finished processing the 2-acre crime scene, we received FBI reports from two of the officers who had been stationed inside the Jeppesen house. The reports indicated that the agents had seen Jonathan Swapp shoulder his weapon right at the same time that rounds started striking their location. We were excited to finally have witnesses who could confirm Rick Crum's findings.

Our hopes flagged when we interviewed the first agent. No, he hadn't actually seen much of anything, and certainly not enough to establish that Jonathan had fired his rifle during the shootout.

Then we brought in the second agent. He told us that he was standing at the window in the living room of the Jeppesen house looking through binoculars when the shooting started. He saw Jonathan Swapp up on the north corner of the Singer house, firing his gun towards the Jeppesen house, at which point the agent yelled for everybody to get down, just as rounds began striking the home.

When we interviewed the agent, we knew exactly where Jonathan must have been standing, thanks to Rick Crum's fine reconstruction work. When we asked the agent to put an "X" on the diagram, he put it dead center in Rick's "cone of firing." We finally had an actual eyewitness!

With each new piece of evidence falling into place, we were getting nearer to our goal: to be able to re-construct this complicated case in court – two courts, actually, since charges involving the bombing and assaults against federal officers would be tried in federal court, and charges relating to the killing of Lt. House, a Utah state officer, would be tried in state court.

The federal case was coming up first, and we were in a race against the clock to be ready for trial, which was scheduled less than two months from when we finished processing the scene. Could we really be ready in time?

CHAPTER 11

Prosecuting the
Singer-Swapp Case

WITH THE FEDERAL TRIAL LOOMING, and in order to most effectively prosecute both the federal and state cases, I was deputized as a Special Assistant United States Attorney to assist in the federal prosecution. In return, the U. S. Attorney's Office agreed to allow Dave Schwendiman[34] to be cross-designated as a Special Assistant Attorney General, so he could help me prosecute the murder trial later in the fall. It was a good arrangement and provided important continuity between the state and federal prosecutions.

The federal trial of Vickie Singer, Addam Swapp, Jonathan Swapp and John Timothy Singer for the bombing of the church, assault of federal officers, and attempted murder of federal officers took place in the spring of 1988. The case went to trial so quickly that we barely had adequate

---

[34] Dave went on to have the most amazing career of any prosecutor I know. His accomplishments and awards would require an appendix. He has prosecuted some of the highest-profile cases in Utah history, was the legal coordinator for all matters pertaining to the 2002 Winter Olympic Games in Salt Lake City, served as Assistant Inspector General/Director of Forward Operations for the Special Inspector General for Afghanistan Reconstruction, and has served as an International Prosecutor in the Special Department for War Crimes of the Prosecutor's Office of Bosnia and Herzegovina. He is presently Lead Prosecutor of the European Union's Special Investigative Task Force investigating crimes against humanity in Kosovo.

time to prepare. Federal Judge Bruce Jenkins, who had been assigned the case, set an initial trial date of April 6. At the time, we expected that the defense would ask for more time to prepare, because the case involved complicated issues and evidence, there were more than 100 potential witnesses, and we still hadn't received all the witness reports and lab test results.

While the defense attorneys did want more time to prepare, the defendants insisted on the April 6 trial date, because April 6 was not only Addam Swapp's birthday, but it also had other special significance to the group. It was the date of the official founding of the Mormon Church, as well as, reputedly, the actual day Christ was born, according to Mormon belief. So it looked like providence to the defendants, and they weren't about to agree to delay the trial. We asked Judge Jenkins for more time to prepare our case, but he denied our motion for a continuance, saying that we'd all "just have to do the best we can."

For the federal case, I joined the trial team, which consisted of Dave Schwendiman, Richard Lambert, and the U.S. Attorney for Utah, Brent Ward. We had the invaluable assistance of case agent Ron Miller and paralegal Sharon Fleck of the Attorney General's Office, both of whom did an outstanding job of keeping track of the evidence and helping us organize our case at trial.[35]

Going to trial on the federal charges so quickly – a little more than two months after the shootout – created some unique challenges. We had to move at a breakneck speed, both in trial preparation and during the course of the trial. When we divided up trial duties, I got the draw to handle some of the more technical aspects of the case, including questioning Rick Crum, the FBI ballistics and crime scene reconstruction expert.

Midway through trial, Rick flew in the night before he was to testify, and I spent many hours with him going over the exhibits, diagrams, photos

---

[35] Ron was the case agent and Sharon the paralegal for both the federal and state trials.

and other evidence, and organizing his testimony. We worked past 2:00 a.m., so I didn't get much sleep that night. The next day by mid-afternoon, it was time to put Rick on the stand.

His testimony was crucial to our case, establishing where the shots were fired and where they impacted. My questioning drew a lot of objections from the defense attorneys. How could Rick give these opinions? How accurate could they be? Didn't he just have a simple protractor that he used at the scene as he tried to reconstruct the trajectory of the shots during the shootout? The back-and-forth with defense counsel was getting tiring, and I realized that the pace of the trial and the lack of sleep were catching up with me. About an hour into Rick's testimony, I looked down at my own notes and was having difficulty tracking what I had written.

At about that time, Judge Jenkins started to lose patience with it all, and tried to get me to wrap up the witness's testimony. Jenkins, a well-respected and imposing figure, pointedly told me, "Either put your next question to the witness or SIT DOWN," with a clear emphasis on the second option. I put my next question. The defense attorneys objected, and Judge Jenkins sustained the objection. Jenkins then said to me again, "Either put your next question to the witness or SIT DOWN," with even more emphasis than before.

I was exhausted and frustrated, and might have taken the not-so-subtle invitation to end my questioning, but I still had points I wanted to make, and my prior experience with Third District Judge Ballinger stood me in good stead. Having so regularly been raked over the coals in those early years by the good judge, I was more used to it than many, and had developed a rather thick skin when it came to judicial batterings. Despite repeated invitations from Judge Jenkins, I didn't sit down until I got all the testimony I felt I needed from Rick.

After the federal trial was over and the defendants stood convicted of the federal offenses – bombing the church, assaulting federal officers, and attempting to kill federal officers – we were pleased with the result and relieved that we had been able to pull our case together in such a short time frame. I remembered hearing from one of the defense attorneys just before trial that the defendants hadn't thought we could be ready to go to trial so quickly, which was another reason they had opposed any postponement of the trial.

While it was a relief to be done with the federal case, I knew that Dave Schwendiman and I didn't have much time to rest, because now we had to gear up for the state murder trial. As part of our trial preparation, we asked Ron Miller to talk with some of the federal jurors to see what insights we might gain. It wasn't unusual to check with jurors after a big case to get an assessment of what we had done right and what we could have done better, and it seemed like a particularly good idea to do it now, as we were going to be presenting essentially the same evidence to a second jury in the state murder trial.

Shortly afterwards, Ron returned to the Capitol with some troubling news: One of the jurors he had spoken with said that during the early stages of the deliberations when the other jurors were ready to convict, he had been a holdout. He told Ron that he had only changed his mind after talking to a friend of his who was a police officer. The juror also claimed he'd conducted legal research on his own. If true, both of those things would have constituted a violation of his oath as a juror, since jurors are instructed not to talk to anybody about the case, except other jurors during deliberations, and not to seek outside information. They're supposed to make their decision based on what is presented in court, including the law as explained to them by the judge.

Ron and I knew we had a big problem, and we immediately called to set up a meeting with the federal prosecution team – U.S. Attorney Brent Ward, Richard Lambert, and Dave Schwendiman – to discuss what we should do. Soon we were all in Brent's office. It was a tough situation. We had all just been through a lengthy and intense high-profile trial, and we knew that this juror information had the potential of unraveling it all, as the defense attorneys would certainly use it to try to overturn the verdicts and ask for a new trial.

While I regretted sending Ron out to talk to the jurors, we all felt there was only one ethical thing to do now – disclose the information. The only question was whether to disclose it initially to Judge Jenkins alone, or whether at the same time we should notify defense counsel for the Singers and Swapps.

Someone made the point that, since we were all in agreement that we had an ethical obligation to disclose the information to the defense, why should we wait? So we decided to notify the judge in writing and send copies to all defense counsel. I say "we" decided because we all agreed on what should happen, but in truth, the decision was U.S. Attorney Brent Ward's to make.

As predicted, John Bucher, Addam Swapp's attorney, made a motion for a hearing to take testimony from the juror, in hopes of getting evidence of juror misconduct that could result in setting aside the guilty verdicts. At this point, it seemed quite plausible that we might have to retry the entire case.

Judge Jenkins decided to bring the juror into chambers, with all counsel present, and question him under oath about any outside contact or research he may have done during the trial. To our surprise, the juror reported that he had not actually done either, which put the matter to rest. We were of course relieved at having dodged a bullet. When we'd made the decision to disclose the information about the juror, we knew we could be facing a much different result.[36]

After the federal trial ended, it was time to proceed with the state trial for the killing of Lieutenant Fred House. Whom should we charge, and with what level of homicide? Midway through the federal trial, after Addam had testified and maintained his defiant stance that everything he

---

[36] Given the high stakes involved, I was pleased that Brent Ward did not hesitate to take the ethical path, no matter the consequences.

had done was justified, we had made our decision: All three – Addam Swapp, Jonathan Swapp, and Tim Singer – would be charged with second-degree murder.

While it was clear that Tim Singer had fired the fatal shot, it didn't seem right that he alone should be held accountable for Fred House's death. After all, Addam was clearly the leader of the group and in control of all decisions on the property. Tim was a follower and only at that window with a rifle because Addam had told him to cover them that morning as they went out to milk the goat. Addam was the one who had insisted on playing the deadly cat-and-mouse game with law enforcement officers, and he, more than anyone else, had set in motion the series of events that resulted in Fred's tragic death.

So while the evidence of intentional killing was weak – evidence that would be necessary in order to prove capital murder – we felt that we could hang our hat on another provision of Utah's homicide law, called "depraved indifference to human life." If we could prove that Addam and the others had acted with depraved indifference to human life, we could convict them of second-degree murder, punishable by five years to life in prison, without having to prove that they intentionally caused Fred's death.

This theory of murder – depraved indifference – wasn't dependent on who fired the fatal shot. In fact, it was conceivable that the jury might find Tim guilty of manslaughter, a lesser degree of homicide, for recklessly causing the death of Fred House, but still find Addam guilty of murder on a theory that he acted with a depraved indifference to human life. It also fit the conduct of Jonathan Swapp, who had also, we now knew, fired three shots during the shootout. Jonathan was Addam's right-hand man throughout the 13-day standoff, and he encouraged and aided in the events leading to the tragic death of Lt. House.

By charging under this theory of murder, we could argue to the jury that it was predictable that the standoff would result in the death of an officer, given the group's continual use and threatened use of deadly weapons. We felt that was enough to demonstrate that the defendants acted with depraved indifference to human life, and it would allow us to hold accountable all three who participated in the deadly shootout.

The state trial for the murder of Fred House was held in the old Summit County Courthouse in Coalville, Utah, in late 1988, before Third District Judge Michael Murphy. It began just after Thanksgiving and ended a few days before Christmas.

Not all the drama occurred inside the courtroom. We got word, just as the trial was about to begin, that a jail inmate claimed he had overheard Addam and Jonathan Swapp plotting a jailbreak, allegedly with the help of a motorcycle gang. We didn't worry too much about it, but the Sheriff beefed up jail security just in case. We gave it slightly more credence when Ron Miller went to drop some documents off at one of the defense attorney's offices, and there were several motorcycles parked outside – likely just a coincidence, and, fortunately, there was no escape attempt during the trial.

Dave Schwendiman and I divided up the witnesses and put on the case, which had a lot of the same witnesses and evidence as the federal trial. During the defense case, we took the trial outside into the parking lot for a demonstration, and the FBI was required to simulate the noise they blared toward the compound during the standoff.

Towards the end of the trial, one of Fred House's relatives who was watching the proceedings reported that he had heard someone in the hallway threaten me – something along the lines of "If someone is going to take care of Horton, they ought to do it quickly before the case is over and it's too late." I didn't take it too seriously, although I did mention it to Ron Miller, who was armed and staying in the motel room next to mine. It was the only time during my career that I was made aware of any threat, and this one was pretty oblique.

When both sides were through with the evidence, we made our final arguments, and then the case was in the hands of the jury.

Under Utah law, killing with depraved indifference and killing recklessly are closely related concepts, and the jury ultimately gave Addam Swapp and Tim Singer the benefit of the doubt and convicted them of manslaughter rather than murder.[37] Jonathan Swapp, who was neither the leader of the group nor the one who fired the fatal shot, was convicted of negligent homicide, a lesser offense.[38]

While we were disappointed that the jury had convicted Jonathan only of negligent homicide, and hadn't convicted Addam of murder, we did feel that justice had been done in one respect: Addam had been convicted of the same level of offense as Tim, and nothing less. Plus, given the fact that Addam had been convicted of all federal charges and sentenced to a long stretch in federal prison – and that Judge Michael Murphy had ordered his state sentence to be served at the end of his federal sentence – Addam would likely spend decades behind bars for his crimes.

During the many months I was immersed in this case, there were times when I felt an almost overwhelming sense of sadness for what had happened up in Marion that January. It was heartbreaking to see the effect of this crime on the House family, and I felt so bad for Fred's widow, their children, and his brothers and sisters.

While it wasn't unusual for me to empathize with victims' family members, I must confess that I also felt sympathy for those whom Addam had led astray through his religious posturing, his escalation of violence, and his unwillingness to listen to reason and end the standoff. It was heartrending to see his own young children crying and saying goodbye to their father as he was led away to prison following his federal convictions. He was given so many chances to end the standoff and avoid this tragedy. In his letter, Governor Bangerter had virtually begged Addam to end it, if only for the sake of his own children. But Addam was not willing

---

[37] Murder carried a maximum sentence of life in prison, while manslaughter carried a maximum term of 15 years.

[38] Negligent homicide, a misdemeanor, carried a maximum sentence of one year.

to budge from "his stand," and in the process, he created so much grief and heartache for so many – not only in Fred House's family, but also in his own.

And then there was Tim. While Addam had brought about his own ruin – had virtually insisted on it – Tim was in a much different position. In a sense, he was also one of Addam's victims, for without Addam's provocative and dangerous posturing, I doubt that Tim would have ever been at that window with a rifle in his hands that morning.

By this point in my career, I had spent eight years prosecuting homicide cases, and Tim Singer stood apart from the many vicious killers I had prosecuted. He was raised by parents who were constantly at odds with the "outside world." He was brought up with strident fundamentalist Mormon beliefs, and isolated from others in the community. In television news interviews, his father, John Singer, had forcefully asserted his right to use deadly force against those in authority who might try to take any action against him. When things finally came to a head and officers tried to serve him with an arrest warrant, John Singer pulled a gun on them and was shot and killed.

Tim was a young boy at the time, only 11 years old, and he watched it happen outside his window. He was then raised by his mother on a catechism of hatred against church and secular authorities, neighbors, and other "enemies." She constantly reinforced the message that John Singer had been "murdered" by state officials.

Then, as I understand it, when he was about 16 years old, Tim started to rebel and break away somewhat from the family. But shortly afterwards, he was injured in a logging accident and paralyzed from the waist down. His mother reinforced the notion that his injury was due to his having broken away from the family's correct teachings and way of life. After the accident, he became more dependent on the family and more socially isolated.

And then Addam Swapp came onto the scene, held himself out as a "savior," and led members of the family, and Tim specifically, into an armed resistance of officers after bombing the church and declaring holy war on the world – "church, state and nation." And to cap it off, Addam taught that all this destruction and death would not only be God's will, but would also lead to the resurrection of Tim's father, John Singer.

It seemed to me that Tim Singer had never had much of a shot at life, and when the trial was over, Dave Schwendiman and I wrote him a letter in prison. We told him that while he had to pay for the part he played in the tragic death of Fred House, we as his prosecutors did not see him as a bad or vicious person, and wished him well.[39]

This was the only time I ever sent a convicted prisoner a letter of encouragement. Dave and I never heard back from Tim.[40]

---

[39] In 2002, I attended a seminar at the University of Utah on the topic of "Restorative Justice," which emphasizes the possibility of reconciliation between offenders and victims' family members, through face-to-face encounters. I couldn't help but think of Tim. After the seminar ended, I wrote a letter to a member of Fred House's family explaining the concept, and enclosed a copy of the letter Dave and I had written to Tim. I offered to arrange a meeting where they could sit down and talk with Tim, but I later heard back that the family was not then inclined to take that path.

[40] Tim Singer was released from prison in October of 2006, having completed both his federal and state sentences. From the time of his arrest, Addam Swapp spent over 25 years in federal and state custody, prior to his release on parole in July of 2013. Jonathan Swapp was released in 1997 after serving his federal and state sentences.

CHAPTER 12

The *Bloundt* Case:
Prosecuting a Child Killer, Getting Cross-Wise with a Supreme Court Justice

ON SUNDAY, AUGUST 7, 1988, in Vernal, Utah, 6-year-old Victoria Lassen went out to play and never came home. When her parents discovered her missing, they frantically called the police, who started canvassing the neighborhood. Officers spoke to several people in the area who said they'd seen Victoria earlier in the day. One of them was Robert Bloundt, a 16-year-old neighbor boy and friend of Victoria's older brother. Bloundt told one of the officers that he had seen Victoria earlier in the day when he was on the roof of a shed behind his house. He said he had no idea where she was now, and offered to assist the police in their attempts to locate her.

After several agonizing days of searching by the police and the community, there was still no sign of Victoria. With no leads, the police decided to go back and take complete statements from the people who said they had seen her the day she disappeared. It was now Friday, August 12 – five days after Victoria had disappeared. One of the officers was assigned to go over to Robert Bloundt's house and ask him to come in for additional questioning. Bloundt answered the door and agreed to come down to the station with the officer and make a complete statement.

The interview was recorded, and during questioning, Bloundt appeared nervous and changed some of the details of his story. The officer became suspicious and gave Bloundt his Miranda warnings. After waiving his right to remain silent, Bloundt agreed to talk, and eventually admitted that he had kidnapped, sexually abused, and murdered Victoria. He also agreed to take officers to a mountainous area known as Little Brush Creek, to show them where he had hidden her body.

When they got to the scene, officers found Victoria's body under some brush inside a pillow case, with a sock tied around her neck. Officers then began the grisly task of processing the scene and recovering the child's body, while others drove Bloundt back to the station. There, they took a videotaped statement from him, in which he described in detail what he had done to Victoria.

In that statement, he told the police that he had seen the victim out in the alleyway that day, and invited her to come inside his house. Since he was a friend of her older brother, Victoria trusted him and agreed to accompany him inside. After spending about 90 minutes together in the house, Bloundt forced Victoria into his mother's car and drove her up into the mountains. During the 12-mile drive, Victoria was crying and begging to go home.

When Bloundt got to Little Brush Creek, he took Victoria out of the car by forcing her into a large pillowcase, carried her a distance, and then repeatedly sexually molested her. He first tried to kill her by bludgeoning her over the head with sticks and choking her with his hands, but when he let her go, she regained consciousness. He then took one of her socks and tied it like a tourniquet around her neck, pulling it as tight as he could, until he strangled her to death. When she finally stopped struggling, he placed her body back in the pillowcase and tried to hide it under some brush. He then jumped into his car and drove back home in time to speak to officers who were looking for Victoria that afternoon. At that point, he pretended he wanted to help them find her, and joined in the search.

After taking the videotaped statement, officers arrested Bloundt and called the Attorney General's Office, bypassing the local county attorney who had no experience handling murder cases. It was the summer of 1988, and I had just finished the preliminary hearing in the Singer-Swapp murder case, which was going to go to trial in Summit County later in the year. Since Bloundt was in custody, we needed to move quickly to file criminal charges.

Detective Rick Hawkins of the Vernal Police Department drove to my house in Salt Lake late on a Friday afternoon to drop off all the police reports, lab reports, crime scene photos and witness statements, so I could review them and prepare the charging documents over the weekend. He also brought with him a photo of a beautiful little girl – a picture of Victoria taken a few months earlier. It was a heartbreaking case, and while all the murder cases I handled were tragic, the ones involving child victims like Victoria were always the hardest.

The following Monday morning, Attorney General David Wilkinson and I drove to Vernal to file the charges. Even though Bloundt was a juvenile, Utah law allowed us to file charges against him in the adult system, because he had passed his 16th birthday and was charged with serious felonies, and these were as serious as they got – capital murder, child kidnapping, and aggravated sexual abuse of a child.

Having reviewed all the police reports, witness statements, lab reports, and the audio and video tapes of Bloundt's confession, I knew the police had done a good job investigating the case. I also knew that the attorney assigned to represent Bloundt would likely file motions to suppress his statements as well as the physical evidence that resulted from his statements, but I was confident that the evidence would all eventually be ruled properly obtained and admissible.

After filing the charges, I met with Chief Robert Downard of the Vernal Police Department, Detective Rick Hawkins, and the officers involved in the investigation. I told them two things I was pretty sure of:

First, we were going to be able to convict Bloundt of capital murder, and second, even though the crimes he committed were horrific, Bloundt would never be executed, because he was barely 16 years old at the time of the murder.[41]

Bloundt's lawyer had a couple of cards to play – that Bloundt should be tried in juvenile court rather than in adult court, and that the evidence should be suppressed because Bloundt was a juvenile and shouldn't have been interviewed by the police without having one of his parents or his lawyer present.

Sure enough, the first motion the defense filed was to transfer the case back to juvenile court. While Utah law allowed the direct filing of capital charges against a 16-year-old, it also had a provision that allowed a juvenile court judge to recall the case to the juvenile court system. If the case were to go through juvenile court, the most that could happen to Bloundt would be secure confinement in a juvenile facility for about 5 years, until he turned 21, at which time the juvenile court would lose jurisdiction over him.

Because of the defense motion to recall the case to the juvenile court, it was assigned to Judge Leonard Gustavson of the Eighth District Juvenile Court, a judge I had never encountered before. Before the hearing began, the judge called both counsel into his chambers, and told us that given Bloundt's age, he intended to recall the case to the juvenile court. He said that I could later go through the process of trying to certify Bloundt to stand trial as an adult, if I chose to do so. I asked the judge if he would at least allow me to put on my evidence before making a final decision on the recall. He said he would, but suggested I was wasting my time.

I had reviewed the videotape of Bloundt's confession, and felt that if

---

[41] Not long before this murder was committed, the United States Supreme Court had forbidden the execution of offenders who were under the age of 16 at the times their crimes were committed. *Thompson v. Oklahoma,* 487 U.S. 815 (1988). Seventeen years later, the Supreme Court prohibited the execution of all juveniles who committed their crimes when they were under the age of 18. *Roper v. Simmons,* 543 U.S. 551 (2005).

I could play it for the judge, he would see that the crime was so heinous that there was no way it should be recalled to the juvenile court system. I had seen a lot of confessions to murder, and this was one of the most chilling and cold-blooded, notwithstanding Bloundt's age. It was a monstrous crime.

I put on the evidence, and it changed Judge Gustavson's mind. He ruled that there would be no recall to juvenile court, and that Bloundt would stand trial as an adult. It was a huge setback for the defense. Because the evidence of Bloundt's guilt was overwhelming, the defense's only hope for lenient treatment was to get the case moved to the juvenile court system. Faced with the possibility of a death penalty if Bloundt stayed in the adult system, his lawyer appealed Judge Gustavson's decision.

During the next year and a half, while we continued to fight the legal battles over the admissibility of the evidence and the appropriateness of trying Bloundt as an adult, my personal circumstances changed. I got married, and my first daughter was born in July of 1989, about a year after Victoria was killed.

Prosecuting murder cases does affect you psychologically. Every time you drive by a location where you know a murder took place, you can't help but note it. Although we lived near some beautiful canyons, I tended to avoid going up certain ones, because I knew where people had been killed and where bodies had been recovered. And because of my experience handling the Bloundt case, when my daughter turned six, I was particularly uneasy about her safety, and I felt some sense of relief when she made it to her 7th birthday without anything bad happening to her. It wasn't particularly logical, but it was an almost unconscious reaction to knowing that another little 6-year-old girl hadn't been so lucky.

In the *Bloundt* case, it took about two years to resolve all the preliminary legal issues. In addition to the issue of whether Bloundt should be transferred to the juvenile court system, the defense also wanted the judge to suppress the statements Bloundt had made to the police confessing to the murder. If they had been successful in suppressing the confessions, it would have meant that all the evidence obtained as a result of the confession had to be excluded as well, including possibly even the victim's body, so the stakes were high.

The day before the suppression hearing, I drove out to Vernal to meet with all the officers whose testimony I would need for the hearing. Since I was going to be gone a couple of days, I decided to drop my wife and daughter off at my in-laws' house in Coalville. The car was loaded pretty full with baby equipment such as playpens and the like. After I dropped them off, I headed over the mountain to Vernal. About two hours later, I got the sinking feeling that my suit wasn't hanging up behind me in the car. I had totally forgotten to bring it. I was going to have to scrounge something up in Vernal. At least I had a day before the hearing to come up with something.

The next day, I had interviews with the various Vernal officers who were involved in taking Bloundt's confessions and recovering the evidence from the crime scene. I put the word out that I was looking for something that would pass as a suit to wear in court the next day. One by one the officers came in, and while they were all willing to lend me what they had in their wardrobes, they were all pretty big guys, and I was going to look really silly wearing their clothes. Fortunately, the last officer I interviewed that day was about my size, maybe a little smaller. Next morning, he brought in some clothes for me to wear that didn't fit too well or match too well, but at least I had something other than Levis and a T-shirt to wear in court. After a day-long suppression hearing, the judge ruled that the confession and evidence were all properly obtained, and that they would be admissible at trial.

Over the next several months it became clear that Bloundt's lawyer wasn't going to win any of his motions, and that Bloundt would inevitably be convicted. In June of 1990, he agreed to plead guilty to capital murder, child kidnapping, and aggravated sexual abuse of a child, in exchange for our agreement not to seek the death penalty. It was clear at the time of the plea that the entire basis for our agreement not to seek the death penalty was the fact that Bloundt was barely 16 when he committed the crime. While it was true that, having reached the age of 16, he was eligible for the death penalty, we factored in that he had only turned 16 a few days before the murder.

On November 14, 1990, Eighth District Judge Patrick Smethsted sentenced Bloundt to a term of up to life in prison for capital murder, a term of 15 years to life for child kidnapping, and a term of 9 years to life for aggravated sexual abuse of a child. The judge also ordered that the sentences run consecutively – that is, one after the other – rather than concurrently. It meant that Bloundt would have to serve a minimum of 24 years in prison before he could be paroled by the Utah Board of Pardons and Parole. At the sentencing hearing, Judge Smethsted told Bloundt it could well mean that he would spend the rest of his life in prison, and that, in the judge's opinion, given the cruelty and depravity of the crime, that sentence would not be too severe a punishment for what he did.

After sentencing, I sent a letter to the Board of Pardons, describing the crime and its devastating effect on the Lassen family, and recommending that Bloundt remain in prison for the rest of his life. At that point, it appeared that the case was over, but it wasn't. Little did I know that something I had done the year before – something totally unrelated to the case – might play a part in what would happen next.

Cut back to December of 1988, about four months after I was assigned to the Bloundt case. I happened to read an article in the *Utah Bar Journal*, the official publication of the Utah State Bar, by Justice Michael Zimmerman of the Utah Supreme Court, entitled "Professional Standards Versus Personal Ethics: The Lawyer's Dilemma." While the focus of the article concerned the need for ethical practitioners in the area of civil litigation, Justice Zimmerman did mention criminal defense attorneys, and seemed to suggest that they could operate free of ethical constraints.

It concerned me, not only because my inspiration for becoming a lawyer was the portrayal of an ethical defense attorney, Atticus Finch in *To Kill a Mockingbird*, but also because I knew several ethical members of the defense Bar in Salt Lake who were troubled by the article. I thought these ethical defense lawyers should be the ones held up as role models for young lawyers – not less ethical practitioners interested in winning at any cost.

After speaking to two more ethical defense attorneys who told me they were very offended by the article, I decided to send a letter to Justice Zimmerman. If this many ethical defense attorneys were also troubled by what Justice Zimmerman had said, maybe it was time for someone to speak up and say something to him.

My first draft of the letter used phrases such as, "I take issue with your characterization that criminal defense attorneys may operate free from ethical considerations." I decided the tone was too confrontational, so I worked on a more diplomatic approach. Maybe I was misinterpreting his words. Maybe the *Bar Journal* took his statements out of context. It did say at the beginning of the article that it contained excerpts from a law school commencement speech that Justice Zimmerman had given.

Besides, I didn't want to offend him. I just wanted him to clarify his article and reinforce the idea that defense attorneys should be ethical. After all, the purpose of his remarks was to encourage ethical behavior among members of the Bar, and I doubted that he really intended to sanction less-than-ethical conduct by criminal defense attorneys, although his words were being taken that way by many.

I worked the draft over until I felt reasonably comfortable with it, although I recognized the danger of lecturing a Supreme Court justice on ethics. Still, this was a private communication between the two of us, so how much trouble could I really get into? Either he would agree that his words could be misinterpreted and clarify that portion of his article, or he would tell me he thought my concerns didn't merit any response on his part. Either way, I could live with the outcome, and would have at least informed him of a concern that was widespread in the legal community, albeit one that no one seemed willing to broach with him, I suppose for fear of alienating a Supreme Court justice.

By late January of 1989, after hearing yet another defense attorney express displeasure with Zimmerman's article, I sent the letter. About a month later, I received a letter in reply, which was very professional, but seemed to me to have an undercurrent of annoyance to it. He said he was hard-put to understand how anyone could have so misinterpreted his comments, and went on to say, "I suppose, however, that those who do not like the role criminal defense lawyers must play under our system, or who think that certain members of that group violate the Code of Professional Responsibility, might read the article and leap to the mistaken impression that I was granting them license to do as they please."

I took the first part of the sentence as a bit of a jab. Perhaps I just didn't like the role criminal defense lawyers played in the system. I guess he assumed I might be an overzealous prosecutor, rather than one who not only appreciated the role criminal defense lawyers played in the system, but who had started out with aspirations of playing that role myself.

The last paragraph of Justice Zimmerman's article surprised me. He said, "In the event that others might share your concern, I am taking the liberty of forwarding a copy of your letter and of my reply to the *Utah Bar Journal*. If they conclude that there is a real danger that my views can be read as you suggest, then I will request that they publish our correspondence."

While this could potentially move the discussion from the private to the public arena, I knew there was virtually no chance that the *Utah Bar Journal* editorial staff would agree with me that there was a real concern, when Justice Zimmerman had declared that the issue I raised was of no real consequence. I knew the score. The letters would never be published, and that was probably for the best. After all, had I wanted to engage in a public discourse, I could have simply sent a letter to the editor to the *Bar Journal*, rather than sending a private letter to Justice Zimmerman.[42]

So the matter was closed. Or so I thought. But several months later I ran into an old friend, Max Miller, and in casual conversation I mentioned to him my concern about the statements in Justice Zimmerman's article. Max was very interested to hear about it, and told me that he was the Chair of the Government Law Section of the Utah State Bar. He said that several members of that section were upset with the article, and had talked about doing something about it themselves. I told him about the exchange of letters, and Max said he didn't think it was fair that I should be characterized as an overzealous prosecutor with an overactive imagination, when so many other lawyers felt the same way. At Max's request, I gave him a copy of the letters.

Shortly after our discussion, I heard back from Max. The Government Law Section of the Bar wanted to ask the *Utah Bar Journal* to publish the letters which Justice Zimmerman and I had exchanged. Max said he would first send a letter to Zimmerman informing him that several lawyers Max had spoken with had concerns similar to those I had expressed, and asking for Zimmerman's permission to have the *Bar Journal* publish the letters. Max kept me informed of what the Government Law Section was doing, and I didn't object. At this point, I was convinced that there were enough people concerned about Zimmerman's article that the issue shouldn't just be brushed aside.

So in June of 1989, Max sent the letter to Justice Zimmerman, asking for his permission to publish the exchange of letters. Justice Zimmerman responded quickly, saying that he had suggested initially that the *Bar Journal* might want to publish the correspondence. He went on to say, "Apparently, they chose not to do so. However, you have my permission to take another

---

[42] I must admit, though, that after continuing to hear attorneys voice the same concerns about Zimmerman's article, I considered sending a letter to the *Bar Journal,* encouraging the editors to publish our exchange of letters. I had even drafted one, but in the end decided not to send it.

try at it." And so in the August/September 1989 edition of the *Utah Bar Journal*, the letters that Justice Zimmerman and I had exchanged were printed side by side, with a statement at the top from the editors that they were publishing the letters at the request of the Government Law Section of the Bar – lest it appear, I suppose, that they themselves had made the decision to publish them.[43]

After the letters were published, I got feedback from other lawyers that generally fell into two categories: 1) Thanks for being willing to step up and tell Justice Zimmerman what so many people were thinking but reluctant to say; and 2) If Zimmerman is annoyed or embarrassed by the incident, it might not bode well for you in your next oral argument before the Supreme Court. One of the lawyers in my division re-printed the page with our letters and superimposed at the top a title from an unrelated article later in the publication, called, "Lessons from a Drowning Dog." It was clever, and I got a kick out of it, but it also made the point: How can you take on a Supreme Court justice in public and not pay a price?

I had to admit that, in my enthusiasm to see if I could persuade Justice Zimmerman to clarify his remarks, I hadn't really focused on how it could affect any future appearances I might have before the Supreme Court. Trial prosecutors generally don't do appeals, and I didn't do any when at the D.A.'s Office – nobody did. All appeals from felony cases throughout the state were handled by the Attorney General's Appeals Division. But now that I had joined the Attorney General's Office, I was able to handle the appeals from my own trials. Our Appeals Division didn't seem to mind, and I enjoyed the experience. I had appeared before the Utah Court of Appeals a few times, and once before the U.S. Court of Appeals for the Tenth Circuit, in Denver. But I had yet to appear before the Utah Supreme Court.

---

[43] I don't know if my letter had anything to do with it, but I did note with interest an article in the *Salt Lake Tribune* the following May, when a new batch of lawyers was being sworn in. The article said that Justice Zimmerman spoke at the ceremony, and told the new lawyers that criminal law cannot function without lawyers zealously defending clients, but lawyers must be more than "amoral hired guns." and "have an equally important role as ethical human beings whose ultimate aim is to serve justice." I liked the sound of it. It had a nice Atticus Finch ring to it.

So how was this going to play out? I certainly hadn't set out to embarrass Justice Zimmerman. But had I? I re-read my letter. I had to acknowledge that it was pretty much a lecture on ethics to a Supreme Court justice. Maybe I should have toned it down. Did I really need to quote precedent from the United States Supreme Court about the ethical duty of defense attorneys? And maybe I should have told Max Miller I preferred to let sleeping dogs lie, rather than encourage the Government Law Section to charge up the hill behind me, to vindicate that I was not the only one concerned about the issue. In any case, it was too late now. What was done was done, and I'd just have to deal with it, if and when I ever appeared before Utah's high court.

Which brings us back to the Bloundt case. As I mentioned, after Bloundt pled guilty in 1990, Judge Smethsted sentenced him to a term of up to life in prison for capital murder, 15 years to life for child kidnapping, and 9 years to life for aggravated sexual abuse of a child – all consecutive sentences. A few weeks later, Bloundt's lawyer filed a notice of appeal to the Utah Supreme Court, alleging that the sentences were excessive, given the fact that Bloundt was only 16 when he committed the crimes.

Oh boy, it looks like I'm going to be seeing Justice Zimmerman in court, and sooner than I anticipated. Since my office was at the Capitol, where the Supreme Court was also located, I occasionally saw the various justices coming and going, and had developed a passing rapport with a couple of them, but Justice Zimmerman had always kept to himself. Since the *Bar Journal* had published our letters, I had seen Justice Zimmerman a couple of times in the elevator at the Capitol, and it had been pretty chilly in there.[44] I wondered how chilly it would be in court.

When the day for oral argument arrived, I was excited and a bit nervous to be making my first appearance before the Utah Supreme Court.

---

[44] While my exchange of letters with Justice Zimmerman created a distance between us at the time, a few years later we were both invited to participate in a symposium which brought together experts in philosophy, behavioral genetics, and law to comment on the possible use and misuse of genetic information in the criminal justice system, and we actually became friends.

I had been present for oral arguments involving some of my cases, including the Arthur Gary Bishop capital murder case, but this was to be the first time I would be appearing as lead appellate counsel for the State.

It was a short walk from my office on the second floor of the Capitol out into the Rotunda and up the broad marble staircase to the ornate courtroom on the third floor where the Utah Supreme Court heard cases. The room itself was steeped in history, with a high bench where the five justices sat, surrounded by large paintings depicting scenes from Utah's pioneer past.

I had prepared the State's brief in opposition to the one Bloundt's lawyer filed, in which he complained that Judge Smethsted hadn't sufficiently considered Bloundt's young age when he sentenced him to consecutive minimum mandatory terms totaling 24 years, on top of the life sentence for capital murder. I felt confident that the sentences were justified, given the enormity of the crimes Bloundt had committed against a helpless 6-year-old girl. The only thing that really concerned me was whether my public dialogue with Justice Zimmerman might somehow become a factor.

At oral argument, Bloundt's lawyer went first, and made his pitch to the Court – the judge must not have adequately considered Bloundt's age when he gave him long consecutive sentences. Then it was my turn. I felt my argument was going pretty well when, near the end, Justice Zimmerman interrupted me and, peering down over his glasses, said, "Counsel, we don't see sentences this severe in Utah."

It struck me as an odd statement. After all, since he was 16 when he committed the crimes, Bloundt was constitutionally eligible for the death penalty, as it existed at that time. I wondered if Justice Zimmerman was really challenging my position, or if he was actually lobbing me a softball. It was the perfect lead-in to drive home how terrible the crime was and how much little Victoria Lassen had suffered.

So I recounted the facts of what Bloundt had done – how he had forced Victoria into his car, driven her against her will twelve miles to

Little Brush Creek as she cried and begged him to take her home; how he had tried to get her out of the car as she kicked and screamed until he finally forced her into a large pillowcase and carried her to a location where he sexually abused her, then carried her to another location and abused her again; how he had struck her repeatedly on the head with large branches and choked her with his hands, trying to kill her; how she had continued to regain consciousness despite his attempts to kill her through choking and bludgeoning her; and how he then took one of her socks, tied it around her neck, and twisted it like a tourniquet, until he finally succeeded in strangling her to death.

As I was driving home these points, I thought I saw in the faces of some of the other justices a recognition that not only was the case horrific enough to justify the sentences given, but that Bloundt was lucky he never faced a jury that might have been inclined to sentence him to death. I couldn't really read Justice Zimmerman's reaction, and I knew enough about the process to realize it's generally a losing game to predict case outcomes based on oral arguments anyway. Too often in the past, cases that appeared to be sure winners or losers for one side or the other had been decided in ways no one had anticipated. Still, I left the Supreme Court that day feeling pretty good. I'd made the points I wanted to make, and had even been aided in the process by Justice Zimmerman's implied question as to what could justify such severe sentences. Now we just had to wait for the Court's decision.

It came in January of 1993.[45] In a 4 to 1 decision, the Utah Supreme Court vacated Bloundt's sentences on what appeared to me then, and still appears to me now, to be a slender reed. The majority said that Judge Smethsted, in imposing consecutive sentences, abused his discretion "in failing to sufficiently consider the defendant's rehabilitative needs in light of his extreme youth and the absence of prior violent crimes." Since the

---

[45] 846 P.2d 1297 (Utah 1993)

one and only reason the State had agreed not to seek the death penalty was Bloundt's age, and since there were numerous attempts by the defense to move the case over to the juvenile court system, by what stretch of the imagination could the judge have overlooked the fact that Bloundt was 16 when determining what sentence to impose?

At the time of sentencing, Judge Smethsted had received a pre-sentence report from Adult Probation and Parole, which concluded that, notwithstanding his young age, Bloundt was an extreme danger to the community, with poor prospects for rehabilitation. Although it was obvious that the judge was aware of Bloundt's age, he did not make an express finding that Bloundt's youth at the time of the crime was a mitigating factor, which the Supreme Court seized on in striking down the sentences. Under Utah law, a particular aggravating or mitigating factor does not control the sentencing outcome, which is based on a judgment call, not on any set formula. So Bloundt's age, standing alone as a mitigating factor, would not have mandated more lenient sentences than the ones that Judge Smethsted imposed.

While I found it odd that the Supreme Court had struck down Blount's sentences on the basis that Judge Smethsted hadn't made a specific finding that Bloundt's youth was a potential mitigating factor, what I found even more anomalous about the decision was the Supreme Court's other holding: That on resentencing, if the trial judge were to again impose the longest minimum mandatory terms for the crimes of child kidnapping and aggravated sexual abuse of a child, "all three terms should be ordered to run concurrently." So they essentially took away from the trial judge the discretion, upon resentencing, to make an independent judgment as to whether the sentences should be concurrent or consecutive.

Appellate courts don't generally substitute their judgment for that of trial judges. If they find an error in the sentencing process, they generally send the case back to the trial judge with instructions to resentence a defendant using the correct standard. By dictating the final sentence, the justices showed that their decision in this case had more to do with their disagreement with the result than with the process, although it was the process that they ostensibly found wanting.

I wasn't the only one who thought the reasoning was flawed. Chief Justice Gordon Hall filed a dissenting opinion[46] in which he said that he found it *"unthinkable that the trial court was not aware of defendant's age or that it was overlooked at the time of sentencing."* He also said, *"In the instant case, since defendant could have been constitutionally subjected to the death penalty, the sentence he did receive was clearly not excessive. Rather, it was wholly consistent with the magnitude of the offenses committed and the accompanying cruelty and depravity."* And finally, he pointed out that the decision whether to impose consecutive sentences *"lies within the discretionary authority of the (trial) court."* But here, curiously, the majority had simply substituted its judgment for that of the trial court, taking away from the trial judge the discretion to decide the appropriate sentence.

So did my public disagreement with Justice Zimmerman affect the outcome of the Bloundt decision? I have no way of knowing what happened in the private deliberations of the justices – what give-and-take took place in their chambers after the oral arguments ended. The opinion was written by Associate Chief Justice Richard Howe, so it wasn't authored by Justice Zimmerman, although he concurred in the majority opinion. All I know is that it seemed like an anomalous decision, particularly when it robbed the trial court of its discretion in the resentencing process.

But the decision had been issued, and in July of 1993, according to the Supreme Court's directive, Bloundt was resentenced, and received concurrent, rather than consecutive, sentences for child kidnapping and aggravated sexual abuse of a child.

After being sent to prison, Bloundt appeared before the Board of Pardons and Parole. The Board of Pardons has the discretion to decide just how much time an inmate will actually spend in prison, within the

---

[46] *Id* at p. 1302

bounds of the sentences legally imposed. The Board reviewed the case and issued its decision, giving Bloundt a sentence of "natural life," meaning that he will spend the rest of his life in prison. The practical effect of that determination was to re-instate Judge Smethsted's original sentence. And, unlike the trial judge's, the Board's decision on the matter was final.

Creighton's father, Creighton C. Horton, M.D.

Creighton's uncle, Robert Horton, who, in the late 1950s and early 60s, starred as scout Flint McCullough in the popular TV series, Wagon Train.

Creighton's bandmates in Ragtime trio, "J.C. Munns & His Boys," 1974
From left, Jay Munns, Dave Ellsworth.

Creighton and Professor Paul Boland at UCLA Law School graduation, 1976.
On right, Creighton's brother, Joe.

Creighton as a rookie prosecutor, 1980.

Creighton's mentor, Dick "Shep" Shepherd, 1980.

Creighton during capital murder trial of Joseph Paul Franklin, 1981.

Prosecution team during capital murder trial of Arthur Gary Bishop, 1984.
From left, after unidentified court official, Robert Stott, Creighton, Tom Vuyk.

Creighton and fellow prosecutor Dave Schwendiman during the
Singer-Swapp murder trial, 1988.

Performing gag songs at a prosecutors conference, 1994.
From left, Creighton, Ginny Christensen and Paul Boyden of the Salt Lake
DA's Office, and Assistant Attorney General Mike Wims.

Assistant Attorney General Rob Lunnen, 1994.

Utah Attorney General Jan Graham at "Honk and Wave" event, campaigning for re-election, with enthusiastic young supporter, 1996.

Comparison photos of Creighton and his look-alike, Tully Cathey, guitarist, composer, and retired music professor, University of Utah. From a training conference presentation, to highlight the fallibility of eyewitness identification that can lead to wrongful convictions.

*Creighton and Mike Wims, playing Ebenezer
Scrooge and Bob Cratchit in a skit for the
Attorney General's Office, December, 1997.*

*Ceremonial signing of Senate Bill 16, Exoneration and Innocence Assistance,
April 15, 2008. From left, Robert Yeates (Executive Director of
Utah Commission on Criminal and Juvenile Justice), Creighton,
Utah Governor Jon Huntsman, Jr., Kirk Torgensen (Chief Deputy Utah
Attorney General), Heather Harris and Katie Monroe (Director of Rocky
Mountain Innocence Center).*

157

The Salt Lake Tribune

Local News TV Today, Page C-11
Theaters

Thursday Morning
September 24, 1981

Section B   Page: One

After Escape Attempt

Franklin Given Life Sentence

By Con Psarras
Tribune Staff Writer

Joseph Paul Franklin will be sentenced to his in prison for the murders of two black joggers gunned down near Liberty Park on the night of Aug. 20, 1980.

A jury of seven men and two women deliberated for about two hours Wednesday before deciding they could not sentence Franklin to death for the murders of Ted Fields, 21, and Dave Martin, 18.

The deliberations began about an hour after Franklin escaped from a courthouse holding cell during a brief recess in the sentencing hearing. The jurors waited for about 20 minutes before frantic lawmen found Franklin hiding near an elevator two floors beneath the crowded courtroom.

The judge said a formal sentencing hearing will be held next Monday when Judge Banks will decide whether Franklin should serve the life prison terms for each killing consecutively or concurrently.

Sits Quietly, Smiling

The 31-year-old defendant sat quietly, smiling, as the court clerk announced that the jury was unable to agree unanimously on the death penalty. Under Utah law, the jury's decision leaves Judge Jay E. Banks with the duty to sentence Franklin to life in prison.

For about 15 shocking moments Wednesday, court officials wondered whether Franklin would receive any sentence at all. The defendant, moments after one of his lawyers finished pleading for mercy, sneaked into a prisoner elevator which links the courthouse to the county jail, and, after hot-wiring elevator controls, descended two floors into another courthouse holding area.

Try to Remove Door

A jail guard captured Franklin as the defendant was attempting to remove pins on hinges to a door leading from the holding area, which connects to the elevator to the public hallway in the courthouse.

Salt Lake County Sheriff Pete Hayward said Franklin used a small metal file to pry apart the elevator door and get it on the third floor of the holding cell, in which he crossed electrical wires to open the jail elevator door and take it to the third floor of the courthouse, two floors beneath Judge Banks' courtroom.

Hundreds of policemen scoured the three block area surrounding the courthouse, searching all moving and parked cars. Courthouse security guards scampered up staircases and down public elevator shafts in a search of the defendant.

Jail guard John Merrick, who had sat behind Franklin during the 15-day trial, found the rangy defendant crouched inside the third-floor holding area a while the jurors sat alone and perplexed in the courtroom, waiting patiently for the proceedings to resume.

Franklin was returned to the courtroom by an angry Sheriff Hayward who sat behind the defendant during the final moments of the day-long sentencing hearing.

Shortly After Speeches

Franklin's escape attempt occurred shortly after speeches by prosecutor Robert L. Stott — who demanded Franklin be sentenced to death — and defense lawyer David E. Yocom, who pleaded for mercy.

Following the attempted escape defense lawyer D. Frank Wilkins delivered a brief statement against capital punishment and Mr. Stott followed with a rebuttal speech, again demanding that Franklin be executed.

The jurors were not told of Franklin's attempted escape, and they were sent into deliberations at 3:30 p.m. returning with their decision against the death penalty at about 6 p.m.

Jury foreman James McCoy said the jurors were unaware of the escape attempt when they deliberated. "We learned of it afterward," he said.

Mr. Stott argued forcefully for the death penalty, raising his voice and slapping the courtroom podium as he described the "horror and brutality" of the sniper murders.

"The joggers, the young victims, were kidding, they were laughing, they were kibitzing, they were just enjoying their lives. They didn't know what hit them, they didn't know who hit them, and they didn't even know why they were hit," he said.

"From the moment that Joseph Paul Franklin stepped into that field and had behind that mound of dirt with a rifle, he himself made the decision to subject himself to the death penalty — nobody forced him to make that decision," the prosecutor argued.

He attacked Franklin's claim that he was accused of the murders in Salt Lake at the time of the murder and because of his racist views, only because he was: "The true victims of circumstance in this crime were Dave Martin and Ted Fields — they were the one's who happened to be in the wrong place at the wrong time with the wrong people," the prosecutor claied.

Prosecutor Begins

In beginning his speech, Mr. Scott told the jury, "You have already locked the

See Page B-2, Column 1

Joseph Paul Franklin smiles as jurors leave courtroom, having decided against death penalty.

Joseph Paul Franklin's courtroom escape | Stott, left, and Creighton C. Horton, | Doug Jigstead. Franklin escaped custo-
is explained to prosecutors Robert L. | right, by jail transportation officer | dy for 15 minutes Wednesday afternoon.

158

The Salt Lake Tribune

Local

Saturday Morning—May 7, 1988
Section B Page 1 Sports is on B-3

Judges Hand Lafferty, Bishop Dates With Death

Killer of Two to Face Firing Squad June 24?

By Paul Rolly
Tribune Staff Writer

PROVO — While condemned murderer Ronald Watson Lafferty peppered the court with obscenities and insults Friday, 4th District Judge J. Boyd Park ordered him to die by firing squad June 24.

Lafferty, a self-proclaimed prophet who received the death sentence for the 1984 ritualistic slashing murders of his sister-in-law, Brenda Lafferty, and her 15-month-old daughter Erika, refused to choose his mode of death, so the judge eventually settled on a firing squad.

"That's one hell of a choice, isn't it," Lafferty sneered at the judge when asked if he would like to die by firing squad or by lethal injection. "I guess old age isn't a choice, huh?"

The law states that if the defendant fails to make a choice, the default method of execution is lethal injection," Deputy Utah County Attorney Craig Madsen told the court.

"Yeah, well f... your lethal injection," Lafferty said. "And f... you too, you jerk . . .," he said to Mr. Madsen.

Noting that Lafferty had earlier indicated he preferred the firing squad to lethal injection, Judge Park ordered the firing squad as the mode of execution.

He signed the death warrant after legal defender Mike Esplin said Lafferty had indicated he no longer wanted to be represented by Mr. Esplin. The attorney said perhaps Lafferty needed some assistance of counsel because he is locked up in death row at the Utah

See B-2, Column 4

'Ready, Anxious' Child Killer To Die by Injection June 10

By Mike Carter
Tribune Staff Writer

Child killer Arthur Gary Bishop, saying his "soul grieves" for the families of his young victims, Friday was ordered to die June 10.

Bishop stood stoically before 3rd District Judge Frank G. Noel while the death warrant was signed and sentence pronounced as his trial defense attorney, Jo Carol Nessel-Sale, wept silently behind him.

Before the sentence was passed, Bishop read a statement again apologizing for the kidnappings and sex-related murders of five young Salt Lake County boys and announcing he was "ready and anxious" to die in hopes that his execution will somehow ease the pain of those families. (See related story).

Bishop, answered several questions posed by the judge in a firm voice and spoke clearly when he stated he preferred lethal injection as the mode of execution. His voice broke once and his hand shook, fluttering the single piece of yellow legal paper, as he read his statement to the judge.

After the statement was read, Judge Noel announced:

"It is the order of this court that the judgment and sentence in this case be . . . executed by the warden of the Utah State Prison on the 10th day of June, 1988." He then signed the death warrant.

Following the 15-minute hearing Friday morning, defense attorney Walter P. Bugden Jr. said there is

"no doubt" about Bishop's sincerity or his conviction to go through with his execution.

"That was a gutsy and courageous thing he did in there," Mr. Bugden said.

Mr. Bugden, who has agreed to represent Bishop in his quest for execution, said it is also unlikely that any third-party actions could successfully stop the execution without Bishop's expressed approval.

The Utah Supreme Court lifted the stay of Bishop's execution and remanded the case to district court for a new death warrant after psychiatrists found him competent to make that decision. He had asked to end his appeals and be allowed to accept his five death sentences after his appeal was denied last January.

Bishop told Judge Noel Friday he does not want to die. But he said he believes he should be executed for his crimes.

Mr. Bugden said Bishop was impressed by statements made by the families of the victims in the Ogden Hi-Fi killings after the August execution of Dale Pierre Selby. He hopes his death will have the same affect on the families of the five boys be murdered.

"He feels that if [his death] will help those people, then so be it," Mr. Bugden said ". . . It is his hope his death will add finality to the nightmare of these families. He truly believes it is the appropriate sanction in his circumstances."

Child murderer Arthur Gary Bishop reads a lengthy letter in court | before being granted his wish and given a June 10 execution date.

Ceremonies To Salute

'I Wish I Could . . . Change What Happened,' Says Bishop

Here is a verbatim transcript of . . . offer some acceptable excuse for my . . . now. Only now am I beginning to re- . . . that in giving my life, these five inno- . . . die. Though a prison existence seems

Singer-Swapp Trio Is Arraigned on Murder Charges

Police Arrest Singer Guest in Arson Try

By Mike Carter
Tribune Staff Writer

COALVILLE, Summit County — Three members of the polygamous Singer-Swapp clan were arraigned Tuesday on charges of murdering Department of Corrections Lt. Fred House following a 13-day standoff at their ranch last January.

Meanwhile, Summit County lawmen were investigating an apparent attempted arson at the Marion LDS Stake Center the clan bombed Jan. 16 as the first salvo of the religious battle they believed would end in the resurrection of slain patriarch John Singer.

Summit County Attorney Robert Adkins confirmed deputies arrested a 34-year-old Salt Lake City man who had been staying on the Singers' Marion, Summit County, compound after a burglary alarm sounded in the church Monday night about 11 p.m. No formal charges were filed Tuesday.

Addam Swapp, 27, his 21-year-old brother, Jonathon, and John Timothy Singer, 22, the brother of Addam's two wives, were arraigned on second-degree murder charges.

Third Circuit Judge Maurice D. Jones set a tentative preliminary hearing for the three defendants for Sept. 27.

The men are being held without bail in the Salt Lake County Jail. Judge Jones said he would hold bail hearings if requested, but noted those proceedings would be "academic."

All three defendants have been convicted in U.S. District Court for Utah on charges of attempting to kill FBI agents and the church bombing. Addam Swapp has been sentenced to 15 years in a federal penitentiary; Jonathon and John Timothy received 10-year sentences. Vicki Singer, the group matriarch, was given five years in prison for her role in the standoff and bombing.

Each could now receive an additional term of five years to life in prison, with enhancements for using a firearm during the commission of a felony.

Judge Jones appointed attorneys for the men and entertained a state's motion stipulating future circuit court hearings would be held in Salt Lake City. He said he would grant the motion only if all of the attorneys and their clients agreed to those arrangements.

The judge appointed the same attorneys who handled the cases in the monthlong federal trial — William Morrison and John Bucher representing Addam Swapp and G. Fred Metos as John Timothy's attorney.

In the only surprise to come out of the brief hearing

Tuesday, Jonathon Swapp fired the attorney who represented him and insisted on hiring his own lawyer, even though he said he has no money.

He presented to the court L. Charles Spafford, who along with his father, Earl Spafford, have taken over his defense.

He told the court that he had a "problem" with the representation of Park City attorney Bruce Savage. "It's a conflict," he told the court.

Judge Jones seemed surprised by Swapp's insistence that he be allowed to provide his own lawyer. Some family members in the courtroom mumbled uncomfortably when he told the court he would hire a lawyer.

"Mr. Savage is an excellent attorney," the judge told the defendant, noting Swapp's request is an unusual one given that he is indigent. He made it clear to Swapp that he would have to pay for the lawyer himself. Swapp had told the court he had no assets.

"It's your dilemma, Mr. Swapp," Judge Jones said. "And yours," he said to Mr. Spafford.

And he made it clear to the defense attorney that, "if you're in, you're in. . ." For the duo to resign as Swapp's attorneys, the judge said it would require "a highly unusual set of circumstances."

Mr. Spafford told the judge that he and his father were "committed to [Jonathon Swapp's] cause."

After the hearing, Mr. Spafford declined to discuss how or if he will be paid. "I just don't think that's important," he said. "Further comment would be inappropriate."

Summit County Attorney Robert Adkins said the coun-

See B-4, Column 4

John Timothy Singer   Jonathon Swapp

Addam Swapp is escorted into court Tuesday for arraignment. Swapp and brother Jonathon, and John Timothy Singer, are charged with murdering Lt. Fred House.

—Tribune Staff Photo by Al Hartmann

CHAPTER 13

Prosecuting
White-Collar Crime:
A Tale of Two Cons

IT WAS 1989, AND I HAD MY HANDS FULL with a couple of interesting homicide investigations, as well as the Bloundt murder case, when my supervisor told me that I was being assigned to handle an insurance fraud case. I would be helping out the Cache County Attorney, in northern Utah, who had requested our office's assistance.

My initial reaction was that it was going to be hard for me to get very excited about the case, since it would likely distract me from the much more compelling cases I was working on. While I had handled a few white-collar cases in the D.A.'s Office, they weren't my forte. If I was being assigned to help out because our office had special expertise in complex white-collar cases, I wasn't sure they were sending the right guy.

THE SELIGMAN CASE: HOW TO MOTIVATE A VIOLENT
CRIME PROSECUTOR TO DO WHITE COLLAR CASES

Dick Seligman was an insurance agent who lived in Logan, a mid-sized town in Northern Utah, and attended an LDS Ward there, presenting himself as a faithful member of the Mormon Church. By doing so, he gained the confidence of many elderly members of the congregation and then talked them into buying annuity policies.

One of his victims was a woman who had been a waitress for more than 30 years. She had saved for her retirement out of the money she made from waitressing and from the tips she received. At Seligman's urging, she had purchased an annuity policy to provide her a guaranteed monthly income for the rest of her life.

Another of Seligman's victims was an elderly man, a widower who lived in a modest house across the street from the Mormon Temple in Logan. When Agent Ron Miller of our office and I went to interview him, he put it succinctly.

"Dick screwed me," he said.

Indeed he had, just as he had an elderly couple across town, who also lost tens of thousands of dollars.[47]

And then there was the woman whose husband had recently died in a nursing home. Shortly before the man died, Dick went to the nursing home and knelt at the bedside of the dying man to pray with the soon-to-be widow. After saying a prayer, Dick told the woman that he didn't want her to end up like her poor soon-to-be departed husband, and thus, he had taken out a hefty annuity policy for her. Now all she needed to do was pay him for it. When she became alarmed and told him she didn't have that kind of money, Seligman persuaded her to go down to her bank and withdraw money she had in a CD so she could "reimburse" him for the new policy.

The church connection wasn't the only way Seligman gained the trust of his victims. There was the woman he befriended whose husband with Alzheimer's disease had recently died. Seligman professed a great interest in helping her raise money for Alzheimer's research. Along the way, he also persuaded the woman to part with her life savings to purchase an annuity policy.

---

[47] Most of Seligman's victims lost $30,000 to $40,000.

While it was bad enough that Seligman was engaging in high-pressure tactics to induce elderly people to purchase insurance, that wasn't the worst of it. Instead of forwarding the money that he received from the victims to the insurance companies, Seligman deposited the funds – more than $123,000 – into his own accounts. To lull the victims into a false sense of security, Seligman sent them monthly "annuity checks" referencing their policy numbers – checks which were purportedly from the insurance companies, but were actually from accounts he controlled. Seligman's scam came to light when some of his victims contacted the insurance companies about their investments, and were told they had no policies.

As Ron Miller and I met with victim after victim and heard their stories, we became more and more incensed at the tactics Seligman had used to rob these people of their financial security. I no longer viewed the case as a distraction from my "more important" cases. My motivation to bring Seligman to justice for what he had done to these people only increased when I found out he had pulled similar insurance scams against elderly victims in Illinois, just before he moved to Utah.

Even after his scheme was uncovered, Seligman still wasn't through scamming. For one of his victims, he created a phony loan document, claiming that the victim had signed it (it was an obvious forgery) and had given him $30,000 as a personal loan, rather than for an annuity policy.

It strengthened our case that so many victims had similar stories, demonstrating a clear pattern, which headed off the defense many scammers of the elderly use – that the victims are so old and mentally compromised that they can't reliably recall the details of how and why they parted with their money.

After floating some bogus defenses and filing motions to try to get his case dismissed on technicalities, Seligman could see that things were closing in on him. He ultimately pled guilty to six counts of felony communications fraud in a Logan courtroom, and was extradited back to federal prison in Illinois to start serving out his sentences there.

After the Seligman case, I was much more interested in handling white-collar cases, even though they "only" involved the loss of money, rather than physical injury or death. While many of the violent crimes I prosecuted were committed by people who lost control and lashed out because of anger, jealousy, rage, or other strong emotions, or because they were under the influence of drugs or alcohol, white-collar criminals who prey on vulnerable people and steal their financial security are among the most calculating of criminals, and deserve more punishment than they usually receive at the hands of the criminal justice system.

Judges often tend to cut white-collar criminals slack because, after all, how much harm do they really do, compared to violent criminals? It just takes one Dick Seligman to change your perspective on that. But white-collar criminals often have families and support systems to aid in their rehabilitation, not to mention "respectable" friends to write letters of recommendation on their behalf. Also working in their favor is the fact that judges know that the prisons are already crowded, and there is a need to have beds available for all those vicious murderers, kidnappers, and rapists.

Oh, and the trump card many white-collar criminals play is their professed remorse and stated desire to pay restitution, which of course requires that they stay out of prison so they can make money to repay their victims, although few of them ever do. Sometimes, even with million-dollar restitution orders against them, these criminals end up paying just a few hundred dollars a month, total. As a result, many elderly victims hardly ever see anything approaching full restitution before they die.

In Seligman's case, the victims were lucky. Although he had already squandered and spent the money he stole from them by the time we caught up with him, he was an authorized agent of the insurance companies whose policies he "sold." Under the law, those companies were obligated to pay the victims for the losses they incurred through the misdeeds of their agent. Although some companies were initially reluctant to do so, such as the case in which Seligman cooked up the phony loan document, Seligman's pattern of deception was so strong that the companies couldn't really deny their responsibility. So our victims were more fortunate than most in that they were able to get their money back, which is unusual in white-collar crime cases.

One other positive thing did come from the case: While Seligman was awaiting trial in Utah, I spoke with the federal prosecutor who was handling the case against him in Illinois. Through those conversations, I learned that Illinois had a law enhancing penalties for criminals who prey on elderly victims. After seeing how Seligman had taken advantage of his victims and wiped out their life savings, I felt it would be a good idea to have a law like that in Utah. I drafted such a bill and testified in support of it before the Legislature, highlighting the *Seligman* case. While the idea met with ridicule the first time I proposed it – some of the legislators themselves were over 65 and said they could take care of themselves just fine – eventually Utah did enact a law enhancing penalties for those who take advantage of vulnerable adults.

The final word on Dick Seligman must go to the federal judge who sentenced him in Illinois. Here's the account I got from the federal prosecutor there: At the sentencing hearing, the prosecutor commented that he hoped there was a special place in hell reserved for Dick Seligman for what he had done to the elderly victims he'd befriended and then swindled. Seligman's attorney jumped up and objected, and if what the federal prosecutor told me is accurate, the judge replied, "Well, it wouldn't be worth the powder it would take to blow Mr. Seligman to hell."

THE SCOOTER CASE: CONNING A CON MAN

I don't know where Len Scooter is now. Maybe he's reformed. Maybe he's a model citizen. But in the 1980s, he was a consummate con man, a man with a gift for taking advantage of other people by gaining their confidence and taking their money.

I first learned of Len Scooter when I was working at the D.A.'s Office and a Salt Lake City detective came to my office to screen a theft case. He said a guy had spent about a week in the Travelodge in downtown Salt Lake, had run up a whole bunch of extra expenses for meals, phone calls, movies and the like, and then skipped out on his bill. Eventually the cops tracked him down and arrested him. His name was Len Scooter.

It seemed like a routine case, but one thing was unusual. The detective had done his homework and had brought with him an article from a Texas magazine, entitled "The Elusive Scooter." There was a cartoon of Len in a ten-gallon cowboy hat, riding in a Thunderbird convertible with a longhorn hood ornament and money blowing out of the back of the car.

The article went on to discuss Scooter's antics in Texas, as well as in other states. He had conned a lot of people into thinking he was raising money to build a stadium and bring some big-league team to town, taken hundreds of thousands of dollars from investors, and then fled with the cash. The detective noted that, based on the description in the article, Scooter had such a way of charming people out of their money that he could have made a fortune doing legitimate promotions, if he had been inclined to "go straight."

I charged Scooter with felony theft for skipping out on his hotel bill. Although he had spirited away hundreds of thousands of dollars from hapless victims over the years, he informed the court that he was indigent, and so Sue Ann Fisher, an attorney in the Salt Lake Legal Defender's Office, was appointed to represent him.

While the case was pending trial, Sue Ann approached me on more than one occasion about reducing Scooter's bond. After all, it wasn't a violent crime. Why not reduce his bond and allow him to get out of jail? Scooter wasn't going anywhere. He was anxious to have his day in court. Sue Ann assured me that he would not be a flight risk if he were to be released, and that he could be supervised by Pre-Trial Services.

I told Sue Ann that I wouldn't agree to reducing the amount of bail, given Scooter's record and history of skipping town when things got hot. Why should I trust him?

Of course, Scooter had a line. It was all a big misunderstanding. Someone else was supposed to pay his hotel bill. From researching his background and M.O., I knew this was classic Scooter, trying to talk his way out of a jam.

As the trial approached, I learned that one of the hotel witnesses we would need to call at trial was somewhat flaky. Although our case was still strong, I knew of Scooter's reputation, and wondered if he might try to sweet-talk the jury, who wouldn't be informed about his history of scamming people out of their money. Without that context, I wondered if he might be able to talk his way out of yet another con.

I ran into Sue Ann later that week, and she pitched once again the idea that Scooter really wanted to get out of jail, and would promise to make all his court appearances if I would just give him a chance.

It was at that point that I came up with a new approach. Scooter's history was a road map of what he would do if he had half the chance – get out of Dodge as fast as he could. I knew his assurances were worthless, but I also knew he wanted badly enough to get out of jail that he might bite at a proposal. So I told Sue Ann that if Scooter pled guilty to felony theft, I would agree to his immediate release on his own recognizance, and he could stay out of jail pending his sentencing, which would be a month or so down the line. Sue Ann said she would relay the offer, and thought he would probably want to take the deal.

I figured the way it would play out would be that Scooter would probably bolt at the first opportunity, just as he had in Texas and other places. He would fail to appear for sentencing and the judge would issue a bench warrant for his arrest. When he eventually got picked up and returned for sentencing, he would likely get the prison term he had managed to avoid for so long.

I heard back quickly from Sue Ann Fisher. Yes, Scooter would like to take the deal, plead guilty, and get out of jail pending his sentencing hearing. And I had his word that he wouldn't bolt.

The next day, we took his plea, and I stipulated to his immediate release pending sentencing. Later that day, when I got back to the office, I had a message from Scooter, thanking me for believing in him and telling me he wouldn't let me down.

He didn't. As soon as he got out of jail, he was gone. When we got the word of his disappearance, Sue Ann was dismayed, and assumed I would be upset as well. She may have wondered why I took it all in stride.

A bench warrant was issued for Scooter's arrest, and he was picked up a few weeks later in another state and returned to Utah. At his sentencing hearing, the only question before the judge was whether Scooter should go to prison or be put on probation. Since he had pled guilty, it was too late to talk his way out of the charges, and by fleeing the jurisdiction, he had already proven to the judge that he wasn't a good candidate for probation.

The judge sentenced Scooter to prison, and the "Elusive Scooter" was finally behind bars. Contrary to what his lawyer thought, he had not let me down.[48]

---

[48] After I finished writing this chapter, I googled Scooter to see if I could find anything about his recent activities. I found many posts from folks he had recently swindled, lamenting that he is still on the loose and not behind bars for his fraudulent schemes. One victim said Scooter set up a company and sold shares in a gold mine. In an attempt to verify the legitimacy of the investment, the man had verified that the company was registered with the state. Trouble was, while the company may have been real, the gold mine was not.

CHAPTER 14

Ninety Years of
Convictions Up In Smoke?

The Indian Jurisdiction Cases[49]

I DON'T REMEMBER WHERE I WAS when I first heard about it. But I do remember where I was when I first told my wife Jo about it. It was early 1994, and we were on the road to Vernal, in eastern Utah, where I was handling a case, and on the way out to the Uintah Basin, we passed through the town of Roosevelt and the Uintah/Ouray Indian Reservation. I told her that the U.S. Supreme Court had recently redefined the boundaries of the reservation, and now there was a possibility that decades of federal convictions might be thrown out, because the events had actually occurred on state rather than federal land, as newly-defined. I told her that at the time the cases were prosecuted, everyone had believed that the crimes occurred on reservation land, where the federal government had exclusive jurisdiction, and that a federal judge had even entered an injunction preventing the State from prosecuting crimes there. Now it looked like the whole thing was going to unravel.

As I explained the situation to Jo, she turned to me in the car and said,

---

[49] I use the term "Indian" rather than "Native American" because state and federal courts still use that term in referring to legal issues such as jurisdiction.

"That makes no sense. Only lawyers could think of something like that." It hit me that she was right. What sense did it make to throw out decades of settled convictions where there were no claims of innocence, lack of due process, or unfairness in the trials? Was this really what the law required? I had always thought that the law should make sense, and if it didn't, it ought to be changed, either through legislation or fresh court interpretation, notwithstanding the importance of precedent in the law – the legal doctrine that courts should not lightly depart from well-settled legal principles and interpretations.

I had always harbored the ambition of knocking down irrational precedent, and even had a literary reference at the ready. In *Huckleberry Finn*, there was a paragraph that seemed to fit. Referring to the Widow Douglas, who had taken him in to "sivilize" him and make him respectable, Huck says:

> *After supper she got out her book and learned me about Moses and the Bulrushers, and I was in a sweat to find out all about him; but by and by she let it out that Moses had been dead a considerable long time; so then I didn't care no more about him, because I don't take no stock in dead people.*

In my imagination, I would quote Huck, and then make the argument: "Now, your honors, the decisions that appear to require this nonsensical result were written by jurists who have all been dead a considerable long time, and I don't think we should put too much stock in them." As events surrounding the Supreme Court's boundary redefinition were to unfold, I was to keep this argument in my back pocket.

At the time, I worked under Attorney General Jan Graham, Utah's first and still only woman Attorney General, and in my view, one of the most effective we've ever had. I worked in her office from 1992 to 2000, and these were the best years of my career. Not only was Jan an outstanding Attorney General, but she had also appointed Reed Richards as her Chief Criminal Deputy. Reed had served for eight years as the elected Weber

County Attorney up in Ogden, and was also an outstanding attorney with great experience and judgment.

Here's the set-up: A year or so before, Jan had spearheaded an appeal to the United States Supreme Court to bring to a head the thorny question of the proper interpretation of the boundaries of the Uintah/Ouray Indian Reservation in Duchesne County, Utah, which had been the subject of some confusion. The question centered on whether the reservation had been diminished when Congress had decided to open the reservation to non-Indian settlement in 1905. If it had, then Congress had made the reservation smaller, and the town of Roosevelt was no longer part of the reservation, so crimes committed in Roosevelt were subject to prosecution in state courts. If it had not, Roosevelt was still part of the reservation, and subject only to federal jurisdiction.

Jan took the case to the U.S. Supreme Court, arguing that the town of Roosevelt was within state rather than federal jurisdiction, and therefore the State could prosecute crimes that occurred within its boundaries. The U.S. Department of Justice argued that it was not, and opposed Utah's position before the high court. The Court issued its opinion in February of 1994 in *Hagen v. U.S.*, 114 S.Ct. 958 (1994), and, in a 7 to 2 decision, held that Roosevelt was in fact not within the territorial area of the Indian Reservation, and hence it was subject to Utah's jurisdiction.

While it was a great victory for Utah, the celebration was short-lived, as we soon learned that the U.S. Attorney for Utah, Scott Matheson, Jr., might be about to take the position that all convictions should be vacated for persons still in federal prison whose crimes had occurred in these areas of newly-designated state lands, and that these convicted defendants should be released from federal prison.

By the time we learned about it, the train had left the station, as Matheson had already sent a letter in March of 1994 to Chief Judge David K. Winder of the U.S. District Court, with copies to all known convicted defendants and their attorneys. This letter suggested that the U.S. Attorney's

Office might be prepared to join in a motion to vacate all convictions, leaving to the State of Utah the decision of whether to bring charges against the defendants.[50]

It was a staggering proposition. Many of these convictions went back decades. Many involved very serious crimes – murders, rapes, child abuse and the like. The prospect of successfully putting together prosecutable cases in state court was remote at best, and likely to re-traumatize the surviving victims and their families on a massive scale.

I figured there had to be a better way, so I placed a call to a friend of mine, an Assistant U.S. Attorney, and asked what was going on and what the Attorney General's Office could do to help. To my surprise, he was quite emphatic that our office should just stay out of it – that the U.S. Attorney's Office had analyzed it from every angle and there just didn't seem to be a way to save the convictions. Lots of really smart people had already grappled with the issue, including Scott Matheson himself, and while they would be the first to defend the convictions if they could, they just didn't see how it could be done, given the state of the law.

Since we were going to be left with the fallout if the convictions were vacated – we would be the ones trying to figure out how to pick up the pieces and make something out of decades-old cases – it seemed only fair that we be allowed to collaborate with the U. S. Attorney's Office on possible solutions. But my friend suggested that there were still some ongoing discussions in their office and some differences of opinion as to how to proceed, and that it might even be counterproductive for the Attorney General's Office to inject ourselves into the process. Knowing what a tenacious prosecutor my friend was, I inferred that he was probably among those who were still advocating to save the convictions, but that he was in the minority.

---

[50] Although the letter from Matheson stated that the *Hagen* case may have created a jurisdictional defect requiring vacating the convictions, it didn't entirely concede the point, stating "… if there is a legitimate legal or factual argument to support any conviction, we will make it."

We had been given a clear signal to stand down. Still, there was so much at stake, and with no real indication that the train was going anywhere but to the end of the line, we weren't willing to just stand down. I briefed Reed and Jan, and asked Mike Wims, an experienced prosecutor in my division, to spearhead the legal research and prepare a memo with his analysis of whether the convictions were salvageable. Mike brought a wealth of experience to the table, having been an Air Force JAG Officer for twenty-two years – experience that included being a prosecutor, defense attorney, judge, appellate counsel, and administrator. He was also a brilliant trial lawyer and strategic thinker.[51] I figured if anyone could come up with theories to save those convictions, it would be Mike Wims.

Mike found cases that suggested courts would be willing to stretch in order to avoid throwing out decades of otherwise valid convictions based on a shifting boundary line. He prepared a memo in which he opined that "if indeed no precedent exists for wiping out decades of prior convictions obtained according to the jurisdictional boundaries then recognized as valid by the courts, that alone should cause great concern about conceding in a matter of first impression where the consequences of the concession are so far-reaching and drastic."

By April 20, we had Mike's memo, as well as one from the Criminal Appeals Division of our office. Division Chief Chris Soltis, herself a former federal prosecutor with extensive experience, reacted the same way we did to the position taken by the U.S. Attorney's Office: *There must be some argument they can make. Have they really thought of all the possibilities?*

Mike's memo focused on one theory of how to preserve the convictions: *res judicata*, the legal doctrine that a final judgment is conclusive as to all matters that were litigated or could have been litigated in court. The memo prepared by the Criminal Appeals Division of our office focused on another, related theory of how the convictions could stand:

---

[51] Mike taught me a lot about effective trial advocacy.

that the *Hagen* case should not be applied retroactively to convictions that were already final before it was decided. Both memos cited as authority *O'Callahan v. Parker*, 395 U.S. 258 (1969) and *Gosa v. Mayden*, 413 U.S. 679 (1973).

In *O'Callahan*, the U.S. Supreme Court held that military courts lacked jurisdiction to try individuals for non-service-connected crimes. Defendants who had been convicted of non-service-connected crimes then appealed their convictions, arguing that since the courts that tried them had no jurisdiction to do so, their convictions should be invalidated. In *Gosa*, the U.S. Supreme Court disagreed, refused to apply its *O'Callahan* ruling retroactively, and rejected the argument that all prior military court convictions should be voided "ab initio" (from the start). It seemed like pretty good precedent to us.

On April 20, I sent the two memos over to Scott Matheson and requested that we meet with him in his office. Within a short time, I heard through the grapevine that the U.S. Attorney's Office was not happy with Mike's memo. While Mike's memo emphasized the case law and policy arguments in favor of preserving the convictions, including how much the victims would suffer if the convictions were thrown out, the U.S. Attorney's Office apparently interpreted the memo as a lecture to their office. When we called to set up a meeting with Scott and his key assistants to discuss the issue, we were told that it would not be necessary for Mike to attend the meeting.

So on April 25, 1994, Jan Graham, Reed Richards and I met with Scott Matheson in his office. Also present was Barbara Bearnson, an Assistant U.S. Attorney who had at one time worked in my division of the Attorney General's Office, in our Child Abuse Unit. Barbara was the point person assigned to the Indian Jurisdiction case, and an able lawyer.

During the meeting, Scott told us that his office had analyzed the issues from all angles, and that it was their legal conclusion that nothing could be done to save the convictions. He said they were already aware of and could distinguish every case our office had provided in favor of preserving the convictions – that none of them were directly on point, and that they were hence ultimately not helpful. He also said that the U.S. Department of Justice would not allow him to make such an argument, having likewise concluded that the convictions were not salvageable. This struck me at the time as potential payback to Jan for having taken on and beaten the Department of Justice in the *Hagen* case. It seemed a bit like, "Be careful what you wish for ..."[52]

Scott then pulled out the trump card. He told us that Ron Boyce, the federal magistrate who would recommend action to the federal judge, had already let the U.S. Attorney's Office know that Boyce felt the convictions were unsustainable for lack of jurisdiction, and that he was in fact somewhat impatient to move things along to get the prisoners released.

Boyce was undeniably an impressive figure – universally admired and *the* authority on criminal law in the state of Utah, having literally written the (text)book and taught criminal law at the University of Utah College of Law for decades before becoming a federal magistrate. He had an encyclopedic knowledge of the law, and could cite by name and volume not only Utah state decisions but decisions from other state and federal courts as well. Most of the criminal practitioners in the state had studied criminal law at the knee of Professor Boyce – at least, all those who had attended the University of Utah's College of Law. In criminal law circles, as long as anyone could remember, often all one needed to say to win an argument was that Ron Boyce shared the same opinion.

I knew Boyce well, and liked him, but having gone to law school in California rather than Utah, I may have been a little more inclined to question his opinion than most, and I had at times (although rarely) disagreed with him on interpretations of law, as well as on legislative proposals.

Still, for Scott, I'm sure it was a powerful reinforcement that Ron Boyce

---

[52] I knew this wouldn't be Scott's approach, but I wondered about the Department of Justice. Why wouldn't the Department even allow Scott to make an argument to preserve the convictions?

believed the convictions could not stand. After all, Boyce would be passing along his Report & Recommendation to Judge David Sam, the federal judge who would ultimately decide the case, and no one could recall a time when Judge Sam had *not* followed Ron Boyce's recommendation.

I knew Scott well, respected him, and liked him. But on this issue, I couldn't agree with him. I remember telling him that while the cases we'd cited may not have been definitive authority for the proposition that the convictions must stand, likewise none of the cases his office cited was definitive authority for the opposite proposition – that ninety years of settled convictions must be thrown out because a court decision changes a boundary line.

Scott told us he understood our concerns, and that he didn't like the result any more than we did. He knew how difficult it would be to re-try the cases, and he too was concerned about the effect on the victims. He told us that he would make arguments in favor of preserving the convictions if he felt he could legally and ethically do so, but he just felt that he could not. In fact, he said he couldn't make an argument to uphold the convictions with a straight face. I remember telling him, "Scott, you can not only make this argument with a straight face, you can win this argument." He looked down and just shook his head.

I decided to try one more approach, which perhaps bordered on impertinence. After all, I wasn't the Attorney General or even the Chief Deputy Attorney General, so who was I to lecture the U. S. Attorney? But I felt strongly about it, and knowing Scott was a decent and reasonable guy, I went ahead anyway in the hope that it might make a difference.

I told Scott about an experience I had while I was a law clerk for a private law firm, when I was fresh out of law school. I had been given an assignment to find precedent that would be helpful to one of the firm's clients in defending a civil action that would otherwise result in hundreds of thousands of dollars in fines. I researched the issue and reported to the senior partner that there was no helpful precedent, and that he should just advise the company to pay the fine. At that, the attorney told me to keep looking, and that if I thought there was no precedent that could help them, I hadn't looked long enough. At the time, I was rather put off, and felt like the attorney was pressuring me to cook up some type of bogus argument, which I didn't like and wasn't willing to do. Reluctantly, and with some resentment, I agreed to look again to see if I could find any helpful precedent. To my surprise, I did find some cases that supported the client's position.

After relaying that experience to Scott, I told him, "Scott, if you think there's no legal precedent that could allow you to argue that these convictions should be preserved, you haven't looked long enough." I recognized I was pushing the envelope, but I was trying in any way I could to get him to reconsider his position. He listened, but it soon became apparent that we weren't making any headway, and that further attempts to persuade him would be futile.

At that point, Jan Graham turned to Scott and in a very calm voice said, "We understand your position, and we don't want you to do anything you don't feel you can ethically do. Please let us know when the hearing will be held, and we will come in and intervene on behalf of the victims, because somebody has to speak for them."

It was clear from Scott's reaction that he was not expecting this approach from Jan. I don't know that I was expecting it myself. While I don't recall Scott's exact words at that time, the prospect of having the Utah Attorney General intervene in support of preserving the convictions seemed unsettling to him. As we wrapped up the meeting, there was some discussion of the U.S. Attorney's Office reconsidering its position, and we were invited to provide any additional input and authority we might find.

And we did. On June 1, we submitted another memo to Scott and Barbara in support of upholding the convictions. In the meantime, we were in the process of preparing arrest warrants and charging documents, in case we had to prosecute the defendants in state court. We dreaded the prospect, but felt we had to be ready. We figured there were about twenty convicted criminals still in federal prison who might be released if the decision went against us. The oldest case dated back to 1977, and the prospect of prosecuting a case that was almost twenty years old was daunting.

Mike Wims and I were particularly sensitized to the challenges of trying "stale" cases. We were in the process of preparing for the retrial of Ron Lafferty, who had been convicted of two counts of capital murder ten years before. His convictions had been reversed by the U.S. Tenth Circuit Court of Appeals on a competency claim, and the case had landed in our lap because the Utah County Attorney's Office had a conflict of interest. While reconstructing a decade-old case had its unique challenges, we couldn't even imagine how we'd be able to successfully resurrect a case that was even older.

So we were relieved and surprised when, a short time later, we got a call from the U.S. Attorney's Office telling us that Scott had decided to have his office go ahead and make arguments before Magistrate Boyce in favor of preserving the convictions. Boyce would consider all the legal memoranda and arguments and make his Report & Recommendation concerning the matter, which would then go to Judge David Sam, who would make the final decision.

I was pleased with the turn of events. It showed a willingness on Scott's part to listen and consider all points of view, even after he had taken such a strong position with us during the meeting. I also recognized that, whatever pressure Scott might have felt from us, he must have felt even more pressure from the Department of Justice not to not buck their initial decision to give up on the convictions. Somehow Scot had still come to the conclusion that he should. I knew he was concerned about the effect on the victims if the convictions were invalidated, and wondered if that might have ultimately affected his decision.

In any event, from the message we received that his office would be making arguments before Magistrate Boyce, I took it that Scott had changed his position for principled reasons, and had somehow convinced the Department to reverse its position, and authorize him to fight to maintain the convictions. From what I know of bureaucratic entrenchment, it couldn't have been an easy sell.

While I was pleased that Scott was going to fight for the convictions, I wasn't particularly optimistic. There was no getting around the fact that Boyce, the most respected authority on criminal law in the state of Utah, had telegraphed that he believed the convictions could not stand and must be vacated. If that was what Boyce was going to recommend to Judge Sam, how could Scott overcome it?

Months passed, and I worked on other things, knowing that we'd done what we could and the case was in good hands. Then on July 26, 1994, Magistrate Boyce issued his "Report and Recommendation" in *Cuch v. U.S*, and it wasn't good news. His view was clear – the case must be vacated because the defendant was tried in federal court, and federal court never had any jurisdiction to try him. The conviction was "void ab initio" – void right from the start. As a result, he recommended that Cuch be "forthwith discharged from the custody of the United States." Since this was the test case, we knew that if Boyce's recommendations were followed, the game would be over and the prison gates would be opened for all similarly situated convicts.

Now it was on to Judge David Sam, who, we were reminded, had never departed from a recommendation by Magistrate Boyce. At that point, Barbara and Scott were not very optimistic about winning before Judge Sam, but they were committed to continuing with the arguments in favor of preserving the convictions.

About six months later, in January of 1995, after considering Magistrate Boyce's "Report and Recommendation" and reviewing the memoranda and legal arguments of counsel for both sides, Judge Sam issued his ruling, and it defied the odds.

Citing policy arguments similar to those in Mike's memo, and citing

O'Callahan and *Gosa* as authority,[53] Judge Sam decided not to apply the *Hagen* decision retroactively to cases that were final prior to the issuance of that decision.[54]

The upshot was that 90 years of settled convictions were not going to be declared "void ab initio." I suspect that Judge Sam, who had at one time been a state court judge out in the Uintah Basin, understood on a visceral level what it would mean to invalidate all those convictions, and decided to take a common-sense approach. Near the end of his ruling, Judge Sam said this: "The rule of law is strengthened when courts, in their search for fairness, giving proper consideration to the facts and applicable precedent, allow the law to be an instrument in obtaining a result that promotes order, justice and equality."[55] Sounded good to me.

It was a great victory for the U.S. Attorney's office, but it would be some time before we all knew if it would stand, as the defense attorneys would certainly appeal the case to the next level – the U.S. Court of Appeals for the Tenth Circuit. Although the U.S. Attorney's Office had prevailed before Judge Sam, it was by no means a foregone conclusion that the Tenth Circuit was going to agree. The case law was, after all, equivocal at best.

Cut now to the spring of 1996. Mike Wims and I were in Provo, starting the double capital murder re-trial of Ron Lafferty for the murders of his sister-in-law and her 15-month-old baby. We got a message from Barbara Bearnson, and it was very good news. On March 21, 1996, two years after we first learned that the U.S. Attorney's Office was contemplating joining in vacating the convictions, the Tenth Circuit Court of Appeals issued its decision in *U.S. v. Cuch,* 79 F.3d 987, affirming Judge

---

[53] I do not mean to suggest that our office's memos were submitted to the Court, or that the U.S. Attorney's Office just copied and pasted our memos and gave them to the Court. The issues were more complex than that, and the U.S. Attorney's Office prepared extensive pleadings in favor of preservation, and by all accounts, did an excellent job.

[54] *U.S. v. Cuch,* 875 F. Supp. 766 (D. Utah 1995)

[55] *Cuch,* 875 F. Supp. at 772

Sam's ruling and preserving the convictions. A second victory for the U.S. Attorney's Office, and a great moment of relief for us all![56]

The last recourse for the defendants was to the U.S. Supreme Court, and their attorneys filed a petition for certiorari, asking the Court to hear the case. When the Supreme Court refused to review the case, the Tenth Circuit's opinion became the final word.

At last, the convictions were safe. We could finally tear up all the criminal complaints we had prepared at a point when it looked almost certain that we would have to use them to try to prevent convicted murderers, rapists, and child molesters from being set free.

It was a very good day.

---

[56] I later learned from Dave Schwendiman, who was present during the oral argument, that the 10th Circuit Court of Appeals seemed initially inclined to strike down the convictions, but that Scott did an excellent job arguing the case, and turned the Court around.

CHAPTER 15

Wooly Bully:
The Jeremy Clawson Murder Trial

IN JUNE OF 1993, two Indiana teenagers, 18-year-old Jeremy Clawson and his 16-year-old passenger, Paul Rafferty, stole Rafferty's mother's red Thunderbird, loaded up the trunk with Clawson's guns, and drove west. When they ran out of money, they stole gas and food, and on June 16, they committed a gas skip at a convenience store along a remote stretch of I-70 in Thompson Springs, Grand County, Utah, and started a series of events that would end in tragedy.

Not long after the theft was reported by the attendant at Thompson Springs, a deputy sheriff from Grand County saw a Thunderbird matching the description of the car involved in the gas theft, and tried to pull it over. Clawson, who was driving, sped away, and the chase was on. The deputy requested backup from other officers in the area, and soon several Utah Highway Patrol troopers joined the chase, as the Thunderbird proceeded west at a high rate of speed on I-70, across one of the most picturesque landscapes in the West.

Trooper Blake Sands of the Utah Highway Patrol joined the pursuit and soon drove the lead vehicle. As the cars sped west past the town of

Green River, they crossed the line into Emery County.

During the chase, Clawson shouted at Rafferty to grab the wheel of the car and steer, as Clawson leaned out the driver's side window and fired several rounds back at the pursuing officers. Several police cars took rounds, and one penetrated the windshield of Trooper Sands' car and struck him in the eye. Sands somehow managed to pull his car off the freeway before losing consciousness.

The other officers continued the chase. They spiked the tires of the fleeing car, causing it to veer off the interstate and roll. Officers converged at the scene of the crash site and took both Clawson and Rafferty into custody at gunpoint. At that time, the arresting officers had no idea what had happened to Blake Sands.

Back where Trooper Sands' car sat off the highway, officers and bystanders found him unconscious behind the wheel with a bullet wound to the head. In a tragic coincidence, Trooper Sands' wife, an EMT, was on duty that evening and was dispatched to the scene of the shooting. As she was en route, officers who realized her husband was the victim radioed for her not to come to the scene. Although Trooper Sands was rushed to a hospital in Price, he died a short time later.

Not long afterwards, Clawson and Rafferty were charged with aggravated murder, a capital offense, as well as felony fleeing and attempting to kill other officers who had taken part in the pursuit that day, and whose cars had taken rounds. As per Utah law, both defendants were appointed capital-qualified defense counsel, some of the best in the state. Tom Evans was appointed to represent Clawson, and Rod O'Connor was appointed as Rafferty's lawyer.

As frequently occurred when capital cases happened in rural areas, Emery County Attorney David Blackwell asked the Attorney General's Office for assistance. I went out to Emery County to team up with Dave, a very able and steady prosecutor, and a true gentleman. Rounding out the team was a young prosecutor in my division of the Attorney General's

Office named Rob Lunnen, a rising star in our office who proved invaluable during the trial.[57]

Some months prior to trial, Rod O'Connor approached us about a negotiated plea for Paul Rafferty. We felt it was justified, given Rafferty's age and the fact that he was clearly the less culpable of the two. Rod said that Rafferty was also willing to give us a full statement and to testify against Clawson. We debriefed Rafferty, who gave important details that helped establish Clawson's intent to kill – details that would counter Clawson's assertions that he had never aimed at or intended to hit anyone, and was just shooting blindly to try to get the officers to back off.

Even with the plea agreement, Rafferty's "deal" was pretty stringent. He pled guilty to murder rather than aggravated murder, and also pled guilty to two counts of attempted murder based on shots fired by Clawson at other officers during the chase. The sentence for the murder charge alone was 5 years to life in prison, a staggering concept for a teenager. As we prepared for trial, we divided up the witnesses and decided that Dave Blackwell would question Rafferty on the stand.

On June 19, 1995, Clawson's trial began in Castle Dale, the county seat of Emery County, before Judge Joseph Canby. During jury selection, defense counsel Tom Evans re-positioned counsel table so that Clawson was seated directly in front of the prospective jurors. At the time of the trial, Clawson, now 20, looked much younger than his age. He was clean-cut and baby-faced – like a boy scout. I leaned over to Dave Blackwell as court was about to begin and whispered, "The jury's going to have a hard time convicting this kid of capital murder."

What made a capital conviction more likely was the decision we had made a few months before to take the death penalty off the table, without requesting any concessions from the defense. While we felt it was clearly

---

[57] Rob later moved to the U.S. Attorney's Office and went on to distinguish himself in multiple capacities. Among his many accomplishments, he served the Department of Justice in Colombia and later in Afghanistan. He is currently Chief of the Criminal Division of the U.S. Attorney's Office in Utah.

a capital case – the intentional killing of a police officer – it was not a compelling case for the death penalty, given Clawson's age and relatively minor previous criminal record. We also felt that having the specter of death hanging over the jury's deliberations would reduce the likelihood that they would convict him of aggravated murder. With the death penalty off the table, the sentencing options would be either life in prison with the possibility of parole, or life without parole.

After jury selection was complete and the proceedings adjourned for the day, Rob Lunnen and I spent some time with Dave, and he went through a dry run of his opening statement. We talked about our theory of the case. Anticipating Clawson's defense that he hadn't intended anyone to get hurt and that it was a one-in-a-million fluky shot that killed Trooper Sands, Dave emphasized his theme that Clawson had "fired over and over and over again" at the pursuing officers.

Next day, after Dave gave a very effective opening statement, Tom Evans stood up to address the jury. During his opening statement, he portrayed Clawson as a meek, clean-cut kid, and said: "There sits Jeremy Clawson, never having been in trouble with the law before …"

Later, in chambers, we argued to Judge Canby that Evans had opened the door for us to put into evidence the fact that not only had Clawson been in trouble with the law before, but it was because of that trouble that Clawson had convinced Rafferty to steal his mother's car so he could get out of Indiana. Some months before, Clawson had been caught selling a PCP-laced cigarette to an undercover cop. He was supposed to work as a "snitch" for the police in order to avoid being prosecuted for the felony drug charge, but he hadn't been following through. And that wasn't his only brush with the law. I told the judge I thought we should be allowed to present to the jury the truth about Clawson's past run-ins with the law.

Evans countered that what he had meant was, "There sits Jeremy Clawson, *looking like* he's never been in trouble with the law before." Really? Judge Canby mulled it over and then said he would allow us to get into some of the details of Clawson's legal troubles in Indiana, which shed light on why he was so motivated to get away from the police in Utah. Clawson hadn't wanted to get caught because then he would have to go back to Indiana and face the music on the drug charge.

The first day of trial went well. We had testimony from the gas station attendant in Thompson Springs where Clawson and Rafferty had done their gas skip – the event which had resulted in the report to the police, the attempt to pull them over, and the eventual high-speed chase. Other Highway Patrol troopers who took part in the pursuit also testified: Bruce Riches, Steve Rapich, and Richard Haycock. We demonstrated how rounds fired by Clawson struck the patrol cars of officers besides Trooper Sands, rounds which could have resulted in their also being injured or killed.

As we rolled along, all seemed to be going well, until the evening I got a call from Dave Blackwell as I was preparing some exhibits at the courthouse for the next day's proceedings. Dave had left an hour earlier to do his final run-through of the facts with Paul Rafferty, who was scheduled to testify the next morning. Dave told me on the phone, "We have a problem. Paul is now claiming he can't remember anything, even the things he's said in prior signed statements and even when I play him portions of his own taped statements. He's also saying it doesn't matter anyway, because he's already been sentenced and there's nothing we can do to him if he doesn't cooperate."

Dave went on to relay that Rafferty's counsel, Rod O'Connor, was in Colorado on a case, and no one could reach him or knew just when he would be available. So Rod couldn't have a heart-to-heart with Paul and tell him there would be serious consequences if he failed to cooperate after getting a plea bargain based in part on his promise to testify for the State.

My immediate thought was, "Oh no, this kid is making a huge mistake, and someone needs to set him straight." Clawson had damn near ruined his life already, and I knew that Rafferty was wrong if he thought there would be no adverse consequences for reneging on his agreement. It

187

seemed clear to me that Paul didn't understand the stakes, and somebody needed to level with him. I also knew, of course, that if he didn't change his mind, it could negatively impact our case. I told Dave I would come over to the jail right away and have a "Come to Jesus" meeting with Paul.

When I got to the jail, I sat down with Paul and told him it was vital that he tell the truth, and that if he didn't, there would be consequences. Although he'd already been sentenced, the amount of time he served was up to the Board of Pardons. It could be 5 years. It could be life. It could be somewhere in between. But if the Board believed he'd gotten a plea bargain in a capital case by pledging to testify truthfully and then hadn't delivered, they could decide to hold him for a very long time.

I also told him that we as prosecutors were required to write a letter to the Board with a recommendation on each inmate committed to prison, and that the letter we wrote on whether he cooperated could have a large impact on the amount of time he actually served in prison. Having spent far too many hours in the company of undercover cops and adopting their vernacular on double-crossing witnesses, I said to Paul, "You don't want to do that. It's called pissing backwards" (an expression I would never use in ordinary conversation).

During the whole time I talked with him, Paul sat quietly and seemed to be taking it in. I thought I was getting through to him, and felt good that I was able to give him the straight story, since his lawyer wasn't available to talk with him. Talking to him brought home to me again how young Paul was, and I genuinely felt bad for him for what Clawson had gotten him into, and what he was facing as a consequence. I left the meeting with Paul and reported to Dave that I thought he would follow through and testify truthfully the next day.

Next morning, June 29, was not my best day. When I got to the courthouse, Dave said that Rod O'Connor had unexpectedly shown up, having just returned from Colorado. We went into Dave's office, and Rod confirmed that he had just spoken with Paul, and that Paul had gotten over the jitters and was willing to testify truthfully. I figured that Rod had reinforced what I had told Paul the night before, and I was glad things were back on track. Then, just as we were getting up to head to the courtroom, Rod threw out, "Oh, by the way, Paul feels like you threatened him yesterday, and he told that to Tom Evans." I was surprised, since I thought the conversation had gone well, but Dave and I were at least glad to get the heads-up from Rod so we wouldn't be blindsided.

We walked into the courtroom, and Dave put Paul on the stand and covered the essential points of his testimony. Of particular importance was the fact that when Trooper Sands had first passed their car, Clawson had tried to fire at him point-blank, but the shotgun hadn't been primed and had just clicked. Clawson quickly pumped it and pulled the trigger again. This time it fired, but by then Trooper Sands' car had pulled ahead, and the shot blasted out Sands' backdoor window but didn't strike him.

After Dave had covered all the details, he asked Paul whether he had ever felt threatened during conversations with the prosecutors, in an attempt to deflect whatever hay the defense might try to make out of it. Paul said yes, but then agreed with Dave that at no time had any of us ever told him he should testify to anything other than the truth.

Then it was Evans' turn, and he went right there: *Who was it that threatened you?* (Paul pointed and I raised my hand.) *What did he say?* (Yes, the colorful colloquial phrase came out.) I sat there thinking, "Oh, brother, how did it come to this?"

After Paul Rafferty finished his testimony and the jury left the courtroom, Evans moved for a mistrial based on prosecutorial misconduct. Oh, great. I wasn't worried the judge would grant the motion, but I knew the reporters were going to jump on it. I usually avoided the press mid-trial when possible. Now, I had a decision to make. Should I just slip out the back door after the proceedings ended, or face the press and make a statement in my own defense?

The quote that came to my mind was from *A Man for All Seasons*, when Cromwell is trying to get Sir Thomas More to give him information that More refuses to disclose. At one point during an interrogation, when Cromwell threatens More, More says, "You threaten like a dockside bully." Cromwell asks, "How should I threaten?" More says, "Like a Minister of State, with justice." At which point Cromwell says, "Oh, justice is what you're threatened with," and More replies, "Then I'm not threatened."

I thought about saying, "All I did was threaten him with justice," but how was that going to come across as a sound bite, particularly without the context of the dialogue from *A Man For All Seasons*? I didn't know, but in the meantime, now that Rafferty had finished testifying, we were arguing another, more substantive motion. Judge Canby ruled in our favor on that motion and then, almost as an afterthought and without asking us to address the issue of whether what I had said to Paul was improper, said to Evans, "Oh, and Mr. Evans, your motion for mistrial is denied."

As the proceeding ended, I realized I'd made no formal response to the allegation on the record, so the press had only heard one side of the story. In retrospect, I think I should have made myself available for a comment to the press, because they were left with nothing but the defense attorney's forceful statements about the shocking conduct of a prosecutor threatening a witness. A simple "I just told him he needed to tell the truth" would have sufficed, but I was preoccupied with other trial concerns, was naturally reluctant to make statements to the press, and didn't have the presence of mind to realize I should probably make an exception and not let the allegations stand without saying something in my own defense.

After court ended for the day, Rob Lunnen and I drove back to our hotel in Price, about 30 minutes away. Back in our room, we turned on the evening news. The big story? You guessed it. "Prosecutor Threatens Witness." The low point for me was when the news anchor asked the field reporter if Horton was going to be sanctioned by the Bar. At that point, Rob suggested we not watch the other stations – a good suggestion. We left the motel room and walked around the parking lot and periphery of the hotel grounds, discussing the "slings and arrows of outrageous fortune" and the fact that this too would pass.

The morning after Paul Rafferty testified, the headline in the *Salt Lake Tribune* read, "*Murder-Trial Witness Says Prosecutor Threatened Him.*" In court that day, Emery County Sheriff's Deputy Kyle Ekker, the primary case agent, with whom I'd developed a close relationship, leaned over and handed me a name tag with "Wooly Bully"[58] written on it – a comment, I assumed, on both my deportment with the witness and my rather shaggy hair. I smiled, so I must have been getting over the public skewering.

It was then on to more serious things. Clawson was about to testify in his own defense, and I had gotten the draw to cross-examine him. Evans had it set up nicely, and the first several minutes of Clawson's testimony, he just sobbed. Then, when he gained his composure and could finally speak, he said how sorry he was. He said, "I took a father from his children, a husband from his wife, a son from his parents." The idea conveyed was: Look how bad I feel; I must be telling the truth when I tell you I never intended to shoot Trooper Sands. Clawson tearfully testified that at the time he found out he had shot and killed Sands, he was devastated.

The speech seemed canned to me, and I didn't believe the tears were sincere, at least not for the victim or his family. I remembered being told by Dave that at the preliminary hearing, before I became involved in the case, Clawson had been brought into the courtroom, looked over at Paul Rafferty, and snickered during the proceedings.

On cross-examination, I had Clawson reiterate how sad and despondent he was at learning what had happened to Trooper Sands. I asked him if he had learned about Sands' death before the preliminary hearing, and he had to admit that he had. I then said, "But you didn't cry at that hearing, did you?" No. "But then there was no jury there, was there?" His lawyer didn't like the question, but it made the point.

---

[58] "Wooly Bully" was a popular novelty song in the 60's, sung by Sam the Sham and the Pharaohs.

After we finished all the evidence and Dave Blackwell and Tom Evans made their closing arguments, the jury went out for deliberations. Six hours later, they returned, and announced that they had found Clawson guilty as charged of aggravated murder, two counts of attempted aggravated murder, and felony fleeing.

The case then moved to the penalty phase, which would determine what sentence Clawson should receive. At that time, Utah law gave a convicted defendant the choice of whether he wanted the penalty hearing to be heard by the judge or the jury, and the prosecution didn't have any say in the matter. Clawson opted to waive the jury and have Judge Canby alone decide whether the sentence should be life with parole or life without parole. Judge Canby was a likeable judge, but he had a reputation for being lenient on defendants. More than once I had heard him referred to as "Let 'Em Go Joe."

Trooper Sands' family members testified at the penalty hearing about their grievous loss, including the fact that Blake's young son wore his dad's T-shirt at night just to feel nearer to him. Blake was a terrific guy, and it was very emotional, gut-wrenching testimony.

After hearing the testimony of the witnesses and the arguments of counsel, Judge Canby announced his decision. Jeremy Clawson would be sentenced to life with the possibility of parole. Given Clawson's age, the decision was neither unexpected nor unreasonable, and many judges would have done the same. What made it more difficult, especially for Blake Sands' family and the Highway Patrol, was that in announcing his decision, Judge Canby choked back tears, saying, "I can't give up on Jeremy Clawson." The headline in the *Salt Lake Tribune* the next day, July 4, 1995, read, "Tearful Judge Gives Trooper's Murderer a Chance for Parole," and contained a photo of Judge Canby wiping away tears while sentencing Clawson.[59]

---

[59] For the next legislative session, we drafted a bill to provide that convicted capital defendants can only waive juries at penalty phase hearings with the consent of the prosecution. We used the article with the photo of Judge Canby wiping away tears to make the point that the system should be more balanced, and the bill passed.

POSTSCRIPT:

Two years later, in 1997, the Utah Supreme Court upheld Clawson's convictions. One of the claims on appeal was prosecutorial misconduct for my "threatening" of Paul Rafferty. The Supreme Court denied the claim, saying: *"Here the prosecutor simply made explicit one of the consequences of a breach of the plea agreement by the witness; the threatened consequence was neither illegal nor unwarranted."*[60] Sounds kind of like "Threatened like a Minister of State, with justice" – the quote from *A Man For All Seasons*. I wouldn't have minded a headline then – *"Horton Exonerated by Supreme Court"* – but it would only happen in my dreams. The vindication of a prosecutor accused of chicanery two years earlier just doesn't make much of a news story.

At about the time that the Supreme Court handed down its decision, it came to my attention that Paul Rafferty, who had been returned to Indiana to serve his Utah sentence, had been given a 30-year rehearing date. It wasn't a parole release date, just a date to re-evaluate his case and set a parole date.

At first I thought it was a mistake. I had seen cold-blooded murderers get similar rehearing dates, but nobody like Rafferty, who was both very young and not the prime instigator of the crimes. I thought maybe they meant Clawson rather than Rafferty. After all, Rafferty was just the juvenile tag-along who probably wouldn't have stolen his mother's car or committed a crime like this without Clawson's prodding. And I knew that the letter Dave Blackwell sent to the Utah Board of Pardons and Parole in 1996 had said we were satisfied with his cooperation in the Clawson case.

I checked with the Board and learned it was no mistake. Rafferty, who had not appeared personally before the Board because he was being housed at an Indiana prison, had been given a 30-year rehearing date, partly

---

[60] Utah Supreme Court, No. 950400, issued August 12, 1997.

because he had fallen in with a hard group in prison and had become involved in an escape plot. While I didn't know the details of that, the thought came to me that if I were a young kid facing the prospect of life in prison, I might try to escape as well. In any event, the 30-year rehearing date seemed disproportionately long to me. So after consulting with Dave Blackwell, I decided to write a letter to the Board. Had we not been clear enough about the relative culpability of Rafferty vs. Clawson?

I penned a five-page letter to the Board to give them more information "which might affect the parole date of Paul Rafferty." I outlined the relative culpability of the two defendants, pointing out that Clawson was older, was the instigator who convinced Paul to steal his mother's car, was the one who took his guns along, was the one who made the decision to flee the police, was the one who fired numerous rounds and killed Trooper Sands, etc. I also pointed out that Paul had pled guilty and had agreed to testify against Clawson.

On the issue of Paul's testimony, I said: "While it was clearly something he was uncomfortable doing, Rafferty did honor his commitment to testify at Clawson's trial. I believe he did so honestly, and even Clawson's attorney didn't attack his credibility."

I later heard back that the Board had modified its decision. Rafferty's rehearing date had been moved up from 30 years to 20 years. It still seemed like an awfully long time to me.

CHAPTER 16

Prosecuting
Religious Extremists:
What's Going On in Utah?

WHATEVER ELSE ONE THINKS about the Mormon Church, it certainly has been fertile ground for spawning some bizarre offshoot groups and individuals, many of whom have committed high-profile crimes – murders, bombings, kidnappings, sexual assaults, armed standoffs, and the like. And many of these folks have characterized themselves as prophets and identified with a verse from Mormon scripture which talks about the "one mighty and strong."[61] If you put together in a room all those who view themselves as the "one mighty and strong," you'd need a mighty big room.

That room would include:

Ervil LeBaron

LeBaron was the leader of a violent Mormon fundamentalist sect in the 1970s and early 80s. He was a polygamist with multiple "wives," many of whom he involved in a series of murders. Over a 10-year period, he orchestrated the murders of dozens of people, including leaders of rival

---

[61] Doctrine & Covenants 85:7.

polygamist groups and disaffected members of his own "church." He also ordered the killing of several members of his own family, including his brother, Joel. Even after being convicted of murder and sentenced to prison in Utah, LeBaron ordered the killing of many more people from his prison cell. Some of his victims were murdered long after 1981, the year he died in prison. He is thought to be responsible for the murders of at least 28 people.

Ronald Lafferty

In 1984, Lafferty, an excommunicated Mormon, claimed to have received a revelation to kill four people, including his sister-in-law and her 15-month-old baby. Through religious rhetoric, he enlisted the help of his brother Dan, and together they forced their way into the apartment of their sister-in-law, beat her, slashed her throat, and then slit the throat of her baby while the infant lay in her crib. (See Chapter 17 and 18.)

Addam Swapp

Swapp dynamited an LDS stake center in 1988, holed up on a 2-acre compound with his extended family, and led a 13-day armed standoff with state and federal officers, which culminated in a shootout that ended with the death of a police officer. (See Chapters 10 and 11.)

Brian David Mitchell

Mitchell was a panhandler and street preacher who donned white robes, changed his named to "Emmanuel," and claimed personal revelations from God. In 2002, after allegedly receiving a revelation to take virgin brides, he broke into the home of 14-year-old Elizabeth Smart, abducted her at knifepoint, and held her in captivity for several months, sexually assaulting her almost daily. (See Chapter 18.)

And that's just some of the men in the "mighty and strong" club.

THE MIGHTY AND STRONG: TRUE BELIEVERS, MANIPULATORS, OR INSANE?

So what's going on here? Some of these extremists started out as regular members of the Mormon Church. Some even served as Church leaders. Ron Lafferty was once a second counselor in a bishopric. Brian David Mitchell was at one time an LDS temple worker.

At first blush, their strange beliefs and those of other religious extremists seem to be "crazy." But upon closer look at their behavior, none of them appeared to be so out of touch with reality as to qualify for a mental defense, either under Utah law or more traditional insanity laws.[62] They all engaged in goal-oriented behavior, and many of them betrayed themselves by blithely violating the tenets of their own professed "faiths." I've found that jurors don't tend to give the benefit of the doubt to defendants who profess religious motivation for their crimes and then act in ways that reveal that they are actually motivated by things such as hatred, revenge, lust, power and self-aggrandizement.

How could jurors take Ron Lafferty's defense seriously – that he was motivated by a revelation from God to kill his sister-in-law and her baby – when he'd made statements to others that the baby had to die because "she'd just grow up to be a bitch like her mother," and about his sister-in-law that "as far as I'm concerned, they can dig the bitch up and kill her again"? And when, as he'd gathered up his weapons on the day of the murders, he'd responded to the question, "What are you going to hunt?" by saying, "Any f___ing thing that gets in my way!"? Religiously motivated crime?

Similarly, how could jurors not convict Brian David Mitchell, who turned on and off his religious rhetoric and bizarre behavior to suit his purposes, and who used a claimed religious revelation to justify kidnapping and raping Elizabeth Smart?

Neither Lafferty nor Mitchell appeared to be true believers; rather, they seemed to be master manipulators who had learned to enlist the aid

---

[62] For more information on Utah's insanity defense, see Chapter 17.

of those around them by professing religious beliefs and authority. Not that they had large followings. Ron Lafferty had his brother, Dan, the true believer. Brian David Mitchell had his wife, Wanda Barzee. Both accomplices were easily manipulated through appeals to their religious beliefs.

One could certainly question whether Ron Lafferty and Brian David Mitchell really believed their own rhetoric.[63] And if they didn't believe it themselves, how could such professed beliefs be the foundation for an insanity defense?

But not all criminals who are religious extremists are like Lafferty and Mitchell. Some of them do seem to be "true believers." Dan Lafferty appeared to be a "legitimate" religious fanatic, and if either of the Lafferty brothers was mentally ill, it would have been Dan. Dan, unlike Ron, was forthright about what he had done. Dan and Ron were tried separately, and during Dan's trial, he represented himself, and essentially made the argument to the jury that although it was hard to understand why God would have ordered his sister-in-law and her baby killed, he had no choice but to carry out the "revelation" his brother had received.

Cases like *Lafferty* and *Mitchell* raise the question of how we can differentiate between religious ideas that may be caused by mental illness, and those that are clearly outside the mainstream, but which, while they may seem bizarre, are not the product of mental illness. Putting aside Nathaniel Branden's view that all religious beliefs are at their core irrational and, hence, delusional,[64] how do we enter into the territory of another person's religious belief and confidently declare it to be "crazy"? It seems to be a rather universal human experience for people to accept the mysteries of their own faith as somehow reasonable and normal, but to look at the "odd" beliefs of others as unbelievable and absurd.

Even the "battle of the experts" typical of insanity cases gets interesting

---

[63] In their competency proceedings, both Lafferty and Mitchell were characterized as "crazy like a fox."
[64] See "Mental Health versus Mysticism and Self-Sacrifice" by Nathaniel Branden, Chapter 2 in *The Virtue of Selfishness,* by Ayn Rand (Signet Books, 1964).

and somewhat murky here. One psychiatrist or psychologist looks at the written "revelations" of a Ron Lafferty or a Brian David Mitchell as the ravings of a madman, while another says their writings are consistent with the scriptures they grew up with, and quite easily understood when put into the proper subcultural and religious context.

A vivid example of this was in the Mitchell case, where a defense expert characterized Mitchell's religious writing as incoherent babblings, and thus evidence of his mental illness. But then a professor of religion from BYU came in and testified for the prosecution that these same passages were lifted almost verbatim from the *Bible* and *Book of Mormon*, with very few changes.

So when is a "fixed false delusion" enough to cross the line into the realm of insanity? How can a person be so steeped in strange religious ideas and rhetoric and not be mentally ill? Isn't it one's initial impulse to say this stuff is so weird that it must be "crazy"?

These questions are certainly fertile ground for expert testimony, as mental health professionals often line up on opposite sides of the issue. In Ron Lafferty's case, for example, nine psychologists and psychiatrists testified at his competency hearing and trial. About half believed he was both competent and criminally responsible, while the other half didn't. Judge Steven Hansen heard all the testimony and was persuaded by the doctors who opined that Lafferty was not mentally ill, and issued a well-reasoned opinion finding Lafferty competent to stand trial. Similarly, at trial, the jury rejected Lafferty's mental defense and found him "guilty," rather than either "not guilty by reason of insanity" or "guilty and mentally ill."

But not all religious extremists run mental defenses. In Addam Swapp's case, there was no indication that he was mentally ill – just incredibly provocative, narcissistic, and inflexible in his stand. He was absolutely certain of the rightness of his cause, which involved blowing up an LDS church building and then engaging law enforcement officers in a protracted deadly standoff. Not even appeals to the safety of his own children could move him off his "stand."

Unlike Lafferty and Mitchell, Swapp did fit the profile of a "true believer," in the sense that he didn't hesitate to boldly proclaim what he had done and why. Right after the bombing of the church building, he planted a pole with writing on it in the snow, making it clear to the authorities that he was responsible. During the standoff, he told his story to an FBI negotiator, admitting what he'd done. He told the story again to a Salt Lake reporter while he was awaiting trial. And he told it to juries in both his federal and state trials.

Before the federal trial, we raised the issue with Judge Bruce Jenkins of whether Addam and his co-defendants might be mentally ill because of their extreme and unreasonable beliefs, and requested mental competency evaluations. The defense attorneys resisted the evaluations, insisting that the defendants were competent and arguing that we were just trying to paint them as crazy because of their unorthodox beliefs.

We weren't. What we were trying to do was to make sure that if we went to trial and convicted the defendants, an appellate court wouldn't later look at these folks without the context of the subculture from which they sprang, and conclude that they must be mentally ill and should have been evaluated for competency. That could result in any convictions we obtained being overturned on appeal, and we didn't want to have to try the case twice.[65] Judge Jenkins created the record we needed by asking Addam and his co-defendants some questions in court that were designed to probe whether there might be issues relating to their mental competency. After those exchanges, the Judge concluded that there was no reason to order competency evaluations.

Some of the religious zealots I prosecuted remind me of anti-govern-

---

[65] In fact, this happened in the Ron Lafferty case. He was originally convicted of the murders in 1985, but the case was overturned by the 10th Circuit Court of Appeals based on the judges' concerns that he may not have been competent to stand trial. The case was sent back to square one and assigned to the Attorney General's Office, and Mike Wims and I re-tried the case in the spring of 1996.

ment extremists who are willing to escalate a minor encounter with a police officer, such as a request for a driver's license, into a deadly event. While these people take extreme stands that sometimes turn lethal, they don't appear to have any major mental illnesses. What many do exhibit are antisocial and narcissistic personality traits, and they cling to beliefs and ideas that seem not only unreasonable but dangerously provocative.

So what causes so many of these extremists to arise from the ranks of the Mormon faith or culture? I'm not sure anybody has a definitive answer, but it may have something to do with the power of the LDS Church's claim that it is the one true church, as well as the way these extremists are able to seize upon three of the Church's key doctrines and use them for their own purposes: First, the concept of personal revelation – the notion that individuals can receive direct communication from God; second, the concept of priesthood – the idea that these men have special authority to act in God's name; and third, the doctrine of polygamy, which was established by Joseph Smith and practiced by Smith and others from the 1830's until 1890, when it was officially abandoned by the Church (although many Mormons continued to practice it well into the 20th century).

While mainstream Mormons understand the boundaries and limitations of both personal revelation and priesthood, extremists recognize no such limitations when it comes to advancing their ends. They are also able to manipulate others from the same background and enlist them in their "cause." And there is no shortage of verses of scripture, both in the Bible and in Mormon holy books, that these extremists can pull out selectively and use for their own purposes.

There's something for everybody in holy writ – peace and love, death and destruction. Most people in major religions, including Mormons, know that there are extreme verses in their holy books, which, if taken literally and without regard to other moderating principles, could justify extreme acts. But they have the ability to maintain balance by seeing the bigger picture, and have the sense not to lose sight of the overarching principles that make religion a positive influence both in their lives and in the lives of others.

I've found that many of the people who go off the rails and commit crimes in the name of God are very literal thinkers who seize on the fiery rhetoric, the war-like passages, to pattern their "revelations" and justify their antisocial acts. None of them cite the Beatitudes. Rather, they "put on the armor of God," and when they do . . . look out for the rest of us.

An example of a passage of Mormon scripture that seems to resonate with many of these extremists is the story of the prophet Nephi in the *Book of Mormon*. In it, Nephi is commanded by God to obtain certain sacred records engraved on brass plates which are in the possession of a wicked man named Laban. When Nephi's brother talks to Laban and asks for the records, Laban runs the brother off and threatens to kill him. Nephi, a man of great faith, decides to return to Laban's house to try to obtain the brass plates.

As he is on his way, he discovers Laban passed out on the ground, "drunken with wine." Nephi is then "constrained by the Spirit" to kill Laban. When Nephi recoils from the idea of murder, the passage continues: "And it came to pass that the Spirit said unto me again: Slay him, for the Lord hath delivered him into thy hands: Behold the Lord slayeth the wicked to bring forth his righteous purposes. It is better that one man should perish than that a nation should dwindle and perish in unbelief." Nephi then takes Laban's sword, grabs him by the hair, and cuts off his head.[66]

It's not hard to understand how fringe personalities might seize on this scripture as justification for blithely disobeying the cardinal rule of the Ten Commandments: "Thou shalt not kill." This passage of Mormon scripture has emboldened more than one extremist to characterize their own personal enemies as God's enemies, and to then target them for destruction through their "revelations."

---

[66] *Book of Mormon,* 1 Nephi, Chapter 4

A vivid example of this occurred in the Lafferty case. When Ron Lafferty was trying to get his brother Dan to help him kill his sister-in-law and her baby, he primed Dan with a "revelation" that these victims had somehow interfered with the work of the Lord, and thus had to be "removed." Lest there be any misunderstanding about what he meant by "removed," Ron came up with another revelation, which spoke of returning to Utah with "slaughter weapons." So the plan to commit murder was clear. But in order to provide Dan with even greater motivation to carry it out, Ron penned the following "revelation," directed specifically at Dan:

"Thus saith the Lord, and to my servant Dan, behold the words of thy Savior, even the Redeemer of the World: thou art like Nephi of old, for never since the beginning of time have I had a more obedient son."

Ron's "revelation" did the trick, and Dan, the obedient, demonstrated his devotion to God by calmly and with perfect serenity slitting the throat of his 15-month-old niece.

Not surprisingly, when defendants like this carry out their "revelations," they fare no better in Utah courts than Nephi would have fared, had he been put on trial for killing Laban as he lay in a drunken stupor. As I emphasized in forensic mental health training presentations through the years, being "egged on" by God to kill someone does not constitute a defense under Utah Law.

And then there's polygamy. All of the home-grown religious extremists I prosecuted in Utah believed in the doctrine of polygamy, and most practiced it. Although the Mormon Church officially disavowed the practice in 1890, Joseph Smith's revelation sanctifying the practice was never disavowed, nor has it ever been removed from Mormon holy writ.[67] Once the practice of polygamy was no longer sanctioned, the Church's

---

[67] Doctrine and Covenants, Section 132

condemnation of plural marriage spawned many offshoot groups, which took up the cause and perpetuated the practice. Many polygamists still flourish today in enclaves throughout Utah, Arizona, Texas, Canada and Mexico.

Since polygamy is illegal, those who practice it are living in violation of the law, and some tend to get into a siege mentality. While it appears that some polygamists manage to obey all laws except the bigamy law,[68] for others, polygamy is only a part of a larger mindset. It can be a volatile mix – pro-polygamy, anti-government, and fiercely religious. And to ratchet up the volatility, these extremists believe that they carry God's own priesthood authority, which they interpret as the power to receive revelations and to act in God's name however they choose. Many feel that they, not the "apostate" LDS Church which has abandoned the eternal principal of plural marriage, are the rightful heirs to Joseph Smith's true brand of Mormonism.

THE ROLE OF AUTHORITY AND OBEDIENCE IN RELIGION

Religions which make bold claims of authority and hold great sway over their members' day-to-day lives are also more likely to spawn extremists than religions which allow their members a wide latitude of belief. I haven't heard of a member of, for example, the Unitarian Church going off the deep end and committing crimes in the name of God or religion.

But the LDS Church holds itself out as the one true church on earth, exerts tremendous influence over its faithful, and requires adherence to its principles and tenets as the only true pathway to God. It emphasizes conformity, obedience to Church leaders and to strict behavioral standards, and the continuing need for its members to sanctify themselves and strive for perfection as the Church defines it.

It's not just a Sunday religion; rather, it strongly encourages its mem-

---

[68] Utah has no crime specifically designated as "polygamy ," although the Utah Constitution specifically bans its practice, forever. Utah Constitution, Article III, Section I.

bers to make Mormonism central to their daily lives, and considers obedience to Church authority a cardinal virtue. With few exceptions, Church leaders do not encourage independence of thought in matters of religion. The Church as an institution has and uses tools such as Church courts to deal with both what it considers misconduct and what it considers dissent or apostasy on the part of its members.[69] It can also make those who fall short of its ideals feel guilty or unworthy.

It's powerful stuff, and while mainstream members of the Mormon Church are some of the finest people you'll ever meet, there have arisen from the fringes of its ranks, and the ranks of its offshoot groups, a handful of people who have used, or, perhaps more accurately, misused, church concepts and doctrines to justify some pretty horrific crimes.

You have to wonder if these people would have carried out their crimes absent the framework of religious justification. While one could never know for sure, my best guess is that most of them, and perhaps all of them, would have, although probably on a less grand scale. But the overlay of religion does add a powerful element to the mix – it both emboldens people to engage in extreme actions and enables them to recruit obedient followers to help them carry out "the Lord's will."[70]

---

[69] Recent LDS Church excommunications include Kate Kelly of "Ordain Women," and "Mormon Stories" blogger John Dehlin. See https://en.wikipedia.org/wiki/Kate_Kelly_(feminist) and https://en.wikipedia.org/wiki/John_Dehlin

[70] For an example of how dangerous that mix can be, see chapter 18 of *Under the Banner of Heaven,* by Jon Krakauer (Doubleday, 2003). It documents the Mountain Meadows Massacre, a tragic event that occurred in 1857, during which 120 members of a wagon train – unarmed men, women and children – were massacred by Mormon militiamen acting under the direction of their local Church leaders.

In 2007, the Mormon Church released a statement expressing profound regret for the massacre, and emphasized that the responsibility for it lay with local Church leaders who also held civic and military positions, and with members of the Church acting under their direction.

See http://www.mormonnewsroom.org/article/mountain-meadows-massacre

The dangerous dynamic that can lead others to blindly follow religious authority can occur in any situation where extreme fundamentalist beliefs exist, and is in no way unique to Mormon fundamentalism. For an in-depth discussion of the characteristics of fundamentalism and its dangers, see *Our Endangered Values,* by Jimmy Carter (Simon and Schuster, 2006).

RELIGION, CONSCIENCE AND CHOICE

During my preparation for the *Lafferty* trial, something striking happened while I was interviewing a key witness – a man who, along with Ron, Dan, and several others, had been a member of "The School of the Prophets," a small group of disaffected Mormons who met regularly to discuss its members' purported revelations – a group which, over time, became more and more extreme. When Ron had taken to the group his "removal revelation," targeting for death his sister-in-law and her 15-month-old baby, this man had rejected it, saying, "Babies don't get in the way of the Lord's work."

While it seemed reassuring that this witness had managed to maintain his moral compass, he told me something at the end of the interview that attests to the power extreme beliefs can have over people who become steeped in the subculture of radical religion. He said that although it seemed crazy to him now, at the time, he had felt some sense of disappointment in himself for not having the faith to carry out the revelation.

The man's statement reminded me of a passage from *Huckleberry Finn*. As Huck and Jim float down the Mississippi on a raft, Huck struggles with pangs of guilt for helping Jim, a runaway slave, escape from his rightful owner – a poor old woman who has never done Huck "no harm." Based on the culture in which he was raised, Huck feels he knows what he must do to be a good, honest, and clean person. He must give up his evil ways and turn Jim in at the next town down the river.

When he momentarily resolves to do the "right thing," he writes a letter on a piece of paper notifying Jim's owner where Jim can be found. He immediately basks in the thought of cleansing himself of his sin and guilt, and realizes how near he's come to "being lost and going to hell."

But then he thinks of how good Jim has been to him, and how Jim thinks of him as the best friend he has in the world. And then Huck starts to lose his resolve. He picks up the paper he has just written to Jim's owner and holds it in his hands:

I was a-trembling, because I'd got to decide, forever, betwixt two things, and I knowed it. I studied a minute, sort of holding my breath, and then says to myself:

"All right, then, I'll go to hell"— and tore it up.

As I listened to the witness in the *Lafferty* case describe his feelings of disappointment in himself for lacking faith to carry out Lafferty's murderous "revelation," I thought of how contorted things can become – how morality can be turned upside down – in this type of extreme religious environment.

I grew up in the Mormon Church,[71] and remember hearing as a boy that one of the Church's tenets is that there should be moderation in all things.[72] From what I've seen over the years, I think we would all be safer if those who were inclined to religious extremism could apply that principle to religious beliefs as well

---

[71] While I was raised a Mormon in Southern California in a family that could trace its pioneer heritage back for generations, I was always skeptical of the Church's claim that it was the only true church on earth. When I was eighteen, I was interviewed by my bishop, and although I was candid about my doubts, I was nevertheless called as a missionary, and served for two years in France and Belgium. Contrary to my bishop's statement that he wasn't concerned about my lack of faith because, like most missionaries, I would gain my testimony in the mission field, that was not my experience. As a result, much of the time I worked as staff in the mission headquarters in Brussels rather than as a missionary in the field, because I wasn't willing to tell people that I knew the Church was true when I didn't. Currently, I am no longer affiliated with the Mormon Church.

[72] The phrase was generally used in connection with the Word of Wisdom, the Church's exhortation against things like drinking and smoking. *Doctrine and Covenants,* Section 89.

CHAPTER 17

Knocking Down
the Insanity Defense

EARLY IN MY CAREER AT THE D.A.'S OFFICE, I was asked by Bob Stott to do a presentation at a prosecution conference on the subject of cross-examining mental health experts. I had no clue how to do it. At most, I'd taken a couple of college classes in psychology, which didn't give me any real idea of how to go about questioning a psychiatrist or psychologist in court.

I decided to contact the Utah State Hospital and see if I could talk to some mental health experts there. I made contact with a young psychiatrist named Breck Lebegue, who gave me some ideas and helped me do a mock cross-examination at the conference. It went well enough, and I gained a little insight into how subjective mental health opinions really are – just educated guesses at best – and how effectively they can be challenged, particularly if they are inconsistent with known facts about a defendant's behavior and background.

I had no idea at the time, but this little exercise was to set me on a course where I became more and more involved with, and interested in, the interplay between mental health issues and the criminal justice system.

Before long, I found myself embroiled in a series of cases involving mental issues, which generally fell into one of two areas: whether defendants were competent to stand trial, and whether they had any version of an insanity or diminished capacity defense.

I quickly learned that these were two very different questions. Competency boils down to whether a defendant can be tried at all. The U. S. Supreme Court had ruled that incompetent defendants – those suffering from mental illnesses that make them unable to have a factual and rational understanding of the proceedings against them or unable to consult rationally with their attorneys – cannot be tried unless they can be restored to competency.[73] The question of competency is a "here and now" determination – whether the defendant is competent to stand trial *now*.

Mental defenses, on the other hand, are "then and there" determinations – whether at the time a crime was committed, a defendant was insane, and thus could be found "not guilty by reason of insanity" or guilty of a less severe crime than the one charged, generally known as "diminished mental capacity."

Within a couple of years of the conference presentation, I became the office expert on mental issues, and found the area fascinating. I also found that cross-examining mental health experts whose opinions were poorly reasoned or based on faulty information – usually just taking at face value whatever defendants had told them about their mental states – was the most fun you could have in a courtroom. I also discovered that some of the opinions offered by mental health experts, even in the most serious murder cases, were ludicrous – weirder than I could have made up if I'd been given free license to let my imagination run wild. More about that later, in Chapter 18, but first, here are some of the cases I handled where mental claims were raised:

State v. Brent Lompart: The Defendant stabbed the victim, his drug connection, 109 times, and claimed diminished mental capacity due to

---

[73] *Dusky v. U.S.,* 364 U.S. 402 (1960)

cocaine intoxication, which allegedly caused him to believe he was acting in self-defense. The jury didn't buy it, and convicted him of murder.

State v. Arthur Gary Bishop: The Defendant kidnapped, sexually molested and killed five young boys over a four-year period, and claimed at trial that he should only be convicted of manslaughter because he was a homosexual pedophile with antisocial personality disorder. We agreed with the diagnosis, but argued that while it may have helped explain his motivation for the crimes, it in no way provided a defense to what he did. The jury agreed and convicted him of capital murder, sentencing him to the death penalty. (See Chapters 18.)

State v. Preston Greer: The Defendant kidnapped, assaulted and threatened to kill his ex-wife, after going to her house in violation of a protective order, taking with him a shotgun, shells, and a bottle of vodka. He told her this would be the last day they spent together, and terrorized her for hours before a neighbor noticed his car in front of the house and called the police. Greer claimed he had mental problems that caused him to have a diminished mental capacity, and that he didn't know what he was doing. The jury didn't buy it.

State v. Norman Newsted: The defendant, who participated in the triple murder in Cedar City, claimed at trial that he had diminished mental capacity due to borderline mental retardation and intoxication through drugs and alcohol. The jury rejected this defense, and convicted him of capital murder. (See Chapters 7, 8, and 18.)

State v. Joseph Charles Gardner, Jr.: The Defendant shot and killed a young woman who was trying to help his girlfriend break away from him. When caught, he claimed that the antidepressant drug Prozac had caused him to suffer temporary insanity, kill the victim and then forget what he did. He didn't get far with the defense. (See Chapter 18.)

State v. Jeremy Clawson: Clawson killed a Utah Highway Patrol trooper in a high-speed freeway chase. (See Chapter 15.) The defense lined up a psychologist who submitted a lengthy report endorsing the view that

Clawson had only fired at officers in an attempt to get himself shot – "suicide by cop" – and that he had never intended anyone else to get hurt.

At our request, the judge appointed forensic psychologist Stephen Golding to talk to Clawson and assess his claim. When Dr. Golding went down to the jail to talk to him, Clawson stopped the interview after Golding asked probing questions that challenged his "suicide by cop" theory. Dr. Golding, who was forensically trained and knew better than to just accept uncritically anything a defendant told him, did what the defense psychologist had not: He probed for the truth, and Clawson didn't like it.

I was geared up to cross-examine the defense psychologist at trial, but the morning she was scheduled to testify, the defense attorneys withdrew their mental defense and sent their expert witness home. Instead, they said they would call Clawson himself as a witness. They were most concerned that we not be allowed to cross-examine Clawson about anything he had said to their psychologist.

Once Clawson testified, it was easy to see why. He made no mention at all of the "suicide by cop" theory, and claimed that when he shot in the direction of the officers, he was just trying to get them to back off the pursuit. Had the defense not decided to change theories mid-trial, the defense psychologist would have been lined up to testify in support of Clawson's "suicide by cop" theory, and we would have asked the jury to disregard her theory as nothing more than her gullible acceptance of his version of events. In the end, the jury didn't buy Clawson's new defense either, and he was convicted of capital murder.

State v. Ronald Lafferty: The Defendant and his brother Dan killed their sister-in-law Brenda and her 15-month-old baby by slitting their throats. (See Chapters 16 and 18.) Lafferty's attorneys claimed at trial that he acted under a religious delusion that he was carrying out a revelation from God, and thus believed he was morally justified (a quirky provision of Utah law which has since been repealed by the Legislature), and consequently should only be convicted of manslaughter. There was plenty of evidence, however, that the defendant had hated Brenda and held her responsible for the break-up of his marriage. The jury didn't buy Lafferty's mental defense, convicted him of capital murder, and sentenced him to death.

State v. Ronnie Lee Gardner. The Defendant killed a bartender, and then later killed a bystander during a courthouse escape attempt. (See Chapter 6.) He was convicted of capital murder for the courthouse shooting and sentenced to death. Years later, his appellate attorneys claimed, on scant evidence, that Gardner suffered from "frontal lobe syndrome," a brain abnormality that somehow either excused or mitigated the murder. They argued that Gardner's attorneys should have raised a mental defense at his trial. After extensive hearings and a "battle of the experts" in federal court, the judge disagreed, and upheld Gardner's conviction.

REFORMING UTAH'S MENTAL DEFENSE STATUTES

By the time I left the District Attorney's Office, I had handled many cases with mental issues, and so one of my duties at the Attorney General's Office was to consult with prosecutors across the state when they had cases involving questions of competency or mental defenses such as insanity or diminished mental capacity. I also put on training presentations on forensic mental health issues at conferences for prosecutors, mental health experts, and judges.

At the Attorney General's office, I became involved in revising Utah's insanity and competency statutes. Utah has one of the most restrictive mental defense statutes in the country, having nearly abolished the insanity defense altogether in 1983 in the wake of John Hinckley Jr.'s attempted assassination of President Reagan. After Hinckley was found "not guilty by reason of insanity," there was public outcry across the nation. Many states looked into revising their insanity laws, but Utah was one of the few to actually radically change its insanity defense statute.

Before the 1983 amendment, defendants could be found "not guilty by reason of insanity" in Utah if they had a mental illness which substantially impaired their capacity to appreciate the wrongfulness of their conduct or to conform their conduct to the requirements of law – a common standard then used in many states. The law was changed in Utah to focus exclusively on whether the defendant had the mental state described in the criminal statutes themselves. For example, in the case of murder, the law focused on whether the defendant acted intentionally or knowingly in causing the death of another. Knowing right from wrong or being unable to control one's behavior was no longer relevant to the question of criminal responsibility.

Utah could change its laws because the U. S. Supreme Court has never ruled that defendants have a constitutional right to any insanity defense. States are free to legislate in this area as they please, and some states, including Montana and Idaho, have abolished the insanity defense altogether.

So now in Utah, even if a defendant kills due to a crazy delusion caused by mental illness, he cannot escape conviction if he knows he is killing a human being. The Utah Supreme Court, which upheld Utah's revised insanity law in 1995,[74] described it along these lines: If a mentally ill person chokes another to death and thinks he is squeezing a grapefruit, he has a defense. If he knows he is strangling a human being, no matter how crazy the motivation or reasons why, he has no defense and is guilty of murder.

While I was not involved in the initial major change to the insanity defense that occurred in 1983, I did become involved later in lobbying for some additional changes. It seemed to me that the "grapefruit squeezing" standard was too stringent. In the 1995 *Herrera* decision upholding Utah's insanity law, the Court pointed out that a mentally ill defendant who kills under the delusion that he is shooting at an enemy soldier during a war would be guilty of murder under Utah's statute. And while the Supreme Court in *Herrera* upheld Utah's stringent insanity standard, it was a narrow 3-to-2 decision, with blistering dissents from two justices who felt the standard was so stringent as to be unconstitutional.

---

[74] State v. Herrera, 895 P.2d 359 (Utah 1995)

So after the *Herrera* decision was handed down, I worked with the Statewide Association of Prosecutors in lobbying for a change that could benefit at least some mentally ill offenders who kill. It wasn't an easy sell, since a mentally ill woman named Rita Kim had recently walked into an office building and, for no apparent reason, shot and killed a receptionist. It wasn't the best time to advocate for leniency on behalf of mentally ill killers, and the senator who sponsored the bill had me address the Senate to explain why prosecutors would support such a measure. I told them that we felt the amendment was fair and that it would be a hedge against the Court striking down our insanity statute altogether, especially since *Herrera* was such a close and hotly-contested decision. One of the senators asked me if I thought the new provisions could be misused by a defendant. I said he could count on it, but that we had drafted the bill narrowly enough that I was comfortable we could defend against bogus claims.

The new law, which was unique to Utah, passed in 1999, and established the partial defense of special mitigation for mentally ill offenders. It applies to mentally ill defendants who kill under the delusion that they are acting in self-defense. For example, if a former soldier suffers from post-traumatic stress disorder and schizophrenia and has a flashback that he is in the war shooting at an enemy soldier, he could qualify for special mitigation, which would reduce the level of his crime by one degree – for example, from murder to manslaughter. However, if he has the same mental illnesses which cause him to suffer a flashback, but he thinks he's killing unarmed "enemy" civilians, the special mitigation law would not apply and he would still be guilty of murder.

The reason for this distinction is that the law says that special mitigation requires that the mentally ill defendant has a delusion such that, "if the facts existed as the defendant believed them to be in his delusional state, those facts would provide a legal justification for his conduct."[75] In

---

[75] Utah Code Annotated, Section 76-5-205.5

other words, if your delusion is that you're shooting at an enemy soldier, that action would be legally justified, so special mitigation would apply. But if your delusion is that you're killing enemy civilians during a war, that action would not be legally justified, and so the special mitigation statute would not apply.

Some critics have argued that there should be no distinction between mentally ill defendants who kill while experiencing major delusions, whatever their nature. But the law has to draw the line somewhere, and this is where the Utah State Legislature drew it when they agreed to expand Utah's very restrictive law.

While I believe Utah's tough mental defense laws made it somewhat easier to convict defendants in the cases I prosecuted, I don't think it made the essential difference. I believe we could have convicted all those defendants using more traditional standards for insanity, such as whether mental illness prevented defendants from appreciating the wrongfulness of their actions.

I'm comfortable with what the federal government and many other states have done in this area. Defendants who claim insanity in these jurisdictions must show by clear and convincing evidence that they had a mental illness at the time of the crime which made them unable to appreciate the wrongfulness of their conduct. While that's a common standard for insanity in most American jurisdictions, in Utah it's no longer a relevant consideration in determining whether a defendant should be acquitted on grounds of insanity or diminished mental capacity.

During the course of my career, there were only two defendants with a documented history of mental illness that I felt were truly mentally ill and might qualify for some type of mental defense: John Callister and Michael Foxworthy.

JOHN CALLISTER CASE

Callister was a former veteran of the first Gulf War who had been diagnosed as having post-traumatic stress disorder. He was also a former postal worker in Spokane, Washington. By the time he committed a homicide in Utah, he had a well-documented history of mental deterioration, strange behavior, and mental illness.

In late October of 1998, Callister left his apartment in Spokane, Washington, and traveled by train to Green River, Utah. He dressed in military fatigues and took with him three different firearms, as well as ammunition, rations, and backpacking equipment. He got off the train in Green River and then spent four nights camping in a remote area south of town. On October 29, he hid in some rocks next to a dirt roadway in a remote area not far from Green River. As the victim, an Emery County employee, drove by in a county road grader, Callister fired repeatedly at his random victim with a .22-caliber rifle, hitting him nine times. He then dragged the victim's body off the roadway and took his keys and wallet.

The Emery County Sheriff's Office solved the crime by tracking Callister from the crime scene to a motel in Green River, where he was apprehended. He was charged with aggravated murder, which carried the potential of the death penalty, and was appointed a team of attorneys headed by experienced capital-qualified defense counsel, Tom Evans.

My old friend, Emery County Attorney Dave Blackwell, knew early on that the case wasn't going to be a "whodunit," but he also knew that it would have lots of mental issues, and so he invited me to assist him on the case. I was pleased to team up again with Dave and the Emery County Sherriff's officers I had come to know so well a few years earlier, when I had assisted in the capital murder trial of Jeremy Clawson, who had shot and killed a Utah Highway Patrol trooper during a high-speed chase not far from Green River. (See Chapter 15.)

When Callister's local defense counsel learned about the newly-passed special mitigation law, he thought he had the perfect case for it. Callister was practically the poster child of a war veteran who suffers a mental breakdown, has a flashback, and thinks he's back fighting in the war. He had the history, and his behavior was bizarre enough that it looked like he might well qualify under the new law. Under that scenario, Callister, who had been charged with aggravated murder, would only be found guilty of the lesser offense of murder, since special mitigation would reduce the level of offense by one degree. The theory seemed plausible enough. Even some of the people who had known Callister back in Spokane opined that he'd probably had a flashback, which had led him to think that the road grading equipment was an enemy tank, and the driver an enemy soldier.

The case seemed perfectly postured for the new defense, but there was just one problem: While Callister appeared to be truly mentally ill, that wasn't his delusion. When the defense attorneys sent in forensic psychologist Nancy Cohn to interview Callister about what had happened that day and why he killed the victim, he readily told her, and his stated motivation had nothing to do with a war flashback. Callister, who had become a Muslim a couple of months before committing the crime, said that he was on a Jihad when he killed the victim, having been directed by Allah to kill non-believers. Callister had brought materials with him from Spokane, including a map of the U.S. with arrows pointing to the West Coast and the word "Jihad" written across the map.

Not only did Callister tell this version to the defense-retained psychologist, but he also made similar statements to a jailor and another inmate. Even when prompted, he would not endorse the idea that he had any delusion about where he was or what he was doing when he killed the victim. He wasn't having a flashback and he didn't think the victim was any threat to him. It could have been anybody, for he said he viewed all people in the U.S. as non-believers, and felt justified in killing them.

In Utah, unfortunately for Callister, being egged on to commit a homicide, even by God, is not a defense – not even a mental defense. As I mentioned above, the touchstone and relevant question under Utah law is whether the defendant intended to kill, not whether he knew it was wrong to do so. And Callister clearly had that intent. So what about special mitigation? It too didn't apply, because whatever delusion Callister had did not relate to a belief that he was acting in self-defense nor that he was a soldier in a war when he killed the victim. What did that leave? "Guilty," or "guilty and mentally ill"(GAMI).

Shortly before his scheduled trial, Callister's attorneys approached us and said he wanted to plead, but would not plead "guilty" since he felt he was morally justified in what he did. He would, however, plead "no contest," because he had no problem admitting that he had intentionally killed the victim, but felt he had done nothing wrong.[76] In exchange for the plea, Callister's attorneys asked us to take the death penalty off the table.

After consulting with the victim's family and law enforcement, we agreed. One of the specific mitigating circumstances in a death penalty sentencing hearing is a defendant's mental illness at the time of the crime, and this was one case where, based on his bizarre behavior and the opinions of mental health experts we respected, we believed that the defendant was mentally ill when he committed the murder.

While Callister knew that if he pleaded "no contest," the judge would find him guilty – the judge made that very clear – Callister did not want to be found "guilty and mentally ill" (GAMI), and he didn't plead that way. I found it ironic that in the one case where it seemed most clearly applicable, the defendant did not take advantage of the GAMI alternative, although some critics have argued that GAMI is only of illusory benefit to most defendants anyway, since it doesn't really limit the judge's sentencing options. Although Callister didn't plead GAMI, we did notify the Board of Pardons about all aspects of the case, including his mental illness, for their information in deciding whether and under what circumstances he should ever be released from prison.

MICHAEL FOXWORTHY CASE

Back in my early prosecution days at the D.A.'s Office, before the 1983

---

[76] A "no contest" plea neither admits nor disputes a charge. It has the same legal effect as a guilty plea, but does not require the defendant to affirmatively admit his guilt.

Insanity Reform Act, I was given the assignment of helping senior prosecutor Charles Marson on a murder case. The defendant was Michael Foxworthy, a mentally ill man who had killed before, in California. Because of that crime, he had been found "not guilty by reason of insanity" and committed to a mental hospital for the criminally insane in California. He managed to escape from the hospital with the help of a woman from Utah, who then passed Foxworthy off as her son and allowed him to live in her home in Salt Lake City.

One night at the woman's house, Foxworthy stabbed and killed a man she had invited over to dinner. Foxworthy was captured and charged with murder, and it soon became evident that the defense was going to claim that he was insane. We geared up for trial, complete with expert witnesses supporting both the defendant's claim of insanity and our position that he was antisocial and not so mentally ill as to not know right from wrong. Back then, in 1980, the relevant question under Utah law was whether he suffered from a mental illness that "substantially impaired his ability to appreciate the wrongfulness of his conduct, or to conform his conduct to the requirements of law."

Partway through the trial, Chuck Marson was concerned that the defendant might "get off" by being found "not guilty by reason of insanity," as he had in California. So he agreed to a plea bargain with Foxworthy, who had been charged with murder, punishable by five years to life in prison. The prosecution would reduce the charge to manslaughter, punishable by up to 15 years in prison, if Foxworthy would plead guilty. That way, at least he would be convicted of a criminal offense and sentenced to prison, and we wouldn't have to risk the possibility that Foxworthy might be found "not guilty by reason of insanity" at trial, which Marson felt was an unacceptable result.

Foxworthy pled guilty to manslaughter and went off to prison, and I didn't think much about him again until almost fifteen years later. I turned on the news one night and here was a story about Foxworthy – history of mental illness, had killed in California, again in Utah, and now approaching the expiration of his sentence. While the Board of Pardons had given him the maximum 15-year sentence for his manslaughter conviction, the Board's jurisdiction over him was about to end, at which time they would have no choice but to release him.

So now the TV news was running the story, and Foxworthy was making statements to the field reporter that weren't very reassuring – something about how he sure hoped he wouldn't kill again – and it struck me that had he been found "not guilty by reason of insanity," he could have been held indefinitely, until he was either no longer mentally ill or no longer a danger to himself or others. The irony was that by insisting on getting a criminal commitment rather than risking a "not guilty by reason of insanity" verdict at trial, we had set up a situation where Foxworthy was likely going to hit the streets earlier than he would have if he had been sent to the State Hospital as an insanity acquittee, rather than to the State Prison as a convicted killer.

CAPITAL PUNISHMENT AND THE MENTALLY ILL

Finally, a word about the death penalty and the mentally ill: During the past couple of decades, the United States Supreme Court has removed certain classes of people from eligibility for the death penalty. For example, they have exempted juveniles who commit murders while they are under the age of eighteen. And in 2002, they prohibited the execution of mentally retarded killers.[77]

Some see this as a general trend that will one day result in the Supreme Court abolishing the death penalty altogether, and it may be. While the Court has not yet prohibited the execution of those who were mentally ill when they committed their crimes, that group may be next, given the rationale the Court used in excluding the mentally retarded from death

---

[77] *Atkins v. Virginia*, 536 U.S. 335 (2002). For an in-depth discussion of the death penalty, see Chapter 22.

penalty consideration: that they have a "lesser degree of culpability." I don't see much reason to limit the application of that principle to the mentally retarded, and not also include those who commit their crimes when they are so seriously mentally ill that they lose touch with reality.

Still, I think it may take some time for the Supreme Court to extend death penalty protection to the mentally ill. The Court has been pretty skittish about providing any nationwide standard on how to deal with mentally ill defendants, other than in the competency arena. But competency is relatively easy compared to criminal culpability, and when it comes to the question of how culpable mentally ill killers are, the Court has left it to the states to decide.

As a result, the Court has declined to rule that any version of an insanity defense is constitutionally required. Further, as the *Hinckley* case showed, cases involving mentally ill defendants who commit acts of violence and then escape punishment in the justice system can be tinder boxes for public outrage. It appears that under the circumstances, the Supreme Court is not eager to take the lead in navigating such tricky waters.

That being said, death penalty judgments are ultimately moral judgments, and I still think the Court will one day in the not-too-distant future exclude from the death penalty those who kill under the influence of severe mental illness, on the theory that they, like mentally retarded killers, have a "lesser degree of culpability." Makes sense to me.

CHAPTER 18

Adventures in Wonderland:
"Those Were Some Crazy Shrinks"

AS A CAREER PROSECUTOR, I handled lots of cases with mental defenses, mostly murder cases, and nearly all of them were as phony as a three-dollar bill. They involved defendants with antisocial personality traits who were often in trouble with the law, but who didn't have any history of major mental illness. The motivations for the crimes were also easily explainable in traditional terms: hatred, revenge, to carry out a robbery or sexual assault, to leave no witnesses behind, etc. When these defendants got caught red-handed and had no other defense available, suddenly they had all sorts of mental problems, and generally could find an expert to support their newfound "insanity."

But most of those experts were pretty easy to discredit, because their opinions were, frankly, absurd. The truth is, in some cases, the craziest thing that happens in the courtroom is what comes out of the mouths of mental health experts on the witness stand.

Let me show you what I mean:

State v. Arthur Gary Bishop

Between 1979 and 1983, Bishop kidnapped, sexually abused and murdered five young boys over a four-year period. At trial, he produced a psychiatrist in support of his claim that he should only be convicted of manslaughter, rather than capital murder, for killing each of the victims. The claim was that he killed under the influence of extreme mental or emotional disturbance, for which there was a reasonable explanation or excuse.

The defense expert testified that when Bishop bludgeoned the last two boys to death and threw their bodies in the raging waters of Big Cottonwood Creek, he did so because he saw the boys as fundamentally unhappy, and that by throwing their bodies in the river, he was "baptizing them and sending them on to a happier life." I looked at the other members of the prosecution team. Did he really just say that?

When it was my turn to ask questions, I blithely violated the cardinal rule of cross-examination – that lawyers should never ask a question they don't know the answer to – because I figured anything the psychiatrist said would just highlight the absurdity of his theory.

So I asked him, "Did Bishop tell you that?"

"No," he said.

"Then how did you come up with that?" I asked, having no idea what he was going to say. He didn't disappoint me.

"By the birthing order of the family!"[78]

Really?? After that, the tenor of my cross-examination was pretty much "just tell me more," and with each new elaboration of his theories, our case just kept getting better.

But as bizarre as that testimony was, it wasn't the strangest mental testimony I would hear – in fact, not by a long shot.

---

[78] Referring to the birthing order in Bishop's family.

State v. Ronald Lafferty

A psychiatrist testified on Lafferty's behalf, and came up with a line of reasoning so bizarre it was later included in *Mondo Utah*,[79] a book which focused on the weirdest of the weird the state of Utah has produced, which sets the bar pretty high.

During pre-trial motion hearings, Lafferty was fond of hurling insults at us and the judge. During one hearing, when my co-counsel Mike Wims was addressing the court, Lafferty blurted out, "F___ you, Wims! Your brains are in your butt!" At trial, the psychiatrist testified that this statement by Lafferty was actually a religious incantation, and that he had said it to try to prevent the evil homosexual spirit Moroni (a reference to a prophet in the *Book of Mormon*) "from invading him from the rear [his anus]." You couldn't make this stuff up! Besides the absurdity of the claim itself, it helped put things into perspective that Lafferty had mentioned to a jailor who asked him about the evil spirits, "Hell, only the doctors believe that crap!" Well, not all of the doctors.

The truth is, had someone asked me to script "wild and crazy" expert testimony for a book or a screenplay, and told me to let my imagination run wild, I would not have come up with stuff as weird as the actual testimony we heard in the *Bishop* and *Lafferty* cases. It's like Mark Twain says: "Truth is stranger than fiction, because fiction is obliged to stick to possibilities. Truth isn't."

State v. Joseph Charles Gardner, Jr.

Gardner had killed a woman in Southern Utah. The victim had allowed Gardner's girlfriend, who was trying to break away from him, to stay at her apartment as a safe haven. Shortly before the murder, Gardner had showed up at the victim's apartment, trying to locate his girlfriend, and the victim had called the police on him.

---

[79] *Mondo Utah,* by Trent Harris (Dream Garden Press, 1996).

Late one night, Gardner broke into the victim's apartment, shot her as she came down the stairs in the dark, loaded her body into her car, drove to a remote location, and dumped her body out in the desert. He then drove back to the apartment, where he cleaned up the car and the apartment before he left.

When the police solved the case and Gardner was arrested, he claimed he couldn't remember what happened, and his lawyer came up with the theory that he shouldn't be convicted because the antidepressant drug Prozac had caused him to suffer temporary insanity and kill the victim. While Gardner had a history of depression, he also had the most traditional of motives: anger and revenge.

For months after he was caught, Gardner kept up his story that he couldn't remember any details of either the killing or his activities of disposing of the victim's body and cleaning her apartment and car. About a year later, Gardner's lawyer filed a motion to use an "involuntary intoxication" defense, based on the idea that Gardner had taken Prozac under the direction of a physician, and it had caused him to have an irresistible impulse to kill the victim.

About the same time his attorney was filing papers in court raising the defense of "involuntary intoxication," Gardner started telling the mental health experts a different story. Suddenly he was able to remember what had happened: He had gone over late that night to the victim's apartment just to talk to her, but he remembered standing in the victim's apartment with a gun in his hand as she came down the stairs, and when he saw her, he had, in effect, an irresistible impulse to kill her. "Kill her now" was the thought that he said came into his mind.

As I prepared for trial, I met with the defense's expert witness, who was a psychologist at the Utah State Hospital. He told me that in his opinion, Gardner was only guilty of manslaughter. When I asked him why he thought it was manslaughter rather than murder, he said, "I don't know. You guys are the lawyers. You figure it out." No analysis – just a conclusion.

Not the kind of analysis one would expect from an expert schooled in both psychology and the law. I looked forward to cross-examining the doctor at trial so a jury could evaluate his reasoning process, or, more accurately, lack of reasoning process. But I never got the chance, because the case never went to trial.

The reason was that the case was effectively decided in the pre-trial motion phase. While we disagreed from the start that Prozac had caused Gardner to kill the victim – his motivation to get even with the victim seemed clear – we also felt Gardner's lawyer had misapprehended the proper legal standard for involuntary intoxication in Utah, and was thinking he could run an irresistible impulse defense, which was a variation of the insanity defense that Utah had abolished in 1983. We made a motion to have the judge declare the proper legal standard for involuntary intoxication, and Judge Philip Eves agreed with our position that Gardner was subject to Utah's insanity law, and could only prevail if, due to a mental illness, he had no intent to kill.

Now the defense had a big problem, because Gardner's "explanation" to the psychologist in support of his irresistible impulse defense turned out not to be a defense at all. Rather, it was a confession to murder, since he had admitted to intentionally killing the victim. With no viable defense to run, Gardner pled guilty to capital murder and appealed to the Utah Supreme Court, challenging the judge's ruling on the legal standard. The Supreme Court upheld the judge's ruling and affirmed Gardner's conviction.

State v. Norman Newsted

Newsted participated in killing three people in Utah, and then within a week killed a cab driver in Oklahoma. (See Chapters 7 and 8.) The defense attorneys painted Newsted as borderline mentally retarded and claimed he was on a run of drugs during the incident. They filed a motion with the Court in an attempt to try to suppress his statements to the police based on his alleged low level of intelligence. In support of their position,

Newsted's attorneys called a psychologist who, in previous cases, almost universally opined that defendants were not responsible for their actions.

After the psychologist testified, I cross-examined him on the basis for his opinion and, in particular, what incentive Newsted had to try to do well on the IQ tests the psychologist gave him. I mean, the only way they were going to do Newsted any good was if he flunked them, right? And weren't they pretty easy to fake? To illustrate that point, I went over specific questions on the IQ test. How hard would it really be to fake a low IQ?

At the end of the hearing, the judge denied the defense motion to keep out Newsted's statements, rejecting his claim of low intelligence. Shortly afterwards, Newsted's attorneys called him to the stand, and it was interesting to see how he navigated his testimony. Newsted came across as quite intelligent, even correcting his own attorneys on some points and sparring ably with me on cross-examination – hardly the picture of mental retardation that the defense psychologist had painted.

My experience with mental health experts – psychiatrists, psychologists, social workers – was that we had the full spectrum in Utah, from some of the best examiners in the country all the way down to examiners who did superficial evaluations – generally just accepting a defendant's version of events without checking with other sources – and then came in with opinions supporting flaky mental defenses.

I have said before that cross-examining mental health experts who do shoddy work can be the most fun a lawyer can have in a court of law – but it was also true that each time one of them testified, it put a knot in my stomach, as I wondered if the jury was buying what they were selling. Invariably, once I got the chance to cross-examine the experts called by the defense and then put on my own experts in rebuttal, my cases got stronger than they would have been without the phony mental defenses.

While some of the mental health experts, the "darlings of the defense Bar," would offer favorable opinions for defendants in almost every case, the clear pattern was that when they testified, defendants generally lost, because their mental claims were not credible. Our task as prosecutors when confronted with frivolous mental defenses was to level the playing field through cross-examination and calling our own rebuttal experts, and then bring the jury back to the facts of the case, which often spoke more to intent than anything else. Once the jurors were able to assess the defense experts' testimony – and realize how subjective these experts' opinions were – they were able to make their own judgments about a defendant's culpability.

But the most common mental health issue in criminal cases wasn't insanity – it was competency to stand trial. As much as mental defenses could complicate cases, competency issues could literally stop them in their tracks, and sometimes even permanently derail them. That's because the U. S. Supreme Court has ruled that it's a violation of due process to try an incompetent defendant – one who, due to mental illness, does not have a rational and factual understanding of the charges against him and/ or the ability to consult rationally with his attorney.[80] Further complicating the picture, the Supreme Court has also ruled that incompetent defendants can only be held and treated for a reasonable period of time, and that if they can't be restored to competency within that time, they have to be released from custody, or civilly committed.[81]

The prospect of a dangerous criminal escaping justice can present a nightmare scenario for prosecutors. An example of this was the Brian David Mitchell kidnapping case. (See Chapter 16.) In 2002, Mitchell kidnapped 14-year-old Elizabeth Smart by abducting her at knifepoint from her Salt Lake City home. He held her in captivity for several months, during which time he repeatedly sexually abused her. After months of searching for Elizabeth, hopes faded that she would ever be found alive, but nine months after she was kidnapped, Mitchell was apprehended, and

---

[80] *Dusky, v. U.S.*, 364 U.S. 402 (1960)
[81] *Jackson v. Indiana*, 406 U.S. 715 (1972)

Elizabeth was with him. There was no question that he had kidnapped and sexually abused her, and with Elizabeth still alive and poised to testify against him, he had no factual defense for what he had done.

Mitchell was initially charged in state court with multiple first-degree felonies, and in short order, his attorneys filed a petition to have him evaluated for competency. He was, after all, a bizarre figure, playing the role of an itinerant preacher dressed in white robes and spouting religious rhetoric. He claimed to have taken Elizabeth pursuant to divine revelation. After a period of observation and assessment, a competency hearing was held, at which several mental health experts testified. They were split on whether Mitchell was competent to stand trial. After hearing the "battle of the experts," the judge found Mitchell incompetent to proceed, so he was sent to the Utah State Hospital to see if the doctors there could restore him to competency. The case could not move forward until Mitchell was declared competent and ready to stand trial.

One of the things Mitchell routinely did during court hearings was disrupt the proceedings by breaking into religious hymns at the top of his voice. While some of the experts saw this as a sign of mental illness, others viewed it as a cynical attempt to manipulate the proceedings and maintain his status as incompetent to stand trial. Since the likelihood of his winning at trial was virtually nil, and the sentence he would probably receive would put him behind bars for the rest of his life, why wouldn't a cagey defendant in Mitchell's position play the incompetency game?

Further fueling the suspicion that Mitchell was faking, or "malingering," as the doctors call it, was the fact that he'd had a minor brush with the law in California during the time he had held Elizabeth in captivity, and there was a videotape of his court appearance there. Far from breaking into song or acting strange, he did a credible job of minimizing his guilt and talking his way out of trouble. There was nothing bizarre about his behavior then. So it looked like he only acted crazy when he thought he needed to. If Mitchell could turn his "symptoms" on and off at will, how could they be a legitimate manifestation of mental illness, rather than the calculated maneuverings of a crafty criminal?

Nonetheless, credible mental health experts were still split on whether he was competent, and after several years of this stalemate, Utah state prosecutors were looking at a nightmare scenario: The clock was about to run out on how long Mitchell could be held under Utah's statute in the status of "incompetent to stand trial," after which he could no longer be legally held on the charges.[82] The specter of Mitchell being released was appalling, not only to prosecutors, but to the public as well. Here was one of the most high-profile defendants in Utah history, one who had been caught red-handed after committing a brazen child kidnapping that traumatized the community, and now he might have to be released or, at most, civilly committed, because he was supposedly still incompetent to stand trial. How could this be justice?

Fortunately, there was another option. Since Mitchell had kidnapped Elizabeth Smart and transported her across state lines for immoral purposes, he could be prosecuted in federal court. While the standard for competency would be identical there, bringing federal charges would provide an opportunity for more time, as well as a fresh round of mental health examiners to evaluate Mitchell's competency. Most importantly, he would not be released into the community in the meantime, nor would the state prosecutors have to try to get him civilly committed as an alternative to criminal prosecution.

That strategy was ultimately successful, and months later, following competency hearings in federal court, Mitchell was found competent, notwithstanding his singing shenanigans in court. In the federal court "battle of the experts," the judge agreed with the examiners who found Mitchell to be competent, finding that his courtroom antics were not the involuntary ravings of a madman, but rather the calculated disruptions of

---

[82] Utah Code Annotated, Section 77-15-6

a master manipulator. Mitchell was tried in federal court, ran an unsuccessful insanity defense, and was convicted on all counts and sent to federal prison.

Throughout my career, I handled many cases where defendants raised what I thought were bogus competency claims and were able to get mental health experts to testify in support of them. At times it was pretty exasperating. It seemed like some defense-oriented "shrinks" could conjure up incompetency practically from thin air, and it took a lot of time and expense to line up good forensic mental health experts to rebut them. It also burned up a lot of resources and delayed trials, sometimes for years, and in the process, undermined public confidence in the justice system.

Sometimes wanting to delay trials seemed to be the main reason defense attorneys raised competency claims. Particularly in high-profile murder cases, the strategy seemed to be to slow the process down, improving chances of working out better plea bargains after things "cooled down." It seemed a fertile ground for manipulation.

An example of this was the *Gardner* murder case in St. George. After the defendant had been declared incompetent and sent to the State Hospital, his defense attorney told me he could arrange to have Gardner found competent any day that we could work out a plea bargain. The attorney said all he needed to do was make a phone call – whether to the defendant or the defense psychologist, he didn't say – but it was pretty clear that the defendant's "incompetency" was feigned and subject to manipulation for strategic purposes.

Given the fact that the Rules of Evidence are designed to assure at least some semblance of reliability before evidence can be presented in court, it always amazed me to see how that principle went out the window once mental health experts were introduced into the equation. "Anything goes" seemed to be the order of the day, and wildly speculative opinions with poorly-supported reasoning often took center stage. I remember thinking that if many of these behavioral experts had to meet the threshold of reliability applied to other disciplines, they could never do it. But since mental health experts have been allowed to testify in court for decades, there is virtually no scrutiny given to whether their opinions are scientifically derived, and they are allowed free rein.[83]

Maybe it's because mental issues generally make judges uncomfortable[84] – and who else can the justice system turn to in order to seek understanding of psychological issues, if not psychologists and psychiatrists? It seemed to me that most judges just figured it was up to the lawyers on cross-examination and rebuttal to help separate the wheat from the chaff, and there was plenty of chaff. I guess for the most part things worked out, because most defendants who ran bogus mental defenses or who tried to evade going to trial by pretending to be mentally ill were ultimately not successful.

Still, with apologies to the many excellent mental health experts I know and count as friends, I can't resist concluding this chapter by quoting the text of an amendment that was introduced in the New Mexico State Legislature some years back:[85]

> "When a psychologist or psychiatrist testifies during a competency hearing, the psychologist or psychiatrist shall wear a cone-shaped hat that is not less than two feet tall. The surface of the hat shall be imprinted with stars and lightning bolts. Additionally, the psychologist or psychiatrist shall be required to don a white beard that is not less than eighteen inches in length, and shall punctuate crucial elements of his testimony by stabbing the air with

---

[83] I say this with due respect to the many good forensic psychologists and psychiatrists I know whose opinions are well-reasoned. My point is that judges generally don't rein in even the wildest opinions by mental health experts, no matter how bizarre.

[84] I found this to be true not only in the courtroom, but also when I did presentations at judicial conferences relating to the issues of mental defenses and competency to stand trial.

[85] It was sent to me by an excellent forensic psychologist who was frustrated by certain poorly-qualified forensic examiners who seemed to find virtually all defendants either incompetent or insane. It drove him crazy, so to speak, because he felt these so-called experts were bringing discredit on the entire profession.

a wand. Whenever a psychologist or psychiatrist provides expert testimony regarding the defendant's competency, the bailiff shall dim the courtroom lights and administer two strikes to a Chinese gong."[86]

No, the bill didn't pass, but I'm pretty sure I dealt with some of those "wizards" in court.

---

[86] *Better Laws in New Mexico.* Retrieved from http://home.tiac.net/~cri/2000/newmexico.html, 1 July 2011

CHAPTER 19

Gone Forever:
A Prosecutor's Lost Night

IN OCTOBER OF 1998, my wife and I decided to take our kids to the Oregon Coast for an anniversary trip. We had eloped there ten years earlier to Cape Blanco Lighthouse, just north of the little fishing village of Port Orford, the oldest port on the Oregon Coast.

As we started out for the coast, little did I know that I was about to embark on one of the most bizarre experiences of my life, shattering what I thought I knew – what I could count on.

My wife and I packed our two young daughters into the family minivan and struck out for our first stop – Gardnerville, Nevada, near Carson City. My wife's sister lived there with her family, and we thought we'd stay a couple of nights with them and celebrate our younger daughter's third birthday with her cousins.

We got to Gardnerville without incident, but just before her birthday party was to begin, my daughter tripped and cracked her head on an end table as she was running through the house. I had just tied her shoes as she lay on the floor of the living room moments before, and she was excited and full of energy. All of a sudden I heard my daughter crying, and then my wife ran into the room carrying her, blood streaming down my daughter's face. I couldn't understand how in a heartbeat she could have become so badly injured. We rushed her to the emergency room for treatment, where they stitched up the wound in her head and placed a large band-aid over her left eye. She seemed to recover quite quickly, and soon afterwards we were back at the house, celebrating her birthday with her cousins, with a "Teletubbies" theme.

Next morning we said our goodbyes, left early and travelled west toward the coast. On the road, we turned on the radio and listened at length to the impeachment hearings in Washington, D.C. concerning President Clinton's affair with Monica Lewinski. We decided to take the long meandering journey up the Coast Highway.

Two days later, we found ourselves in a little two-story motel in Fort Bragg, California, just north of the picturesque seaside village of Mendocino. We had a second-floor room, and shortly before it got dark we decided to walk down by the ocean. We took the path from the motel that led down to the beach, returning to our room later than we had planned, right at the last gray of twilight.

I remember having a snack in our room – we had brought the cooler up from the van. Around 10:30 we played a game and then all settled in for the night. I wondered if the bed, which was soft, was going to give me a backache, and whether I'd make it through the night without having to get up and move around – a common occurrence for me when we stayed at places with beds with saggy mattresses. Still, I was tired from two days of the almost hypnotic meandering drive up the coast highway, and I easily fell asleep soon after I crawled into bed. The traumatic events of three days earlier had all but dissipated from my mind.

The next thing I recall is sitting in a hospital gown in an examining room and being questioned by a young guy I took for an orderly. The clock on the wall showed 4:00 a.m. The orderly was asking me a series of questions about where I was, who I was with, who the President was, and other things I might have found ridiculous but for the feeling I had that something very strange had happened to me. Had I had a stroke? A head injury? Had I been in an accident?

I answered the questions, but not easily. When asked who I worked with, I listed my friends from the D.A.'s Office, which I had left 11 years before, rather than my colleagues at the Attorney General's Office. I was able to name the current President – Bill Clinton – but when asked if he was in some kind of trouble, I didn't have a clue.

It was then that the orderly turned to my wife and asked her to explain what had happened. I was about to hear details of the past few hours of my life that shocked me, and of which I had absolutely no recollection. How could these things have happened, and I not know anything about them?

My wife gave the details to the orderly, as if I weren't in the room. We had all gone to bed around 11:00. Near midnight, she woke up and noticed that I was gone. Her first thought was that I had probably awakened with a sore back, gotten dressed, and gone out for a walk down by the beach. She was annoyed I hadn't told her I was going. She thought about going out to look for me, but didn't want to leave the kids alone in the room. So she waited.

About two hours later, she heard a car door slam outside, opened the door of the motel, and saw me standing down by the van. She closed the door, expecting me to come up the stairs right away, and when I didn't, she opened the door again and saw me still standing by the van. She stood at the top of the stairs and called out my name, at which point I looked up at her with an odd expression of both surprise and relief. She asked me, "Where have you been?" and I looked up at her with a quizzical look on my face and said, "Where HAVE I been?"

At that point, she told me to come up the stairs, wondering what in the world was going on. When I came inside the room, which was dark, she had me go with her into the lighted bathroom so as not to disturb our sleeping kids, and started asking me questions. I kept saying I knew there was something wrong with my memory, but I thought I'd be fine soon. She checked to see if I had a bump on my head, dilated pupils, or some other evidence of injury, but couldn't find anything physically wrong.

She asked me if I remembered what had happened to our daughter three days before, and I told her no. When she told me our daughter had been hurt and we'd had to take her to the E.R. for stitches, I showed shock and concern. I kept telling my wife I thought it best that we just go to sleep, and I'd probably be fine in the morning. But when she asked me several times about our daughter's accident, and each time I registered the same shock and surprise as if I was hearing it for the first time, she realized I wasn't even remembering details of the conversation we were having, and that I needed to go to the hospital right away. She knew I had a real problem, and she also knew that if she allowed me to go to sleep, I might wake up in the morning seemingly fine, and would never believe her account of my midnight wanderings.

She told the orderly that after she insisted that we go to the hospital, I reluctantly agreed, and I packed a small bag of things I might need. She said that during the whole incident, the tone of my voice was odd – I spoke in a higher register than usual – but otherwise, there was nothing unusual about my speech. She also said she had the impression that I could have driven the car, as I appeared otherwise completely functional – not off-balance, staggering, or otherwise compromised. I had even helped navigate our way to the hospital in Fort Bragg by looking at the map while she drove the van.

In the car, our older daughter kept asking me if I knew what had happened to our younger daughter. Each time she told me about the accident in Gardnerville, I turned around, both surprised and dismayed. When we arrived at the hospital, they put me in a gown and brought me to the examining room.

I listened to every detail of my wife's story, and then I turned to the orderly and said, "That's a complete blank. None of that computes at all.

I have no recollection of any of that ever happening." At that time, my wife could tell I was tracking the conversation for the first time, and that I was coming out of the amnesia.

My wife was right about one thing. If we had not gone to the hospital that night and I had awakened in my motel bed the next morning, no one could have convinced me that I had gotten up in the night, put on my clothes, left the motel, wandered around, returned, and had extensive conversations with my wife in the bathroom while she was checking me to see if I had some kind of head injury. How could I have believed such a crazy story? I would have been convinced that she'd simply had a strange dream. Having never experienced anything like this before, I would have "known" that it simply could not have happened.

But here I was, and it was undeniable that I was at the hospital and couldn't remember coming here or what had happened to me. Something was clearly wrong with my memory. I figured our trip was over, and I'd be told to get back home as soon as possible, so doctors could run a battery of tests and figure out what was wrong with me. They ran me through an MRI machine to scan my brain, and I was bracing for some bad news.

While I was waiting for the results, I decided to call my dad, since he was a physician and I always consulted with him on medical matters. I got him on the phone and explained my strange tale, expecting to hear in his voice a great deal of concern. Instead, he was rather matter-of-fact about it, saying that he'd had several patients with a similar condition. He said he thought I had experienced an episode of "transient global amnesia," and told me that the doctors would likely find nothing wrong with me, and the MRI would probably come back perfectly normal. He also told me the amnesia would probably never recur, and that there was no reason we couldn't just go on with our trip as planned.

A few minutes later, the neurologist came into my room, holding up the MRI results and saying, "Let me show you this really boring MRI. It's totally normal. I think what you've experienced is a condition called 'transient global amnesia,' and if I were you I'd just go on with your vacation and not worry about it. It's highly unlikely to recur, and if you don't have another episode within a year, you probably won't ever have another one."

I confess I would have doubted the doctor's competence had I not just heard the same thing from my dad. How could someone have a total blank spot in their memory and have it be a benign condition?

So they discharged me from the hospital, and we continued our trip on up the coast to Oregon and the Cape Blanco Lighthouse. Many of the things I couldn't remember that morning in the hospital came back to me over the next several days – my daughter's injury, the fact that I was in the hospital room with her while she was being stitched up, details of what we had done the day before the midnight episode. I even had a dreamlike impression of walking on the beach, but it was vague. The clearer memory was the thought I'd had the evening before my amnesia, as we were walking back from the beach, that it would make a good place to walk if I couldn't sleep through the night.

But I have never had even a glimmer of memory return as to what happened during those lost four hours that night. At the hospital, the orderly kidded me that I had probably wandered down to the beach and seen an alien spacecraft land, at which point the aliens had to wipe my memory banks clean, similar to what was portrayed in the movie *Men In Black*. I joked about it too.

For me, the entire experience was more fascinating than troubling – a whole new and foreign experience in my life, with an awareness of some mental confusion, but not with any real trauma associated with the events. It clearly shook up what I thought I knew, but once I learned there was no dire diagnosis in its wake, I found the experience more curious than anything else. And I got a kick out of the little alien figure the kids gave me for Christmas that year.

For my wife, however, it was quite a different story. While I was "out," she didn't know if I had suffered a stroke, whether my memory would ever return, and what she would do with two young children eight hundred miles away from home if I didn't recover – and she was traumatized by it. While we continued on up the coast to the Cape Blanco Lighthouse to complete our anniversary trip, it would be a long time before my wife would no longer stack luggage in front of the motel doors at night, just to make sure I didn't wander off again.

When we got back home, I wrote a poem about my experience:

BLACKOUT

I realize I am here because I don't know why I am here
In a hospital gown
Answering questions put to me by an attendant
Simple questions which I don't mind answering

I can't deny that I have no memory of going to the hospital
My first memory is just sitting here, answering questions
Vaguely aware that answering stupid questions makes sense

Jo and the kids are here too
It's the middle of the night
And she explains how I left the motel room
Was gone an hour or two
Probably down to the beach
I came back and she called to me from the 2nd floor stairway
As I was doing something with the car
She said I didn't know where I had been
And that we then talked for two hours in the room
Before deciding to go to the hospital

I turn to the attendant and say
"That's a complete blank"

Not even a dreamlike recollection
Not like the dreamlike recollection I have
Of walking on the beach

I hear Jo say she told me five times my daughter had been hurt
Just three days before
That we had to take her in for stitches
And that each time I seemed to be hearing it
For the first time
Full of alarm and concern
It was then she knew we must go to the hospital

They run tests
I speak with my dad on the phone
"Transient Global Amnesia"
Not so uncommon
No great concern

Later the tests come back
And the doctor tells me the same thing
And we can continue our trip
And we do
But at night, Jo blocks the door and hides my glasses

It's six weeks later
We joke about my being abducted by aliens
I tell all my friends
It makes a good story
But a four-hour piece of my life is missing

"There are more things in heaven and earth, Horatio . . . "

The last line of the poem refers to Hamlet's statement, "There are more things in heaven and earth, Horatio, than are dreamt of in your philosophy." And, I had learned, in mine.

At home, I researched transient global amnesia on the internet, and found that, while the underlying causes are unknown, it often can be traced to an emotionally stressful incident shortly before symptoms begin. I figured in my case it was likely triggered by the trauma I experienced in seeing my daughter seriously injured three days before.

Online information from the Mayo Clinic showed that my case was typical:

> "Transient global amnesia is a sudden, temporary episode of memory loss that can't be attributed to a more common neurological condition, such as epilepsy or stroke.

> During an episode of transient global amnesia, your recall of recent events simply vanishes, so you can't remember where you are or how you got there. You may also draw a blank when asked to remember things that happened a day, a month or even a year ago. With transient global amnesia, you do remember who you are, and recognize the people you know well, but that doesn't make your memory loss any less disturbing.

> Fortunately, transient global amnesia is rare, seemingly harmless and unlikely to happen again. Episodes are usually short-lived, and afterward your memory is fine."[87]

At the time this happened, I had been a prosecutor for 20 years, and had specialized in mental health issues relating to criminal law, including competency to stand trial and mental defenses such as insanity. I had handled many cases where I believed defendants had pretended to be

---

[87] *Transient Global Amnesia*, Mayo Clinic. Retrieved from http://www.mayoclinic.com/health/transient-global-amnesia/DS01022, 1 July 2011

mentally ill, either to get the benefit of a mental defense or to avoid trial altogether by being declared incompetent to stand trial. I knew that people who claimed amnesia to avoid criminal responsibility had a hard time succeeding, and that prosecutors, judges, and juries tended to view such claims with great suspicion.

I had read cases where courts had rejected claims of amnesia as a basis for finding defendants incompetent to stand trial. While they found that amnesia could make it difficult for defendants to defend themselves, they generally held that it would not violate due process to try such defendants as long as they had access to all the police reports and case materials in the prosecutor's files, in order to prepare their defenses. After all, the alternative would be to allow those with claims of amnesia, claims which couldn't be truly medically validated, to escape the justice system altogether by being found incompetent to stand trial.

I had spent a good deal of my career as a prosecutor countering mental defenses, mostly by defendants who were caught red-handed and had no other excuses for their conduct. And I enjoyed cross-examining psychologists and psychiatrists who testified on behalf of these defendants, and showing how their opinions were little more than educated guesses at best. How could anyone really determine with any accuracy what may have been in the mind of another person at some point in the past? I had conducted prosecutor training on how to deal with claims of mental illness, and told prosecutors that cross-examining mental experts is the most fun you can have in a courtroom. At times, when cross-examining mental health experts, I had even made jurors laugh.

And now I myself had experienced a mysterious mental anomaly, and I had to admit that I would be in one hell of a fix if anyone accused me of committing a crime that October night. How could I defend myself, with no memory of anything that happened during those lost hours? One of the most surprising things I had learned from my wife's description of what I said and how I acted during that time was that I was able to engage in rational conversations and goal-oriented behavior. Under those circumstances, how many people would even believe I was telling the truth about my amnesia, rather than making it up? Even if they did believe me, what defense could I really mount, with no memory and no alibi? If I were a judge or juror hearing such a tale, and if I hadn't lived through this bizarre experience, I probably wouldn't believe it myself.

So what do I make of it all now? How has the lost four hours of my life affected my thinking or my attitudes? It's still a great mystery to me – something so strange and so foreign to the rest of my life experience that I still question how it could have happened to me. And while it's now been over seventeen years and it hasn't recurred, who can say it couldn't happen again?

Beyond that, I guess that if nothing else, this experience has made me more receptive to improbable realities, and less likely to quickly dismiss them as obviously untrue. "There are more things in heaven and earth…"

CHAPTER 20

There Oughta Be a Law:
Taking It to the Legislature

DURING THE NINE YEARS I spent at the D.A.'s Office, I didn't give much thought to how laws were made or amended. My job was to enforce the laws on the books. But shortly after I joined the Attorney General's Office, that changed.

One of my first assignments as a new member of that office was to attend regular monthly meetings of the Statewide Association of Prosecutors, or SWAP, as it was called. One of the main things SWAP did was propose and promote changes to criminal law, as well as try to fend off bad ideas for criminal bills that often found their way to Capitol Hill. Over the next few years, I became more and more interested in working at the policy level to improve the criminal justice system. Eventually, working on legislation became one of my main pursuits.

For two decades, I worked closely with Paul Boyden, SWAP's legislative ace, who was the face of prosecution on Capitol Hill. Paul was universally liked and respected by legislators, and he along with Salt Lake Deputy D.A. Chad Platt deftly shepherded the majority of beneficial criminal bills through the Legislature. Several of the prosecutors in my division also assisted in the effort, and during the Utah State Legislature's annual 45-day session, we all scrambled to keep on top of both promoting good bills and heading off bad ones.

Through the process of promoting bills and testifying at committee hearings, I came to know many legislators well, especially those who sponsored bills for our office and SWAP. It seemed to stand me in good stead that some legislators knew I had spent a good deal of my career in the trenches prosecuting cases. And it was handy that my office was located in the State Capitol building, where the Legislature met.

Through the years, I worked on a lot of bills that reflected the "crime du jour" – whatever seemed to be foremost in the minds of legislators. Often, this was based on high-profile crimes occurring in the community. When gangs were on the rise and becoming more violent, I worked on legislation to beef up penalties for gang members who committed crimes; when meth labs blossomed in Utah, I worked to toughen laws relating to meth labs and meth lab precursor chemicals; after 9/11, I worked on anti-terrorism legislation; when internet fraud became pervasive, I worked on anti-phishing legislation; and when non-Indians started using peyote in self-styled "sacred ceremonies" and Utah's Native American tribes rose up in protest, I worked on legislation to tighten up the law relating to the possession or use of peyote by non-Indians, while preserving the rights of Native Americans to use it in their sacred ceremonies, as they had done for centuries.

Most of the cases I handled throughout my career were violent crimes, and since many murder cases involved mental health issues such as competency and insanity, I worked on a number of bills to change Utah's homicide and mental health statutes. As we in the Attorney General's Office prosecuted cases around the state, we often saw problems with the ways the laws were written, and so we took an active role in bringing these problems to the attention of the Legislature, and advocating for better laws. Through the years, most of the bills we proposed and promoted passed into law, although it often took us more than one year to get a bill successfully through the process.

At the time I left the Attorney General's Office in 2009, I was asked by a reporter what I thought was the most significant achievement of my career. I think she expected me to name one of the high-profile murder cases I prosecuted – something dramatic. But instead, I mentioned my work with the Legislature, because when I look back on my career, I think the longest-lasting impact of my work will be in the area of improving Utah's criminal laws. I guess if I were a politician, I'd say "strengthening Utah's criminal laws," but that implies that I always worked to make them tougher, and the truth is that sometimes I worked to make them less tough – but, I hope, more fair and just.

When I retired from the Attorney General's Office, I left half a dozen filing cabinet drawers full of files relating to bills I had worked on over the years. I'd like to highlight just a few, with the stories associated with them, because every bill has a story.

USE IMMUNITY

Let's start with the Use Immunity bill. If you've read Chapters 7 and 8 about the triple murder case against Douglas Kay and Norman Newsted, you already know some of the backstory that led to this bill's existence. The main accomplice to that horrendous murder spree, Janice Fromeyer, walked away from her crimes scot-free, which was the price police and prosecutors had to pay at the time to obtain her testimony against Kay and Newsted. That experience of seeing an accomplice completely escape justice deeply troubled us all – the judge, the jury, the investigating officers, the public, and certainly those of us who prosecuted the cases.

When I joined the Attorney General's Office in October of 1987, Dave Schwendiman, whose place I was taking as he moved from the Attorney General's Office to the U. S. Attorney's Office, told me how he had tried to get the Legislature to amend Utah law to provide for a different kind of immunity, called "use immunity," which had already been approved as constitutional by the U.S. Supreme Court.[88] It was a more limited form of immunity, one that was consistent with the Fifth Amendment, but didn't confer on a witness a complete blanket of immunity, as Utah's statute did at the time. Although use immunity was already the type of immunity that witnesses received in the federal courts and the courts of many other states, it was to be an uphill climb to get it enacted in Utah.

There had been other murder cases in which Utah's arcane immunity laws had led to great injustices, which was why Dave had worked to change the law. One case involved the murder and dismemberment of Karla Hunt, a young college student from Southern Utah, who had been picked up as a hitchhiker and then murdered by two men in Millard County, in Central Utah. The suspect most directly involved in the murder, George Wesley Hamilton, was tried and convicted of capital murder. His accomplice, a man named Bond, had agreed during the investigation to provide information to the police, but only if he were granted transactional immunity under Utah law – the only type then available, which gave him a complete "immunity bath." That meant he could not be prosecuted for anything he talked about, period.

Here's the way Utah's transactional immunity statute worked: Let's say that two people commit a burglary, and, in the course of the burglary, one of them murders someone. There is ample evidence at the scene that both people broke into the house – there are fingerprints and DNA from both suspects. One of the suspects witnessed the murder, but didn't participate in it. The police want his testimony against the murderer. Under Utah's statute, there was only one option, and that was to give complete immunity to the witness – not just for the murder, but for everything connected with it, including the burglary.

---

[88] *Kastigar v. United States*, 406 U.S. 441 (1972)

The transactional immunity statute went beyond what the Fifth Amendment was designed to protect. It was intended to prevent suspects' statements from being used against them personally, not to prevent their statements from being used against others who commit crimes, including accomplices. But Utah's law prevented accomplices from being prosecuted for *any* crime they spoke about pursuant to a grant of immunity, which is why it was referred to as "transactional immunity." It effectively allowed criminals to stand as a block against society, as if they had a collective rather than an individual Fifth Amendment right. Under that system, it didn't matter if the police had an air-tight case against a witness independent of anything that the witness disclosed pursuant to a grant of immunity. The law still barred prosecution.

Another problem with transactional immunity was trying to figure out which of two or more suspects should be offered immunity. What if the prosecutor guessed wrong? Could a killer simply go free? The answer is yes. In one infamous case in Salt Lake County, a witness who was a police informant came forward and told the police he could identify the killer in an unsolved case, if he were granted immunity. The case involved a store clerk who had been shot and killed at a corner grocery store. The man seemed to have inside information about the killing, and the authorities were eager to solve the case, so they granted him immunity. Once he had the grant of transactional immunity in hand, the witness confessed to having committed the murder himself. The result was that he could not be prosecuted, even if the police later developed independent evidence of his guilt.

In the Karla Hunt murder case, it was clear by the time the investigation concluded that Bond had been deeply involved in the events surrounding Hunt's murder, including the dismemberment of her body. In fact, his complicity was so gross that the prosecutors decided not to even call him as a witness in Hamilton's trial. When it was determined that Bond was no longer going to be called as a witness, he was free to go. He hopped a bus out of town and left the state. Reporters interviewed him at the bus station just before he left, and the community was justifiably outraged. How could a man who participated in cutting up a woman's body and burying body parts just walk away from such a reprehensible crime with no consequences?

Dave had highlighted the *Hamilton/Bond* case in trying to persuade the Utah State Legislature to change the law, but had run into stiff opposition, principally from two senators: Lorraine Lacy and Bill Cranston. These senators effectively killed the bill in the 1987 Session of the Legislature, and since he was leaving the Attorney General's Office, Dave passed the baton to me. With help and support from John Soltis, my old friend from the D.A.'s Office and one of the prosecutors in the *Hamilton* case, we gave it another try in the 1988 Session, but ran into the same opposition from Senators Lacey and Cranston, who seemed convinced that the bill would violate the Fifth Amendment and lead to governmental abuses.

Having both had first-hand experiences trying murder cases where accomplices had been able to escape justice entirely, John and I thought we would at least get some opportunity to sit down with the senators and try to change their minds, but they were entrenched and weren't interested in talking with us. John was particularly offended the day that Senator Lacey laid into us in the hallway of the Capitol, saying things like, "You two don't care about justice. You don't care about fairness. You don't care about the constitution." I remember John looking rather grieved, saying, "But Ma'am, you don't even know us."

Despite having the support of law enforcement, the bill stalled once again. Law Professor Michael Goldsmith of BYU, a former federal prosecutor, wrote in an editorial in the *Salt Lake Tribune* that Lacey's "hysterical concerns" were unfounded and not based on any real-world considerations. Still, with such fierce opposition from both senators, we were unable to get enough traction to change the law that year.

Time passed, and I worked on other legislative projects, and kind of forgot about the Use Immunity bill, having gotten knocked down twice.

Besides, nothing as bad as what had happened in the *Hamilton* case or the *Kay/Newsted* case had happened since to bring the bill back to the top of the priority list for our office or for SWAP. There was also the lingering issue of whether the Utah Supreme Court might not uphold use immunity, since a handful of state supreme courts across the nation had ruled that only transactional immunity was sufficient under their state constitutions. Since the Utah Supreme Court had at times interpreted the Utah Constitution differently than the U.S. Constitution, even when both used the very same language, there was at least a possibility that our bill, even if successful, could be struck down by the Utah Supreme Court on state constitutional grounds.[89]

It was years later, while I was attending a symposium about whether a defendant could run a "genetic defect" defense (one had been tried unsuccessfully in a Georgia murder case), that I overhead Chief Justice Zimmerman of the Utah Supreme Court, who had also been invited to the symposium, mention to an official from another state that Utah still had an antiquated form of immunity known as transactional immunity. It didn't sound to me like he'd be inclined to strike down a use immunity bill, if we could get one passed. It got me thinking that it might be time to dust off our bill and take another run at it in the next session. It helped that neither of the bill's vocal opponents, Senators Lacey and Cranston, was still in the Legislature, and a bright new legislator named David Gladwell, a former Deputy Davis County Attorney, might be the perfect sponsor to run it. I pitched the idea to our office and SWAP, and got the green light to run the bill.

With Gladwell's deft sponsorship, the bill made it through both houses of the Legislature and became law in the spring of 1997, which was none too soon, because the next horrific murder case with an immunity issue

---

[89] States have their own state constitutions, generally patterned very closely after the federal Constitution. While the states cannot give citizens less protection than what the federal Constitution provides, they can give their citizens more protection.

was just around the corner. It took place a year later in remote Duchesne County, where two people were murdered and their bodies blown up with explosives.

I first learned about the murders late one Friday afternoon in October of 1998, as I was preparing to leave the office for the weekend. I was packing up my satchel at the Capitol when a call came in from Herb Gillespie, the Duchesne County Attorney. He told me that the police had information from a citizen informant that two missing ranch hands, Jake Potter and May Carter, had been killed by their boss, John Pinder, who had blown up their bodies with dynamite on Pinder's ranch. The informant had been on site and seen body parts. I got Chris Soltis of our Criminal Appeals Division on the line, and together we consulted with Herb and the Sheriff's Office. Afterwards, they obtained a search warrant, and during the search, found body parts strewn all around the field.

At the time, the police didn't know if they were finding parts of one or more bodies. Some pieces were partly buried under the soil, others attached to bushes and branches. While not many pieces were recovered, it was evident that using dynamite had made it difficult for the killer or killers to effectively hide all traces of the crime after the smoke cleared.

The police eventually traced Pinder and his girlfriend, Caroline DeWitt, to Idaho, and learned that DeWitt had told her daughter that Pinder had admitted to killing two people in Utah. DeWitt also told her father that Pinder had killed two people in Utah by shooting them and then blowing up their bodies, and that she had helped him dispose of evidence and wipe down his truck. When the police eventually recovered Pinder's pickup truck, which he had used to transport the kidnapped victims to the murder site, officers found evidence of recent cleaning consistent with DeWitt's statements.

Pinder was charged with two counts of capital murder, but in order to convict him, the State needed to bring in DeWitt as a witness. Under the old statute, which authorized only the granting of transactional immunity, the price for her testimony would have been a complete "immunity bath" for all crimes she participated in, similar to what had happened in both the *Hamilton* and the *Kay/Newsted* murder cases. With the advent of the new Use Immunity statute, however, the State had an effective new tool to obtain her testimony through a grant of use immunity, which prevented her statements from being used against her, but did not prevent them from being used against Pinder.

Once DeWitt received the grant of use immunity, she no longer had a Fifth Amendment privilege not to testify at Pinder's trial. Although she denied everything when called as a witness, her prior statements to her daughter and father were admissible at Pinder's trial. And since there was plenty of evidence of DeWitt's complicity in destroying evidence and harboring Pinder as a fugitive – evidence that was independent of any statement she made after receiving the grant of use immunity – we could still prosecute her for obstruction of justice.

Mike Wims, a highly experienced attorney in my division and a brilliant trial tactician, prosecuted both cases, with assistance in the *Pinder* case from another of our division's senior prosecutors, Scott Reed. DeWitt was tried first, and convicted of felony obstruction of justice. Then Pinder was tried and convicted of two counts of capital murder and related offenses.

The new statute worked exactly as it was designed, by taking a witness who had crucial information about a crime but was unwilling to testify against a criminal confederate, and preventing that witness from protecting the confederate by hiding behind the Fifth Amendment. And in the *Pinder* case, Mike Wims was able to make the powerful point that DeWitt had given her father details only the killer or someone associated with the killer would know – namely, that the victims had been shot before they were blown up.

At the time DeWitt gave this information to her father, no autopsy had yet been performed on the victims' remains, and no one in law enforcement knew that the victims had been shot before being blown up.

How else would DeWitt's father know that detail other than from his daughter, and how else would she have known it other than from Pinder, the killer, just as she had related to her father?

So why did we need the Use Immunity statute in order to present to the jury the fact that Caroline DeWitt told her father that Pinder had killed two people in Utah? Couldn't we have just called him as a witness and had him testify about that directly? The answer is no, not unless DeWitt herself testified at Pinder's trial and was subject to cross-examination. The reason? In court, there are strict rules against hearsay, which is defined by the Utah Rules of Evidence as "a statement, other than one made by the declarant while testifying at the trial or hearing, offered in evidence to prove the truth of the matter asserted."[90] The problem with hearsay is that it violates a defendant's constitutional right to confrontation, the right to question and cross-examine witnesses in court.

It was therefore crucial for us to have DeWitt testify, even though we knew she would likely deny having made statements implicating Pinder in the murders. And once she was granted use immunity and no longer had the legal option of refusing to testify on Fifth Amendment grounds, it opened the door for us to admit her prior inconsistent statements.

While it might seem that those out-of-court statements were themselves hearsay, they were not. Under the rules, prior inconsistent statements of testifying witnesses, like Caroline DeWitt, are classified as "nonhearsay," because the witnesses are present in court and can be questioned about what they said. So once DeWitt was called as a witness and denied making the statements to her father that Pinder had killed two people in Utah, the rules allowed us to call her father as a witness to testify about those statements, and for the jury to consider that evidence in evaluating Pinder's guilt.

Without the Use Immunity statute, there would have been no way for us to both use Caroline DeWitt as a witness (albeit a reluctant one) against

---

[90] Rule 801 (c), Utah Rules of Evidence

Pinder, and also prosecute her for her own criminal conduct related to the murders. She could have simply asserted her right to remain silent and thereby avoided testifying at Pinder's trial. She would not then have been available as a witness to be cross-examined about the statements she made to her father, and so those statements would have been excluded as inadmissible hearsay. The only way we could have forced her to testify would have been to grant her transactional immunity, making it then impossible to prosecute her for anything she did in connection with the murders.

We were glad that the Use Immunity law had been enacted in time to allow both Pinder and DeWitt to be brought to justice. No more Bonds or Fromeyers walking away as if they'd had nothing to do with the terrible crimes they helped facilitate. With the first felony conviction of a witness who was also an accomplice in a murder case, accomplice accountability had finally come to Utah.

EXPERT DISCOVERY

In the "good old days" at the D.A.'s Office, we had to fly blind when it came to defense experts. It was trial by ambush. While the prosecution was obligated to provide to the defense virtually everything the prosecution had, and generally maintained an open-file policy so the defense had full access to police reports, lab reports, witness statements and the like, it was a one-way street. Except for a few things they were required to disclose to the prosecution by statute (notice of alibi, entrapment, intent to run an insanity defense), the defense didn't have to provide the prosecution with much of anything.

The times we most often got blindsided were when the defense called an expert to the stand. Back then, we first learned what the expert's opinion was at the same time the jury did: while the expert was testifying on the stand. We had no time to prepare or to consult with an expert of our own. And even in the area of psychiatric and psychological testimony, we often got stonewalled on the basis that the defendants weren't technically running a straightforward insanity defense (for which they would have been obligated by statute to give us notice), but rather were running some other variation of defense for which they claimed they had no such duty to disclose.

An example of that was in *State v. Bishop*. As you'll recall, in the early 80s, Bishop kidnapped, sexually abused, and murdered five young boys. At trial, the only defense Bishop was going to mount was based on the testimony of mental health experts. When we tried to get access to the experts' reports, the defense objected, saying they were not running an insanity defense, but a version of manslaughter based on extreme mental or emotional disturbance. We took the issue to the Utah Supreme Court just before trial, and Bishop's defense attorneys argued that requiring them to provide even basic information about their defense would be "devastating" to their case, and might interfere with Bishop's due process rights.[91]

By representing that they weren't running an insanity defense, Bishop's attorneys succeeded in preventing us from getting any meaningful information about their experts' opinions before trial. Yet despite this representation, the defense attorney's opening statement focused entirely on Bishop's alleged mental disorders. There was no other defense presented, and they used mental health testimony to try to persuade the jury to convict Bishop only of manslaughter, rather than capital murder, for the deaths of each of the five young boys. As was typical, we found out about their experts' opinions at the same moment the jury did, and had to cross-examine them without an opportunity to prepare. (See Chapter 18.)

We were tired of this game, so in 1994 we proposed a bill to end it. The bill provided that if either the prosecution or the defense intended to call any expert to testify regarding the mental state of the defendant, notice had to be given and reports provided to the other side. We also proposed a similar expert discovery provision to cover any type of expert that either side might call as a witness.

---

[91] After the case was over, I asked one of the defense attorneys what they were alluding to that would have violated Bishop's due process rights, and he said he couldn't remember.

While it was common practice in federal court and many other states to require both sides to provide expert discovery, defense attorneys in Utah liked the status quo of one-way discovery, and so they vigorously opposed the bill. We knew it would be a battle, and told Attorney General Jan Graham that we expected a fight. We already had a lot of ambitious legislation on our plate for the session, and even discussed the idea of holding off and running the bill the following year. Jan, who was not timid in fighting for causes she believed in, considered the issue and essentially said, "No, it's time for this to happen. Let's go for it now. Why have another year of trial by ambush?"

When the bill came up for consideration in committee, the lobbyist for the defense Bar made an impassioned speech that this change was extreme and would trample on the rights of defendants. It lost us a few votes, but the bill came out of committee with a favorable recommendation, and passed the House. In the Senate, its fate was less certain, because we were running out of time, and had hit the last day of the session when all business, by law, must end at the stroke of midnight.

I was in the Senate gallery that night. At 11:58, the expert discovery bill was two down on the board, and the President of the Senate said there was time to consider just one more bill. At that point I walked out of the gallery, and figured the game was over. There would always be next year. A few minutes later I saw Mike Wims in the hall. He had stayed in the gallery, and told me the bill had passed at the stroke of midnight.

It was a good night. Our other priority bill, a revision of Utah's law relating to competency to stand trial, was the last bill passed by the House at the same midnight hour. I remember tripping down the Capitol steps that night on my way home with a feeling of elation. Bills often died on the board in the waning hours of the legislative session as the clock struck midnight – we had seen it happen many times with other bills we were pushing – and to have our two highest-priority bills both pass at the last second was both unexpected and thrilling.

The expert discovery law has been in place a good long time, since 1994, and, contrary to defense predictions, nobody's rights have been compromised. Instead, it has provided for a much fairer and more balanced process that ultimately aids the jury in its truth-seeking function, which is what it's all about. No more trials by ambush.

LIFE WITHOUT PAROLE

Throughout the 1980s, when I was prosecuting capital cases at the D.A.'s Office, Utah had no "life in prison without parole" sentencing option. The only options were the death penalty and life imprisonment, which did not preclude parole. Because these murder cases were so horrific, and the thought of defendants being one day released from prison so repugnant, just about every capital case in those days went to trial. The prosecution felt compelled to seek the death penalty, because nothing else would ensure that these defendants would never be released to kill again. So in most capital cases, there was no realistic way to negotiate a settlement short of trial.

Although a lot of these capital cases went to trial, very few resulted in the death penalty, because Utah had, and still has, one of the strictest legal standards in the nation for imposing the death penalty. First, the prosecution has to prove beyond a reasonable doubt in the guilt phase of the trial that the defendant intentionally or knowingly caused the death of the victim, and did so under one of the specified aggravating circumstances. These circumstances include things like murders in the course of kidnappings, robberies, or rapes; murders for hire; murders to silence witnesses; and murders of police officers. Then, if the defendant is convicted of a capital murder, there is a separate penalty hearing where both sides may present additional evidence and make arguments for and against the imposition of the death penalty.

At the penalty phase hearing, the State has to prove that the totality of the aggravating circumstances outweighs the totality of mitigating circumstances, and further has to show that the death penalty is the appropriate penalty, which is generally interpreted as the *only* appropriate penalty. What makes Utah's law particularly stringent is that it requires the prosecution to prove both of those things beyond a reasonable doubt – a standard generally applied to factual determinations, but in this context, applicable to the judgment call of whether the death penalty is appropriate.

And finally, all twelve jurors have to agree on the death penalty. If just one juror does not agree, the statute requires that the defendant be given a life sentence.

No wonder, then, that while many capital cases went to trial back in the 1980s, few resulted in the death penalty. From speaking with jurors afterwards, we knew that in many of those cases, all but one or two jurors had voted to impose the death penalty, but because there were holdouts, life imprisonment had been the default penalty imposed.

In 1990, Senator Frances Farley introduced a bill that would have repealed the death penalty and replaced it with life in prison without parole. It passed the Senate only after it was amended to retain the death penalty as an option. At that time, only one prosecutor, Millard County Attorney Warren Peterson, spoke in support of the bill, seeing it as a way to bridge the large gap that existed between the two available sentencing options. Still, it was clear what Farley's agenda was, and in the House, where it was defeated, those who opposed it characterized a vote in favor of the bill as a vote against capital punishment.

The more I thought about it, the more I realized that Warren Peterson was right, and so I proposed that we prosecutors in SWAP and the Attorney General's Office take the lead in supporting a bill to add a new capital case sentencing option of life without parole. We lined up support from law enforcement organizations and other key groups, and took the bill to the Legislature with a new twist. Instead of legislation designed to weaken the death penalty, we argued, the bill was actually a "tough on crime" measure designed to ensure public safety.

To support this argument, we gave the Legislature case examples of Utah murderers who had committed horrendous crimes and who had narrowly escaped the death penalty, thus benefiting from Utah's all-or-nothing approach. Because jurors had not been given the option of imposing a sentence of life without parole, some of Utah's most notorious killers were now serving their sentences with the possibility of parole.

They included serial killer Joseph Paul Franklin, multiple murderer Douglas Kay, double murderer Michael Moore, double and child murderers Julio Gary Valdez and Dan Lafferty, sex murderer Ronald Kelly, and torture murderer Lance Wood. Although several of these killers had escaped the death penalty by just one or two votes, we believed that all jurors would have agreed that they should never be paroled.

And so, this time, the bill passed, with just a few legislators opposing it because they were afraid it would effectively end the death penalty in Utah. It didn't, but it has significantly reduced the number of cases that go to trial. Given the reality of how death penalty cases languish on appeal for decades, and seeing the effect of that on victims' families, I think the best thing life without parole does is promote finality so the victims' families can get on with their lives.[92] They don't have to attend parole hearings or worry about, decades later, picking up a newspaper or watching a TV news story reporting that yet another challenge is being made to a defendant's conviction, which might result in reversal on appeal.

And since most capital cases resulting in life without parole sentences are negotiated, it also spares the families from going through the wrenching experience of sitting through trials and reliving the details of their family members' murders. I have found that oftentimes victims' family members who understand the importance of finality prefer the life without parole option. Some even think it's a tougher sentence than the death penalty.

Looking back after more than twenty years of experience with the

---

[92] For an in-depth discussion of the death penalty in Utah, see Chapter 22.

new sentencing option, I think it's one of the best changes we made to Utah's homicide laws.

INNOCENCE BILLS

One of the last bills I worked on before I left the Attorney General's Office was not a bill to strengthen laws or enhance penalties, but rather a bill to help innocent people convicted of crimes they didn't commit prove their innocence. For the details of how I came to turn my attention from putting people in prison to creating an avenue for exoneration and compensation for innocent persons caught up in the criminal justice system, see Chapter 24, "The Reluctant Prosecutor Comes Full Circle – My Involvement in the Innocence Movement."

CHAPTER 21

Prosecuting a "Good Judge"

NOTHING PUT LOCAL PROSECUTORS IN A JAM like learning that powerful people in their communities might have committed criminal offenses. If you're the county attorney, how do you prosecute the judge before whom you regularly appear in court, the county commissioner whose duties include setting your office's budget, the criminal defense attorney who regularly opposes you in court, the police officers you worked closely with on a daily basis, or the elected sheriff of your county?

Politically charged situations like these usually ended up in our office, and for good reason. If local prosecutors declined to prosecute these kinds of cases on the grounds of insufficient evidence, people in the county would suspect they were influenced by political considerations. If they prosecuted them, the defendants could claim they were being persecuted for political reasons. And if they prosecuted them and lost, how could they ever go back to business as usual? It was a no-win situation. They needed an outside, independent prosecutor to handle these cases, and the Attorney General's Office fulfilled that role.

During the 22 years I spent at the Attorney General's Office, we investigated criminal complaints against elected officials, police and probation officers, county sheriffs, criminal defense attorneys, judges, and, yes, even other prosecutors.

Cases we prosecuted included:

- A sheriff, for misusing public moneys;
- A county attorney, for public intoxication and disorderly conduct;
- A county clerk, for misusing public moneys;
- A justice of the peace, for misusing public moneys;
- Another sheriff, for charges ranging from misusing public moneys to obstruction of justice;
- Another county attorney, for DUI;
- A defense attorney, for possession of methamphetamine;
- A police officer and a probation officer, for poaching a bear;
- A county commissioner, for misusing public moneys;
- Another defense attorney, for aggravated assault;
- A jailer, for sexual misconduct with an inmate;
- A deputy district attorney, for fraudulent use of a credit card; and
- A district court judge, for possession of controlled substances.

One of my most memorable cases involving a defendant who was a powerful public official was this last one – the judge – so let me tell you his story:

It was a Monday in July of 2002, and Mike Wims and I were in the courthouse in Heber City, preparing for a post-conviction hearing in the *Pinder* double murder case. I got a call from Utah County Attorney Kay Bryson, who said he needed a favor. Don Townsend, Presiding Judge of the Fourth District Court in Utah County, had been arrested over the weekend on multiple drug charges, and Bryson needed the Attorney General's Office to handle the case.

It was clear that the Utah County Attorney's Office needed an outside prosecutor for the case. Not only was Judge Townsend one of the judges before whom they regularly appeared in court, but he was also one who was well-liked and well-respected by police and prosecutors in the district. Everybody was stunned that Judge Townsend was about to become a felony drug defendant.

But he was, because on Saturday morning, July 13, Judge Townsend's wife Gwen had called the police, requesting assistance. Something was going on at the home. When officers from the Alpine/Highland Police Department and the Utah County Sheriff's Department arrived, there were several people at the home, including the judge, his wife, other family members, and some drug treatment personnel. At the door, the officers were told by one of the family members that everything was under control and that they didn't need the police anymore. But then Judge Townsend stepped forward and asked to speak to the officers, who immediately noticed that he was under the influence of something. His speech was slow and slurred, his balance poor, and he was staggering. One of the first officers who responded to the call had once served as Judge Townsend's bailiff, and he told us later that it broke his heart to see the judge in such an obviously intoxicated and compromised condition.

Gwen Townsend took an officer to a room at the back of the house where she retrieved a white plastic bag from a wastebasket. There were two clear plastic bags inside, with white powder and two straws. Also inside one of the plastic bags were items of drug paraphernalia, including lighters, a spoon, tin foil, and another spoon with burn marks. Gwen told the officers that her husband had been using heroin and cocaine and had been up all night, and that he had been on a drug binge for several weeks. She also told them that her husband had admitted to her that he had smoked crack in a bathroom next to his judicial chambers.

The officers field-tested the white powder, and it tested positive for cocaine. They then drafted up a warrant to search the rest of the premises for drugs, and took it to Judge Denise Lindberg, a Salt Lake City judge, who signed the search warrant. Officers then searched the rest of the premises, including outbuildings and vehicles, and recovered more items of suspected drugs and drug paraphernalia.

We agreed to take the case, and waited for the results from the Utah State Crime Lab in order to determine what charges to file. In the meantime, the press was at the door, calling our Public Information Officer, Paul Murphy, on a daily basis. When was Townsend going to be charged? What would the charges be? When would the test results be available? Paul, a former television news reporter himself, held them off, saying that the investigation was still pending. He assured the reporters that our office would make a public statement at the time charges were filed.

When we got the results back from the Crime Lab, it was clear that the evidence against Townsend was solid. Not only had items taken from his home been tested and found to contain controlled substances, but a sample of his hair had tested positive for both cocaine and heroin. We prepared a criminal complaint charging Townsend with two counts of Unlawful Possession or Use of a Controlled Substance – one for cocaine and one for heroin. Each count was a third-degree felony, punishable by up to five years in prison. No one could remember a time when a sitting district court judge in Utah had been charged with a felony.

Mike Wims and I were both on the case, and Jeff Gold, Townsend's attorney, made an issue of having "two death-qualified prosecutors" going after his client. The implication was that we were somehow unfairly ganging up on Townsend by having two experienced prosecutors handling the case – not Jeff's strongest argument, but he didn't have a lot to work with. When the court scheduled the preliminary hearing for a time Mike was planning to be out of town, I told him not to worry about it – that I guessed just one death-qualified prosecutor would have to do.

After the charges were filed, Townsend steadfastly maintained his innocence and maligned his wife in the media by branding her a liar. He also verbally attacked the police and prosecutors. He boldly proclaimed that he was looking forward to trial, where he would have the opportunity to vindicate himself, and announced that he was confident that justice would prevail.

For a guy who had been caught red-handed with drugs and under the influence of drugs, this was more than a little annoying, particularly when he had been given the opportunity by his family the day the police were called to simply acknowledge he had a drug problem and voluntarily seek treatment. His wife had called his adult children to the house before she had called the police. When the family told him he would have to choose between his family and drugs, he said he chose drugs. At that point, they felt they had no choice other than to turn him in, so he could get help.

This whole incident was all pretty bizarre for those who had practiced before Judge Townsend, as well as the many defendants, including drug defendants, who had appeared before him. He was known as a tough-on-crime judge, and he was as tough on drug defendants as he was on any others. He was no bleeding-heart judge, and the police and prosecutors in Utah County liked appearing before him because of that.

While the criminal case was pending, the Judicial Conduct Commission (JCC) and the Utah Legislature were themselves going after Townsend. Both had jurisdiction to take action against him. He could be disciplined by the Utah Supreme Court upon recommendation from the JCC, and the Legislature had the power to impeach him as a judge. While all this was pending and he was loudly protesting his innocence, he was on judicial leave with pay, which meant that he continued to draw his full salary as a judge while the proceedings were pending against him.

About the only thing Townsend could do by way of a defense was to attack the search, and try to get the drug evidence thrown out of court. So Jeff Gold filed a motion to suppress the evidence obtained through the search warrant. We held a hearing on his claims, and by late January of 2003, the ruling came down – Townsend's motion to suppress was denied. All the evidence was going to be coming in against him.

Then in mid-February, the Judicial Conduct Commission, headed by

Colin Winchester, issued its order recommending Townsend's removal. About the same time, the Utah House of Representatives passed a resolution to impeach him, the first of its kind in Utah history, and sent it over to the Senate for action, where Mike Wims was gearing up to present evidence in support of Townsend's impeachment.

On February 28, 2003, facing the prospect of judicial removal, impeachment, disbarment and a criminal trial, Townsend finally threw in the towel. He resigned his office, pledged never to seek judicial office again, and shortly afterwards pled guilty to drug charges.

As we were considering what charges to allow Townsend to plead to, we felt that although a misdemeanor plea for this type of drug activity might otherwise have been appropriate, we needed to hold the line and make sure Townsend pled guilty to, or was convicted of, felony-level offenses. I remember meeting with Townsend's family members at their request while the case was pending. We told them, as we had told his attorney, that we felt he needed treatment, but we also felt he needed to plead guilty to at least one felony. We also told them that we would agree to a plea in abeyance, which meant that if Townsend successfully completed all terms of his probation, including drug treatment, the charges could be reduced to misdemeanors.

I remember that one of his daughters was quite indignant that we were being unfairly harsh on him "just because he's a judge." Because he was a judge and had betrayed the public trust, it didn't seem too harsh to me.

Once we worked out the terms of the plea agreement with Jeff Gold, we took it to the judge who was handling Townsend's case. The venue had been changed from Provo to Salt Lake, and Third District Judge Lawrence Morgan had been assigned to the case. We arranged to meet with Judge Morgan in his chambers to let him know what we were proposing.

When Jeff described the plea agreement, Judge Morgan said he wouldn't accept a plea in abeyance. He said he didn't care if the plea was to a misdemeanor, but it had to be something for which he could sentence

Townsend immediately to jail. In effect, he found our proposed felony-level plea to be too lenient, and, upon reflection, Mike and I had to agree with him. Judge Morgan told us to come back if we worked out another disposition.

It was clear that Judge Morgan would treat drug misdemeanor pleas very seriously under the circumstances of the case, and it would allow him to impose substantial jail time, probably comparable to anything Townsend would receive if he pled to third-degree felonies. Mike and I had both seen cases in which the most serious misdemeanor offenses, Class A misdemeanors, resulted in sentences as harsh or harsher than third-degree felonies, which are the least serious felony offenses.

And so we negotiated again with Jeff Gold, and on March 3, 2003, Townsend pled guilty to two Class A misdemeanor drug counts, one for cocaine and one for heroin. After he pled guilty, Townsend spoke to reporters and for the first time took responsibility for his actions, apologizing to his family, friends, fellow judges, and citizens. Judge Morgan ordered the Office of Adult Probation & Parole to prepare a pre-sentence report to give him more information about Townsend and the crimes he had committed, and set sentencing for April 28.

After Townsend pled guilty, the press asked Mike Wims for the prosecutors' reaction. Mike and I knew we would be asked whether we were satisfied with the outcome, so we had discussed it before we went to court. Mike told the reporters that all three of the State's goals had been achieved through the plea agreement: Townsend had resigned, had finally accepted responsibility for his actions, and would be facing criminal sanctions when sentenced by the judge. So, yes, we were satisfied with the outcome.

We reconvened for sentencing before Judge Morgan on April 28. Many Townsend supporters had sent letters asking for leniency. Townsend himself asked for compassion and mercy. Judge Morgan was not particularly moved. He rebuked Townsend for disgracing his office and undermining confidence in the judiciary and the criminal justice system, and ordered

Townsend to serve 120 days in jail, 500 hours of community service, a two-year period of probation, and continued drug treatment.[93]

In November of 2004, after receiving the recommendations of the JCC and the Office of Professional Conduct of the Utah State Bar, the Utah Supreme Court disbarred Townsend. The Court said that disbarment was necessary to restore public confidence in the justice system, particularly when Townsend had continued to publicly maintain his innocence and malign his accusers for more than a year. The Supreme Court also mentioned the fact that Townsend had continued to draw his full salary, placing an undue burden upon his fellow judges, and had delayed his decision to resign until the last possible moment, under the threat of both impeachment by the Legislature and removal by the Supreme Court.

Don Townsend lost his job, his law license, his standing in the community, his wife, and his reputation. Oh yes, and some of his liberty. Supporters and family members complained that he was treated too harshly, because any other first-time drug offender wouldn't have taken such a long fall. But that comes with the territory for people in high places, like judges – they do have farther to fall, and when they betray the public trust, they should expect nothing less.

Having said that, people who get caught up in drugs usually do wreak havoc on their own lives as well as the lives of others, and so there's room for compassion, whether it's the kid down the street or a prestigious district court judge. I don't know what Mr. Townsend is doing now, but, as with many of the drug offenders I prosecuted through the years, I hope he's been able to overcome his drug addiction, move on, and recover some good things in his life.

---

[93] Townsend had spent three months in drug abuse therapy at the Betty Ford Clinic in California, during the same time period that he was issuing public pronouncement asserting his innocence.

CHAPTER 22

Handling Capital Cases, and Thoughts on the Death Penalty

I CAME OF AGE AS A PROSECUTOR in Utah in the 1980s, a period when capital cases exploded onto the evening news. Many of the men now on death row in Utah committed their crimes in the 80s, and many of the murderers from that era became household names. One way or another, I was to get involved in most of their cases.

State v. Joseph Paul Franklin

Franklin was an avowed racist and serial killer who was eventually linked to twenty murders across the country. Under cover of darkness, he hid in the back of a vacant field at twilight and shot and killed two young black men because they were jogging with white women in Salt Lake's Liberty Park.

State v. Ronald Lemoyne Kelly

Kelly broke into a young woman's house late at night and killed her with a butcher's knife in a murderous frenzy. When the police found her, the knife had been plunged into her chest with such force that the tip of the blade went completely through her and stuck to the floorboard beneath her body.

State v. Julio Gary Valdez

Valdez had fathered a child with the victim, his former girlfriend. Facing a paternity action and living with a new girlfriend to whom he was engaged, Valdez arranged to meet the victim and her baby late at night after he got off work. He then shot and killed the victim and dragged her body into some bushes, and threw the baby into the Jordan River.

State v. Elroy Tillman

Tillman stalked and terrorized his former girlfriend and her fiancé, then broke into the fiancé's apartment one night, bludgeoned him over the head into unconsciousness, and set his bed on fire.

State v. Frances Schreuder

Schreuder, a New York socialite with expensive tastes living off of her parents' money, prodded her son Marc Schreuder into killing her father and Marc's grandfather, millionaire Franklin Bradshaw, so she could inherit his estate and support her lavish lifestyle.

State v. Michael Moore

Moore killed a business associate up in Millcreek Canyon in front of the restaurant where he worked as a manager. When a delivery man happened onto the scene, Moore killed him also, because, as he later told the police, "Dead men tell no lies."

State v. Arthur Gary Bishop

Over the course of four years, Bishop terrorized the Salt Lake community by kidnapping five young boys, sexually assaulting them, and then killing them. (See Chapter 18.)

State v. Ron and Dan Lafferty

The Lafferty brothers, based on a claimed religious revelation by Ron, murdered their sister-in-law and her baby. (See Chapters 16, 17 and 18.)

State v. Ronnie Lee Gardner

Gardner killed an attorney and wounded a bailiff in a shooting spree at the courthouse in Salt Lake City. (See Chapter 6.)

State v. Douglas Kay and Norman Newsted

Kay and Newsted robbed a bar in Cedar City, and shot to death execution-style two customers and a barmaid as they lay face-down on the floor of the bar. (See Chapters 7 and 8.)

State v. Mark Hofmann

Hofmann was a master forger of historical Mormon documents and a con man. He killed two people in successive bombings and then injured himself when he accidentally set off a bomb in his car as he was attempting to deliver it to an unknown third victim.

MY INTRODUCTION TO CAPITAL CASES

My first capital case assignment came within months of transferring downtown to the main D.A.'s office to handle felony cases. I was assigned to assist lead prosecutor Robert Stott in the prosecution of Joseph Paul Franklin, an avowed racist from Alabama who hated blacks and was particularly enraged by interracial mixing. On August 20, 1980, he took up a position across from Liberty Park in Salt Lake City, at the back of a vacant field. There, shielded by overgrown weeds, he pulled a high-powered rifle out of the trunk of his Camaro and shot and killed Lawrence Johnson and Tom Childs, two young black men, for the "crime" of jogging with two young white women.

The case against Franklin was entirely circumstantial, as no one could directly place him at the scene. We had witnesses who had seen a car in the field similar to Franklin's, and a hitchhiker who placed Franklin in the area of the park earlier in the day, and said he had made racist comments to her. We also were able to show that Franklin had stayed in motels in the area around the time of the killings, using false names and IDs. And we put in evidence that, four years earlier, on the East Coast, Franklin had followed an interracial couple in his car, forced them to pull over, and then sprayed mace in the black man's face as he yelled, "Nigger!"

Franklin was convicted of two counts of first degree murder, and could have been sentenced to death. For the penalty phase of his trial, where it would be decided whether he would be sentenced to death or to life imprisonment, he said he wanted to represent himself, and was allowed to remain alone in a holding cell area near the courtroom. As the penalty phase was about to begin and the judge and jury were in place, the jailor suddenly showed up at the door and gestured to us with an astonished look on his face. Bob Stott and I quickly walked back toward the hallway behind the courtroom where the jailor was standing. As we approached him, he looked around, shrugged his shoulders, and told us in a hushed and urgent tone, "He's gone!"

Franklin had gone up through a ceiling panel in the holding cell, and no one knew where he was. We quickly walked back into the courtroom and asked to approach the bench with Franklin's lawyers. We quietly informed Judge Jay Banks that Franklin had bolted. Banks, a crusty old former prosecutor with a penchant for smoking cigarillos in chambers and telling prosecutors after "not guilty" verdicts how they should have tried their cases, told the jury we'd be in recess without alerting them to Franklin's sudden disappearance.

About 40 minutes later, the police found Franklin hiding above the ceiling in a different part of the courthouse. The trial resumed, this time with defense counsel, rather than Franklin, presenting the evidence and making the arguments as to why he should not be sentenced to death.

Utah law requires all twelve jurors to agree "beyond a reasonable doubt" that the death penalty should be given. If just one doesn't, the jury cannot return a verdict of death. Franklin's attorney argued that since it was an entirely circumstantial case with no confession from the defendant, the jurors could not be absolutely certain of his guilt, and thus should not vote for death. At least one juror was persuaded not to vote for the death penalty, and Franklin was sentenced to life in prison.

MY GROWING DISENCHANTMENT WITH CAPITAL CASES

By the time I finished my third capital case, *State v. Michael Moore*, I decided I didn't want to be involved in any more capital murder prosecutions. There were several reasons for this. I didn't like the fact that capital defendants were given so much attention by the media that they were almost celebrities, and some seemed to bask in the limelight. I didn't like the fact that capital cases that ended in death sentences went on for decades on appeal, prolonging the suffering of victims' families. And I didn't like the fact that political factors could influence the handling of a capital case.

The *Moore* case was an example of that. Given Utah's high standard to obtain the death penalty – all twelve jurors had to vote that death was essentially the only appropriate penalty, and had to be convinced of that "beyond a reasonable doubt" – very few capital murderers were sentenced to death. While the *Moore* case clearly qualified as capital – he had killed two people, which was one of the statutory aggravating factors for capital murder – we knew the odds of actually securing a verdict of death were quite remote. Moore was relatively young and had no prior criminal record: not the type of defendant a Utah jury was likely to sentence to death.

About the same time, another capital case handled by another prosecutor in our office was also pending trial under similar circumstances – the death penalty was a remote possibility at best. Under such circumstances, we generally would explore with the defense attorneys the possibility of having the defendants plead guilty as charged in exchange for our agreement not to seek the death penalty. But word came down the line that we should not even consider exploring the possibility of resolving these cases without the death penalty.

The reason? It was an election year, and Ted Cannon, the Salt Lake County Attorney, didn't want his opponent to make hay out of him plea-bargaining capital cases. He was afraid he would be pilloried for being soft on crime, soft on the death penalty, and he might have been right about that. Being accused of being soft on the death penalty can be the death knell of elected prosecutors, particularly in jurisdictions with high-profile murders, like Salt Lake.

What bothered me wasn't so much that we had to take the cases to trial rather than work out a plea agreement. It wasn't improper to take them to trial or even to seek the death penalty, given what the defendants had done. What I didn't like was that political considerations could so influence the process.

Another factor in my growing disenchantment with capital cases was the experience of my father's cousin, Dr. Harold Horton, who had once been assigned to attend executions at the Utah State Prison, back when the prison was located at the present site of Sugar House Park in Salt Lake City. His job was to declare dead the prisoners who were executed by firing squad or hanging, and those experiences had shaken his belief that a civilized society ought to engage in executions, even of its most vicious criminals. I remember him giving me a book to read called *88 Men and 2 Women*,[94] written by Clinton T. Duffy, who had been the warden of San Quentin Prison in California during the 1940s and 50s. Based on his first-hand experience of presiding over the execution of 90 prisoners, Duffy came to believe the practice to be barbaric and ineffective, and became a strong advocate for abolishing the death penalty.

In any case, after I had been involved in three capital case prosecutions

---

[94] *88 Men and 2 Women*, by Clinton T. Duffy (Doubleday & Company, 1962).

– Joseph Paul Franklin, Ronald L. Kelly, and Michael Moore – I went to Chief Deputy John T. Nielsen and told him I didn't want to be assigned to any other capital cases. We discussed my reasons, and John T. agreed that while I would be assigned murder cases, I would not be assigned any more capital cases.

And then the Arthur Gary Bishop case broke in July of 1983. Bishop had kidnapped, sexually abused, and murdered five young boys over a 4-year period, eventually confessing and leading the police to the victims' remains. By this point, I had become the office's resident expert at countering insanity defenses, and it appeared that mounting a mental defense was about the only way Bishop's attorneys could run any kind of defense. John T. asked me how I felt about joining the prosecution team in the Bishop case. My friend Bob Stott was to be lead counsel, as he had been in the *Franklin* case. I told John T. that I would think about it.

I remember discussing it with my brother, Joe, and coming to the conclusion if there was ever a case that justified consideration of the death penalty, it was the *Bishop* case. The murder of any one of these young boys would have justified capital treatment, but five? Whatever ultimate sanction existed in Utah law, Bishop deserved to receive it. So the next day, I told John T. that I would be part of the team.

Bishop did, in fact, run a mental defense and call mental health experts to the stand. His defense was that as a homosexual pedophile with antisocial personality disorder, he should only be found guilty of manslaughter, rather than murder, because he acted under extreme mental or emotional disturbance when he committed the murders. We agreed with the diagnosis, but argued that while it may have helped to explain why Bishop did what he did, it in no way excused or mitigated his cold-blooded murders. The jury agreed, and Bishop was convicted of five counts of first degree murder and sentenced to death.

After the Utah Supreme Court upheld his convictions, Bishop voluntarily waived any further appeals, saying he preferred execution to spending the rest of his life in prison. He was then examined by a psychologist to determine if he was making a rational choice or was mentally impaired. Bishop was determined to be sane, and on June 10, 1988, he was executed by lethal injection. I had no regrets at the time of his execution about the outcome, or about my role in the prosecution. But it didn't turn me into a "true believer" in the death penalty either.

Fortunately, although I went on to handle other capital cases throughout my career (including several while at the Utah Attorney General's Office), after the *Moore* case, I never felt any of the others were being unduly influenced by political concerns. And in only one other case did I argue in favor of the death penalty: *State v. Ronald Lafferty*. I felt Lafferty, like Bishop, had committed murders so horrendous that the death penalty was appropriate, for there was no doubt that he had orchestrated the execution of his sister-in-law and her 15-month-old baby.[95] Still, there was no sense of triumph or exhilaration when the jury returned the death penalty verdict in the *Lafferty* case. When asked for a comment by the press, I told them that we had done our jobs as prosecutors and the jury had done its duty, but there was no cause for celebration.

When I first transferred from the D.A.'s Office to the Attorney General's Office, one of the first cases I was assigned was a death penalty case in which the defendant, William Andrews, had been convicted of capital murder and was pending execution for his involvement in the infamous "Hi Fi" murder case in Ogden, Utah.

During this brutal crime, Williams and an accomplice named Dale Pierre Selby had gone into an audio store just before closing to commit an armed robbery. There were five victims in the store, and Selby and Williams herded them downstairs at gunpoint and forced them to drink Drano. They also kicked a pen into one man's ear so deep that it caused brain damage, and they raped a teenage girl before shooting her in the

---

[95] Lafferty had also intended to kill two other people on the same day, but one intended victim was out of town, and they missed the turn to the other's house.

head. When the crime spree was over, three people were dead. Two other victims had somehow survived, but with severe injuries.

Torture, rape, multiple murders – it was as bad a crime spree as anyone could remember, the kind that cried out for the ultimate punishment society could mete out: the death penalty. It was a foregone conclusion that anyone convicted of such horrific crimes would get the death penalty, and both Selby and Williams had in fact been convicted of multiple counts of capital murder and sentenced to death.

After I got the assignment to represent the State in fending off attempts to delay Williams' execution, I asked to meet with John Turner, the Chief Deputy Attorney General. I told him that I preferred not to handle the case, and that I had come to the A.G.'s Office partly because I was tired of doing murder cases, and capital murder cases in particular.

I wasn't sure how Turner would react to my turning down one of the first requests made of me as a recently-hired Assistant Attorney General. After all, my background as a capital prosecutor made me the logical choice to handle the case. But instead of pushing the issue, Turner conceded that he himself had been heavily involved in working to fend off last-minute claims on behalf of Dale Pierre Selby, Williams' co-defendant, and that although there was no question in his mind that Selby was guilty or that he "deserved" the death penalty, Turner hadn't quite been prepared for how profound a hollow feeling set in when the execution finally occurred.

It paralleled what one of my other friends had told me. Dave Schwendiman, whom I had replaced when I joined the Attorney General's Office, described a similar feeling. He too had worked hard to be sure that the Selby execution went forward as scheduled. Dave described having to pull over to the side of the road on the way home, when he finally learned that Selby's date with death that he had worked so hard to preserve had actually taken place – again, a profound sense of hollowness at the "victory" of an execution.

It also reminded me of what I'd read in the book by the San Quentin warden that my dad's cousin had given me many years earlier. Apparently those closest to the ground in carrying out executions often question whether their cause is truly a "worthy" one, even if they support the death penalty in principle and have no doubt that it is justified in a particular case.

MY THOUGHTS ON THE DEATH PENALTY

People sometimes ask me how I feel personally about the death penalty. Having had the experience of prosecuting over a dozen capital cases, I favor abolishing it. While I think that those who commit aggravated murders should never be allowed the opportunity to victimize society again, I find more negatives than positives in the capital punishment system. And I don't think it makes us safer as a society.

Deterrence is often cited as a justification for the death penalty. While it's certainly true that an executed person will never kill again, meaning that capital punishment does specifically deter the murderer from committing future crimes, evidence that it deters other potential killers seems lacking.

I suspect that all we can know for sure are the killers who *weren't* deterred, and there seems to be no shortage of them. The capital murderers I prosecuted were certainly not deterred, and it seems to me that people who are capable of committing these aggravated murders are unlikely to not act on their impulses, even if they know they could face capital punishment. Some may even be emboldened to commit crimes in death penalty jurisdictions, due to a warped sense of bravado. I don't know for sure whether this is the case, but it would be consistent with the fact that many states that don't have the death penalty have lower murder rates than those that do.

One of the reasons that deterrence doesn't seem like a compelling argument in Utah is that capital cases can go on for decades before executions occur, if they occur at all. It's hard to gauge any deterrent effect under those circumstances. And who really knows if potential killers would be more deterred by the fear of execution or the fear of rotting in prison for the rest of their lives, with no hope of release? Sounds like hell either way.

Another reason I believe the death penalty is not an effective deterrent is that so few murderers receive it. In Utah, despite all the horrendous murders committed over the past four decades, only nine men sit on death row, a majority of them for crimes committed back in the 80s. Victims' family members often die before these murderers ever exhaust their round after round of state and federal appeals. Judges have no great appetite to move these cases forward, and capital appellate counsel have the opposite agenda. Every day they can delay post-conviction proceedings is another day their client stays alive. Some defense counsel have, apparently intentionally, sat on their hands for years rather than move a case forward.

And with a 2008 Utah Supreme Court decision, *Archuletta v. Galetka*, 2008 UT 76, defense counsel may have increased incentive to do nothing. The Court announced that, if no competent capital defense attorneys are able and willing to handle these cases expeditiously, the Court might have to step in and convert death sentences into sentences of life without parole. Sounds like a road map for defense counsel who can manage to delay post-conviction proceedings long enough for the Supreme Court to step in.

In the end, only the Attorney General's Appeals Division pushes to move death penalty appeals along, generally with very little success. It's gotten so drawn out that several years ago, Fred Voros, then Chief of the Appeals Division, went to the Utah State Legislature and announced that Utah in practice no longer had a viable death penalty system – unless, like Arthur Gary Bishop, a convicted murderer volunteers to be executed after losing his mandatory appeal before the Utah Supreme Court.[96] In support

---

[96] In cases where defendants are sentenced to death, the Utah Supreme Court scrutinizes the evidence and trial record to be sure the convictions and sentences are appropriate. Since a convicted murderer who is sentenced to death cannot waive this process, it is known as a mandatory appeal.

of Voros' statement, family members whose loved ones were killed decades before described their anguish, wondering if they themselves would die before the murderers who killed their family members were executed.

I can't imagine how it would feel to live through the nightmare of having a loved one brutally murdered, endure a trial at which a jury returned the death penalty, and then have to live for decades with the possibility on any given day of opening up the newspaper or turning on the TV and finding out that new claims of error are being asserted by the killer's attorneys. For victims' families, years and years of that recurring nightmare can be torture, and can prevent them from ever achieving finality and being able to move on with their lives.

I have seen cases where victims' family members initially felt that no sentence less than death would be acceptable, but after suffering through years, even decades, of uncertainty in the post-conviction Alice-in-Wonderland world of death penalty appeals, they ultimately reached a point where they just wanted finality, whatever that might mean.

I understand the notion that some crimes seem to cry out for the death penalty – *Bishop* was such a case for me. How could any punishment less than death be appropriate for a serial killer of children? And what about mass murderers? Should they receive the same sentence as people who kill "just" one victim? Or what about killers who are already sentenced to life without parole, and who go on to kill guards or other inmates? Wouldn't another life without parole sentence be meaningless? How could that be justice? Is there nothing that deserves the death penalty?

I wonder if that is the question we should be asking. If it's an issue of proportionality, rather than a moral issue or even a practical one, what do we do with the unavoidable truth that sometimes jurors decide to impose the death penalty on defendants who kill one person, but don't impose it on some who kill many? If proportionality is the key concept, the justice system can't enforce it, and then the proportionality argument starts to cut the other way. If a man who cuts loose in a crowded theatre with an assault weapon and kills a dozen people and wounds 70 more gets life in prison, how do we reconcile the death penalty for a single killer?[97]

I understand that wanting a murderer put to death is a natural human response to having someone brutally take away the life of someone you love, and I would probably feel the same if it happened to me. And so I don't come easily to the view that we as a society would be better off without the death penalty, but I still do come down on that side.

I have a good friend who prosecutes war crimes in Europe – crimes so staggering in scope and savagery that I don't know that I could do what he does. I think it would be too overwhelming. None of the war criminals he prosecutes will ever get the death penalty, because Europe has abolished it. With all he has seen, he still does not think the death penalty is the answer. Maybe there is no answer.

Over the last decade of my career, I came to feel that the most humane result for victims' families who wanted the death penalty was for a jury to return a sentence of life in prison without parole. Whatever dissatisfaction a victim's family might feel with that verdict, no matter how keenly felt, it would be far less agonizing than living with the fallout from a death verdict, which would likely result in their suffering for decades – and in some instances, for the rest of their lives. That terrible uncertainty sometimes included not just the question of whether the murderers might not be executed, but also the question of whether the convictions themselves might be set aside, because capital cases are scrutinized with a fine-toothed comb.

Because of what I've observed through the years, I have become an advocate of full disclosure to victims' families in capital cases, and feel that it's a moral, if not a legal, obligation of prosecutors who handle capital cases. What I mean by full disclosure is this: After spending time building

---

[97] In August of 2015, James Holmes was sentenced to life without parole for his shooting spree at an Aurora, Colorado movie theater – a spree which left 12 dead and 70 others wounded. http://www.cnn.com/2015/08/07/us/james-holmes-movie-theater-shooting-jury/

rapport with a victim's family, I would level with them about the capital case and appellate process, and tell them that I wanted them to know what I would want someone to tell me if I were in their shoes. I wanted them to know the truth. And the truth is, if a case goes to trial and the jury returns a verdict of death, that pronouncement is probably the last satisfaction the victim's family will get for years, if not decades. From that point on, the delays and uncertainties of the death penalty appeals process are likely to take a terrible toll, keeping the wound open and preventing the victim's family from moving on.

Some victims' families decide either initially or as their cases progress that they don't want the death penalty – that the best way of achieving justice is to have the defendant spend the rest of his life in prison. Some even believe that life in prison without parole is tougher on the criminal than the death penalty.[98] Others insist that the only way for justice to be done is through the death penalty.

Either way, the "lucky" ones are those whose cases result in life without parole, rather than the death penalty. In those cases, the murderers go to prison and, for the most part, no one hears about them again. Unlike defendants sentenced to death, those who receive life-without-parole sentences generally don't have lawyers coming out of the woodwork volunteering to take their cases. Nor am I aware of organizations whose sole purpose is to fight against sentences of life without parole. And so the murderers who are sentenced to life without parole serve their sentences in relative anonymity, and victims' families are able to move on with their lives.

So there are many reasons why I favor life sentences over the death penalty. And all of that is even without a final consideration. No system of justice is perfect, and so it's possible that an innocent person could be

---

[98] That's what Arthur Gary Bishop told a psychologist who was assigned to evaluate whether Bishop was making a sane choice by allowing his execution to go forward, and forgoing further appeals. Bishop said he viewed spending the rest of his life in prison as worse than death. The judge found it to be a rational choice, and Bishop was executed.

convicted of a capital murder and executed. This is not currently a factor in Utah, because there is no credible claim of factual innocence for any of the men on death row. But there have been cases in other states of innocent people being convicted of capital crimes, and being sentenced to death.

One of the most notable is the case of Kirk Bloodsworth, a Maryland fisherman who was convicted of the murder of a little girl in 1985, and sentenced to death. Kirk spent several years on death row before his case was reversed on appeal due to errors at trial. He was re-tried and convicted of murder again, but the second time, he received a sentence of life in prison rather than the death penalty. After serving nine years in prison for a crime he didn't commit, Kirk was exonerated by DNA evidence, which also identified the true killer. (For more on Kirk, see Chapter 24.)

And Kirk Bloodsworth is only one of many people around the country who have been convicted of murders they did not commit, and sentenced to death, only to be exonerated years later. But for the advent of DNA technology, Kirk and other innocent people like him could have been executed. When a mistake is made and the wrong person is sent to prison, there is at least the opportunity for exoneration and release. But when the wrong person is executed, there is no remedy or recourse, and the injustice is irrevocable.

FINAL THOUGHTS

In states that have the death penalty and use it frequently, such as Texas, there is no shortage of murders. If the threat of the death penalty really does serve as a deterrent for potential murderers, it's certainly not evident. While it may be that legislatures in pro-death-penalty states like Utah are unlikely to repeal the death penalty any day soon, I suspect that someday the United States Supreme Court will rule it unconstitutional.

The Court has already chipped away at the death penalty by prohibiting it in certain instances – for example, they have banned it in cases of juveniles[99], mentally retarded defendants[100], passive accomplices who don't intend to kill[101], those who commit rape of adults[102], and those who are insane at the time of their scheduled execution.[103] The trend seems to be moving in the direction of one day recognizing a constitutional ban on the grounds that capital punishment violates the Eighth Amendment to the United States Constitution by inflicting "cruel and unusual punishment."

If the Court does decide to put an end to capital punishment in America, it will put the United States in line with the overwhelming majority of civilized nations, which prohibit the death penalty. I would like to see that day.

---

[99] *Roper v. Simmons*, 543 U.S. 551 (2005)
[100] *Atkins v. Virginia*, 536 U.S. 335 (2002)
[101] *Enmund v. Florida*, 458 U.S. 782 (1982)
[102] *Coker v. Georgia*, 433 U.S. 584 (1977)
[103] *Ford v. Wainwright*, 477 U.S. 399 (1986)

CHAPTER 23
_____

From Chief Prosecutors to Criminal Defendants:
Isn't There a Better Way to Elect Prosecutors?

FOR 17 YEARS – more than half of my 31-year career – I worked for elected public prosecutors who themselves eventually faced criminal charges. I worked for Salt Lake County Attorney Ted Cannon for eight years, and for Utah Attorney General Mark Shurtleff for nine. And as I look back on those experiences, I can't help thinking there must be a better way to elect prosecutors to public office in Utah.

TED CANNON, SALT LAKE COUNTY ATTORNEY 1979-1986

Shortly after I was hired at the Salt Lake County Attorney's Office in 1978, Ted Cannon was elected to head that office. He was a rising star in the Republican Party who had made his name as a tough anti-pornography prosecutor in the Salt Lake City Attorney's Office, targeting X-rated movie theaters. As part of his "get tough on crime" platform, he ran a TV ad that featured him in a trench coat on the streets of Salt Lake, standing in front of a police car with its emergency lights flashing.

The prosecutors working in the trenches under Ted Cannon were some of the ablest in the state, and John T. Nielsen, his chief deputy, was

289

as good as they come. There was an explosion of high-profile capital murder cases in Salt Lake during the 80s[104], and those cases were successfully prosecuted by the career attorneys in Ted's office – lawyers like Bob Stott, Dick Shepherd, David Yocom, John Soltis, Ernie Jones, Mike Christensen, T.J. Tsakalos, Greg Bown, David Walsh, Rich McKelvie, Tom Vuyk, Carvel Harward, David Biggs and Gerry D'Elia.

While most of the staff had offices on the third floor of the Courtside Building, Ted's office was on the fourth floor, and as long as he stayed off the third floor and let the staff do their jobs under John T.'s (and later Bud Ellett's) deft leadership, everything ran pretty smoothly. When Ted got more personally involved, not so much.

For example, in the mid-80s, Ted spearheaded a case against Art Monson, the elected Treasurer of Salt Lake County – a Democrat who was charged with running a private business out of his office. Ted Cannon, a Republican, was accused by Monson's attorney of bringing a politically-motivated prosecution. When the case went to trial and Monson was acquitted of all charges, the defense again trumpeted the political nature of the prosecution, and "Unload Cannon" bumper stickers started showing up around town.

In 1986, toward the end of Ted's second term as County Attorney, things got very strange. One of the secretaries in the office accused him of sexual harassment, and he was investigated by a grand jury, which was looking into allegations ranging from official misconduct to misuse of public funds to sexual harassment to libel.

As time went on, we saw less and less of Ted on the third floor, and he became estranged from the staff. Eventually, he was indicted by the grand jury on several misdemeanor charges. He went to trial and was convicted of criminal libel for statements he had made about a news reporter. Then, facing more charges, he threw in the towel, pled "no contest" to some of

---

[104] See Chapter 22.

the additional charges, and resigned as County Attorney. He served 23 days of a 30-day jail sentence.

MARK SHURTLEFF, UTAH ATTORNEY GENERAL 2001-2013

From 2001 until I retired in 2009, I worked under Mark Shurtleff, a Republican who served three terms as Utah's Attorney General. For most of that time, I was Chief of the Criminal Justice Division, and so I attended regular monthly Division Chief meetings. Outside of those meetings, I didn't have much direct contact with Mark: I was not a part of his executive group nor his inner circle. But Mark was always cordial to me. He did not interfere in my cases and I had no conflicts with him.

So I was more than a little astonished to learn after I retired that both Mark and his successor as Attorney General, Republican John Swallow, were being investigated by state and federal authorities for serious misconduct while in office. Then, in July of 2014, state prosecutors brought multiple felony charges against both men. Shurtleff was charged with receiving or soliciting bribes, accepting gifts, tampering with witnesses and evidence, and participating in a pattern of unlawful conduct, commonly referred to as "racketeering."[105]

While the charges are stunning, I have no first-hand information about the alleged incidents, and will keep my own counsel on the question of guilt or innocence until the cases are resolved. But I do have something to say about the process of how prosecutors are elected in Utah.

A BETTER WAY TO ELECT PROSECUTORS

My view is that prosecution and politics should never mix, and so I would like to see non-partisan elections of both county prosecutors and the Attorney General in Utah. Prosecutors enforce the laws; they don't

---

[105] The racketeering count against Shurtleff was dismissed by prosecutors in November of 2014, and in June of 2015, three bribery counts were also dismissed. He is currently charged with five felonies and two misdemeanors.

write them. But in Utah, many candidates for those positions tout their conservative credentials as if they were running for the Legislature.

In the justice system, it should make absolutely no difference whether a prosecutor is a Republican or a Democrat – or, for that matter, a conservative, a liberal, or none of the above. The reason that "Lady Justice" is often portrayed as blindfolded and holding a scale is that justice should be administered in a fair and even-handed manner, without regard to whether those who are brought before it are the most or least influential members of society.

While the law should treat everyone equally, political parties are like clubs. They divide people into categories of "us" and "them." And if a potential defendant's political affiliation means anything at all to a prosecutor assessing a case, then justice isn't "blind," and the integrity of the system is undermined. The bottom line is that any prosecutor who makes decisions based on political affiliation or considerations is, per se, corrupt.

One problem with electing prosecutors on a partisan basis, even ethical ones, is that, if nothing else, the specter of political motivation hangs over every case brought by a prosecutor of one party against a prominent member of another. And regardless of whether the case is politically motivated, that specter undermines confidence that justice is being applied in an even-handed manner.

Ted Cannon's prosecution of Art Monson is an example. In Salt Lake County government, Cannon was a big-time Republican, Monson a big-time Democrat. Cannon brought charges against Monson. Was he politically motivated, as Monson's defense attorneys alleged? The problem was that no one could be sure one way or the other – two guys, two clubs, one going after the other. Would Cannon have prosecuted a high-ranking Republican who had done the same thing, or would he perhaps have given an official of his own party a pass? Again, who knows? And that's the problem. We should get politics completely out of the courtroom and the justice system, and hence out of the election process.

Perhaps the greatest benefit of non-partisan elections would be to increase the likelihood that the most qualified candidate would be elected, rather than the one associated with the most popular party. That's particularly important in a state like Utah, where one party so dominates the political landscape. Utah is so overwhelmingly Republican – just look at the makeup of both its state legislature and its delegation in Washington – that a qualified Democrat starts out at a significant and sometimes insurmountable disadvantage. It's certainly not a level playing field.

One reason for the dominance of the Republican Party in Utah is its close association with the LDS Church. I found out just how much the deck can be stacked against a Democrat when I campaigned for Jan Graham's reelection in 1996. One weekend when I was making calls to people I knew to urge them to support Jan, I decided to call Janice, an old friend from my college days at UCLA. I hadn't kept close contact with her through the years, but we had been pretty close in college, and I knew she lived in the area.

So I called her up and we chatted for a few minutes. I told her what a great job Jan had done during her first term as Attorney General, and that she was the best boss I had ever worked for. Janice seemed receptive and said she'd vote for Jan, but when I asked her if she'd consider putting a Jan Graham lawn sign in her yard, she hesitated. After a moment, she told me that she had recently been called to a leadership position in her LDS ward and was concerned how it would look if she put a sign for a Democrat in her yard. I was astonished.

So how might things play out differently in a system that elects an Attorney General on a non-partisan basis? First, the Attorney General's election would not be subject to straight-ticket voting, the practice of selecting the option in one stroke of voting for every candidate a political party has on the ballot. Second, voters would have to focus on the credentials and qualifications of the candidates, rather than relying upon party affiliations.

What might the result of that be? Let's take a look backwards and see how it might have played out when Mark Shurtleff was first elected Attorney General.

In 2000, when Jan Graham decided not to seek re-election for a third term, the race was on. Mark Shurtleff, who had been an Assistant Attorney General for a few years, a Deputy Salt Lake County Attorney for a brief period, and then a Salt Lake County Commissioner, lined up on the Republican side. I believe that at the time, he had never prosecuted a criminal case in Utah.

His opponent was Reed Richards, who had served for eight years as Chief Deputy Attorney General under Jan Graham, and before that, eight years as the elected Weber County Attorney in Ogden. He was well-respected by the courts, law enforcement, and the legislature, had a wealth of experience prosecuting major criminal cases, and had been an effective leader as Jan's chief deputy.

Reed had also helped establish the Children's Justice Centers in Utah, was actively involved in promoting victims' rights, and had developed and implemented crime prevention programs in the areas of child abuse, domestic violence, gangs, drug abuse, and senior abuse. To top it off, he was a family man, an LDS church leader, and a person of unquestioned integrity. He was, in short, the perfect candidate for Utah's Attorney General in every way, except one: He was a Democrat.

Even assuming every allegation against Mark Shurtleff is groundless, how would he have fared on a level playing field against Reed Richards, based solely on who had the most experience and who was more qualified to be Attorney General?[106]

But since the race was partisan, the decked was stacked, and even those

---

[106] In an editorial in the Salt Lake Tribune dated Feb. 19, 2013 and entitled "Swallow and single-party voting," former Utah Attorney General Jan Graham makes a similar point with the election of John Swallow over Democrat Dee Smith in the 2012 election. Based on all relevant criteria, Smith's qualifications were much more impressive than Swallow's.

Republicans who knew Reed well and thought he was the best candidate for the job could not endorse him without paying a price.

One who did endorse Reed was Mel Wilson, the Davis County Attorney, and a quality guy. As an experienced prosecutor who had worked with Reed for years, Mel knew that party affiliations weren't what mattered when electing prosecutors. Experience, judgment, integrity – they were what mattered. So Mel endorsed Reed as the best candidate for Attorney General, and when he did, he was roundly condemned by the local Republican Party, which set out to unseat Mel at his next election. They came close to doing so, but were ultimately unsuccessful. They then passed a resolution condemning Mel for endorsing Reed, calling him an embarrassment to the Republican Party.

Somebody got that exactly backward. That incident alone speaks volumes as to why we should remove partisan politics from the process of electing prosecutors.

Whatever the outcome of the Shurtleff prosecution, I can say with confidence that had Reed Richards been elected Attorney General in 2000, he would have served with distinction. I can say that because for eight years I interacted with Reed on a daily basis – when he was Chief Deputy and I was Chief of the Criminal Division – and our offices were close together in the State Capitol. I conferred with him practically every day and witnessed first-hand how he approached his job – his commitment to public service, his motivation, and how he dealt with sensitive and difficult ethical and legal issues. And over the course of eight years, I never saw anything from Reed but the highest ethical conduct. Not even once.[107]

During the 2000 campaign, Reed suggested that voters select an attorney general in the same way they would hire their own personal attorneys: by looking beyond political labels and rhetoric and selecting

---

[107] Given the likelihood that some members of the LDS Church did not vote for Reed Richards in 2000 because he was a Democrat, it is ironic that in July of 2014, the same month Mark Shurtleff was charged with numerous felonies, Reed Richards, a former LDS Bishop, was made a member of the presidency of the LDS Temple in Ogden, Utah.

the person with the most experience, knowledge, and legal skill. I would agree with that, and I would also add that voters should select the person with a proven track record of integrity.

If Utah were to adopt a system of non-partisan elections, it might actually be possible for voters to select their prosecutors in the way Reed described. And given Utah's recent history, what have its citizens really got to lose by requiring candidates for Attorney General to stand on their own merits, without the distraction of virtually meaningless party affiliations? Still, I know that entrenched systems change slowly, if at all.[108]

In the meantime, Utah voters would be well-served to disregard party labels when selecting their local prosecutors and their Attorney General. If they could do that, their elected officials would be more likely to spend their time in court sitting at counsel table for the State, rather than at the defense table.

---

[108] I also recognize that, if non-partisan elections still pit a Republican against a Democrat, even if they are not identified as such on the ballot, it's unlikely that anything will change.

CHAPTER 24

The Reluctant Prosecutor Comes Full Circle:
My Involvement in the Innocence Movement

HAVING SPENT MY WHOLE CAREER AS A PROSECUTOR, I had seen my share of cases in which justice had gone awry. I can't remember when I first heard it said of our justice system, "Better that a hundred guilty people go free than that one innocent person be convicted," but my experience, like that of most prosecutors, had all gone in one direction: seeing guilty people go free. And how could it be otherwise? The standard of proof we had to meet – "beyond a reasonable doubt" – was intentionally weighted in favor of acquittal. A finding of "not guilty" wasn't an affirmative finding of innocence. It meant only that the jury was not unanimously convinced beyond a reasonable doubt that a defendant was guilty.

Sometimes we had additional evidence of guilt we could not present to juries because of evidentiary rulings. Sometimes we couldn't even charge people whom we "knew" (or thought we knew) were guilty, because of mistakes the police had made during an investigation. Other times, jurors who acquitted defendants told us after trial that they really thought the defendants were guilty, but they had acquitted them anyway, sometimes for reasons that were bizarre.[109] In short, while their cases were not as high-profile, most prosecutors had their own "O.J. stories."[110] I was no exception.

PROMOTING INNOCENCE LEGISLATION IN UTAH

Still, when I was approached in 2000 by defense attorneys and law professors associated with Utah's newly-created Innocence Project – people who were advocating for a bill that would allow convicted defendants access to DNA testing in support of innocence claims – I had no problem with the concept. They had set up a meeting in our offices at the Capitol to try to convince us to not oppose legislation to facilitate the testing. We met in Chief Deputy Reed Richards' office, and I recall that they seemed somewhat tentative in approaching us. After all, in some other states, prosecutors had fought tooth and nail to *not* open the door to DNA testing that could be used to undermine convictions.

After the Innocence Project advocates gave their presentation, we told them that, far from being opposed to the concept, we were completely supportive of it, and would be glad to help get such a bill passed. We told them that if any innocent people were sitting at the prison, we wanted them identified and released. Anything else would be inconsistent with our responsibility as prosecutors to seek justice.

I had, of course, heard of cases in other states in which defendants convicted of serious crimes, including rapes and murders, had been proven innocent through DNA evidence – evidence that wasn't available at the

---

[109] I had an acquittal in one case where the evidence of guilt was so strong that the judge prevented me from offering more, feeling it was unnecessary and he didn't want the trial to go into the next day. After the jury returned a verdict of "not guilty," the judge was so stunned that he told me he almost told the jurors what he thought of the verdict. Some months later, I ran into one of the jurors on the street, and she told me that they thought he was guilty but didn't convict him because they only got to hear the evidence once, and "nobody can decide anything if they only get to hear it once."

[110] Referring to the trial of O.J. Simpson, who was acquitted in 1995 of the murders of his ex-wife Nicole Brown Simpson and her friend Ronald Goldman. After the verdict, many believed that Simpson had gotten away with murder – an idea that was reinforced when Simpson was sued civilly for the wrongful deaths of his ex-wife and Goldman, and found to be liable.

time of their trials years before – so I couldn't exclude the possibility that it might have happened in Utah. I wanted to remove any impediment, financial or legal, that might hinder an innocent person from obtaining DNA testing that could establish innocence.

So we offered to take the laboring oar in drafting the bill and presenting it to the Legislature. The attorneys from the Innocent Project were pleased and, I believe, a bit surprised at our response. That year, we drafted the bill and shepherded it through the legislative process, and so in 2001, Utah passed "Postconviction Testing of DNA" supported not only by our office, but also by the Statewide Association of Prosecutors (SWAP) and law enforcement groups that we had spoken with to garner their support. The bill established a whole new procedure in which defendants could get a ruling from a judge not just vacating their convictions, but actually proclaiming them innocent – a brand new concept in Utah law.

A few years earlier, we had worked to pass legislation to require felons to give samples so their DNA profiles could be collected and put into a nationwide database. This database helped solve many cases, some of them "cold cases" that had long been dormant. This new bill was the flip side of that one – a way to establish innocence, just in case any inmates at the Utah State Prison had somehow been convicted of crimes they didn't commit.[111]

But it was all still theoretical to me. I knew of no case where we had sent anyone to prison when we had doubted their guilt. And I could point to several examples of people we knew were guilty who had escaped justice – people like Dale Steineke, who initially reported that his 19-month-old daughter had been abducted from his truck, but later confessed to killing her and putting her body in a dumpster in American Fork. After confessing, he led the police to her body, which he had wrapped in a plastic garbage bag and thrown in the dumpster. There was no ques-

---

[111] In the fall of 2001, I wrote an article for the *Utah Bar Journal* about the new law, entitled, "Utah's DNA Actual Innocence Bill."

tion of his guilt. He was convicted of his daughter's murder, but his conviction was later reversed when the Utah Court of Appeals ruled that there had been a defect in his Miranda waiver. As a result, his confession and everything that stemmed from it, including the finding of the victim's body, was inadmissible at trial. Steinecke was released from custody, and walked away a free man.

And then there was the famous case of Robert Kleasen, who had killed two Mormon missionaries in Texas in the 1970s. Kleasen had invited the missionaries to dinner, shot them to death, and then cut up their bodies with a band saw. In a search of Kleasen's house, police had found body parts and one of the missionary's name tags with a bullet hole in it. Kleasen was tried and convicted of murder and sentenced to death, but later, an appellate court reluctantly freed him because the search warrant obtained by the officers was legally flawed.[112]

Every prosecutor was familiar with cases like this, along with other cases where the evidence had seemed compelling, but where jurors had found reasonable doubt. It was exasperating, sometimes maddening, and it resulted at times in people literally "getting away with murder." But it also was the price our system was willing to pay to ensure that no innocent person would be convicted of a crime. Or so it seemed.

Given my early aspirations of being Atticus Finch, of defending and exonerating the innocent, the DNA exoneration bill appealed to me, and I was glad to have played a role in making it happen in Utah. But it wasn't until about six years later, when I came face-to-face with actual people who had been convicted of murder and then exonerated, that I became a passionate advocate for reform. Here's how it came about, and how, during the last few years of my career, I became friends with innocent people who had been convicted of murder, sent to prison, and later exonerated.

---

[112] See *Evil Among Us – The Texas Mormon Missionary Murders*, by Ken Driggs (Signature Books, 2000).

THE ROAD TO FURTHER INNOCENCE REFORM

During the 2006 General Session of the Utah Legislature, it came to my attention that Representative David Litvack was introducing innocence legislation. Since the DNA Actual Innocence law was already on the books, I was curious to find out what Rep. Litvack was proposing. I got a copy of the bill and saw that it would allow judges to exonerate convicted felons even without DNA evidence, if the felons could produce other evidence of their innocence that was similarly compelling.[113] I also noted that the bill would provide some monetary assistance for exonerees.

I decided to attend a legislative committee hearing on the bill, and listened to presentations made by Rep. Litvack and Heather Harris, a University of Utah law student. Heather had developed a passion for the issue while taking a course taught by Professor Daniel Medwed, a leading advocate for the wrongfully convicted, and had approached David about running the bill.

During Professor Medwed's course, Heather had learned that there was a gap in Utah's innocence law, because not all exonerations involved DNA evidence. Sometimes other compelling evidence of innocence existed. Shouldn't there be a way for these people to be exonerated as well? Heather had also learned that most exonerees were released from prison with few, if any, resources and no financial assistance following their years of imprisonment, and she felt profoundly that something should be done to rectify that.

Conceptually, I liked both of the major objectives of the legislation – to provide a mechanism for exoneration in non-DNA cases, and to provide some measure of restitution to those who had been wrongfully convicted and incarcerated for crimes they did not commit.

As I examined the provisions of the bill, however, I knew it needed more work, because it was written too broadly. It would have created

---

[113] An example of a non-DNA exoneration was the case of Scott Hornoff, which is highlighted later in this chapter. Scott was convicted of murder in Rhode Island and spent several years in prison before the actual murderer came forward and confessed to the crime, with information that only the murderer would know.

unintended consequences, such as potentially exonerating and compensating those whose innocence was not clear. It was also based on a tort litigation model, which would require defendants to prove misconduct or bad faith on someone's part in order to recover. The problem I saw with structuring it that way was that I knew that in most cases of exoneration, defendants would be hard-pressed to show that anyone acted in bad faith or intentionally engaged in misconduct. For example, about 75% of wrongful convictions involved erroneous eyewitness identification, where victims and witnesses sincerely believed they were identifying the right suspect, but, tragically, were mistaken.

It was clear to me that, because the way the bill was written, it had no chance of being passed. It would be vigorously opposed by prosecutors, police officers, and victims' rights groups. So I approached David Litvack and told him that I liked what he was trying to do, but I felt the issue needed more study. I suggested he pull the bill until the following year, and in the meantime work with us to carefully craft a bill that would accomplish the same major objectives, but would also have the support of the key players in the system. David readily agreed, and together we embarked on a two-year journey to pass a bill to help exonerate and compensate innocent people who may have been convicted of crimes they never committed.

We started by putting together a committee that included David, Heather, Professors Jensie Anderson and Daniel Medwed of the University of Utah College of Law – both leading advocates for the innocent – and Katie Monroe, newly-appointed as Director of the Rocky Mountain Innocence Center. We soon learned that Katie's passion for the work was very personal, as her own mother, Beverly Monroe, had been convicted of murder and spent several years in prison in Virginia before being exonerated and released.

Rounding out the prosecution side of the committee with me were Mike Wims and Erin Riley, also of the Attorney General's Office. Mike was a master trial lawyer with a wealth of experience, and Erin, herself a former prosecutor, handled post-conviction petitions for our office, which occurred when inmates challenged their convictions.

Initially, I wondered how well this committee of diverse viewpoints and background would gel. To my surprise, it turned out to be the most congenial and productive committee I ever served on. One of the truly remarkable things about the committee's discussions is that we had such a united purpose that no polarization of opinions ever developed. If someone had attended one of our meetings without knowing which of the members were prosecutors and which were defense advocates, it would have been difficult to tell.

Over the course of the next several months, we crafted the bill together, sought support from key groups, and were poised and ready for the 2007 General Session with a decent shot at passing landmark innocence legislation. With the support we'd lined up, we felt our chances of getting the bill passed were good. But we ran into opposition in the House of Representatives, when the Majority Leader stated on the Floor of the House that he would not support any bill for compensation – not one cent – unless fault by some agent of the State could be proven.

This was a major setback, because the House was heavily Republican, and here their leader was taking a stand against the bill. When we were unsuccessful in trying to get the Majority Leader to reconsider his opinion, we spoke individually to as many members of the House as we could, hoping to persuade them to support the bill anyway.

When it came up for final vote, Katie and I were in the gallery, holding our breath. Would the Republican House members break ranks with their leader and vote for the bill? The voting began and we watched the board light up. When the voting was over, the bill had passed the House on an overwhelming 64 to 8 vote.

We were elated, but the biggest hurdle still lay before us. After the bill passed in the House, it was sent over to the Senate for further action.

Before the bill could be voted on in the Senate, it had to be called up for consideration. It wasn't long before we learned that it was bottled up in the Senate Rules Committee — the committee that decided which bills would be placed before the Senate for discussion, debate, and voting. We were concerned because it was getting late in the 45-day legislative session, and time was running out.

On the last night of the session, we had one more shot, if only the bill would come out of the Rules Committee and be placed on the board for consideration. We had spoken to many senators who told us they would support the bill, and we were confident that if we could just get it up for a vote, it would pass.

I learned that at about six o'clock that night, the Rocky Mountain Innocence Center was sponsoring an event at a local restaurant, which featured exoneree Beverly Monroe, Katie's mother. I went over to the event while the Legislature was taking its dinner break, and had the opportunity to meet Beverly, an extraordinary woman. I felt an immediate affinity with her, and believed that she was someone the senators could readily identify with. In fact, I felt that she would be the perfect person to put a human face on the otherwise theoretical idea of innocent people being wrongfully convicted and sentenced to prison.

Beverly's case fit both aspects of our bill: not only had she struggled to win exoneration without DNA evidence, but she had received no compensation for her time in prison. So I asked Beverly to return to the Capitol with us to try to help get the bill onto the floor of the Senate, and she said she would be glad to help. We were able to introduce her to several lawmakers, including Senator Greg Bell, a deft and principled legislator, who pledged to assist us if the bill came up for consideration before the session ended at midnight.

Although we received multiple assurances from House leadership that the bill would be called up for consideration in the Senate before the midnight deadline, it remained bottled up in the Rules Committee, and never saw the light of day. So at midnight when the session ended, the bill died.

Still, the experience of getting to know Beverly, an absolutely wonderful person and one who seemed so unlikely to have ever suffered the indignity of a wrongful conviction, powerfully reinforced my commitment to try again the following year, and to do everything I could to make Heather's vision of a system that could rectify and pay for its mistakes a reality.

MEETING MORE EXONEREES

Beverly was not the only exoneree I got to know that year. Also attending innocence events and speaking at the University of Utah College of Law was Dennis Fritz, who had been convicted of a gruesome murder in Ada, Oklahoma in 1982. Dennis and his co-defendant, Ronnie Williamson, had been convicted of the murder of a young woman named Debra Sue Carter. Dennis got life in prison, and Williamson the death penalty. Thirteen years later, they were exonerated by DNA evidence that proved that the real killer was a man named Glen Gore, who had provided the police with damning false evidence against Williamson and Fritz.[114] Their case became the subject of John Grisham's true-life novel, *The Innocent Man*,[115] as well as Dennis' own book, *Journey Toward Justice*.[116]

Meeting Dennis and hearing about the ordeal he suffered was once again an eye-opening experience for me as a prosecutor. Katie and the Rocky Mountain Innocence Center presented me with a copy of Dennis' book, which I read with great interest. Now I had met two exonerees, and was deeply affected by the experience of getting to know them and learning what they had gone through.

During the time I was trying to promote the innocence bill, I had attended a federal public defenders conference at the Hotel Monaco in

---

[114] Fortunately, the evidence exonerating Williamson and Fritz came to light before Williamson was executed.
[115] *The Innocent Man – Murder and Injustice in a Small Town*, by John Grisham (Doubleday, 2006).
[116] *Journey Towards Justice*, by Dennis Fritz (Seven Locks Press, 2006).

downtown Salt Lake City, where Kirk Bloodsworth was speaking. Kirk was the first exoneree in the nation to be convicted of murder, receive a sentence of death, and later be exonerated by DNA evidence.

As I mentioned in Chapter 22, Kirk was a fisherman from Maryland, and he had been convicted of killing a little girl. Although he had nothing to do with the crime, he became a suspect based on a police sketch done by a witness who said he had seen a man in the wooded area where the crime occurred that day.

Someone called with a tip – the composite drawing reminded them of Kirk Bloodsworth. That's how it started, and Kirk became the victim of mistaken identification. Although he had a strong alibi, he was convicted anyway, and found himself on death row after undergoing the unbelievable experience of being charged, tried, and convicted of a terrible crime he didn't commit. Due to errors in his first trial, Kirk's conviction and death sentence were overturned, and he was re-tried and convicted once again. This time, he got life in prison rather than the death penalty.

After spending years in prison, Kirk read a book about a new technology – DNA evidence – and how it had helped solve a murder case in England. The thought came to him that if DNA can convict you, it can set you free. After he found a lawyer who was willing to take his case and push for DNA testing of his crime scene evidence, Kirk was exonerated.[117]

I was very impressed with Kirk, whom Katie introduced me to at the conference. He was an engaging speaker, a great storyteller, and, like the other exonerees I had met, surprisingly positive and grateful for the good things in his life. These exonerees impressed me because they didn't seem particularly bitter, and it struck me that they had weathered their own private journeys to hell and back far better than I would have, had I been in their shoes. And considering that their past experiences with prosecutors hadn't been so good, they all seemed amazingly open to accepting

---

[117] You can read his amazing story in *Bloodsworth: The True Story of the First Death Row Inmate Exonerated by DNA*, by Tim Junkin (A Shannon Ravenel Book, 2004).

Katie's assurances that I was a prosecutor who believed in the cause of the innocence movement and was trying to make good things happen in Utah.

DISCOVERING COMMON CAUSES OF WRONGFUL CONVICTIONS

What I was learning from the exonerees and their stories was not only that wrongful convictions can and do occur, but also some of the most common causes behind them – things like mistaken eyewitness identification, false testimony by "snitches," (criminal informants), unrecorded or false confessions, junk science, and tunnel vision by police officers and prosecutors.

I was not surprised to learn that many wrongful convictions included testimony by criminal informants, or "snitches." I had always been leery of using them as witnesses, especially criminals trying to cooperate with the police in exchange for lenient treatment, or to "work off a beef." Not only did these snitches have their own agendas, but their cooperation could sometimes result in their avoiding altogether accountability for their own criminal behavior.

I remember attending a homicide seminar once, a joint presentation featuring both a police detective who had handled lots of murder cases and an experienced homicide prosecutor from the Los Angeles D.A.'s Office. After the detective spoke for a couple of hours on a number of subjects, it was the prosecutor's turn. He stood up and said, "Never, ever, ever use a snitch in a murder case." Sounded like the guy had been burned before.

In any case, it wasn't difficult to connect the dots between informants and wrongful convictions. Many snitches had little or no credibility, and I generally shied away from using them, unless I had strong corroboration and could show the jury that, despite their general unreliability, they just happened to be telling the truth in the case at hand.[118]

---

[118] To make the point, I used tell juries that, if the snitch told them the sun was coming up in the east, they should check the window.

I learned that tunnel vision was another common problem associated with wrongful convictions. Tunnel vision occurs when police officers, and sometimes prosecutors, focus prematurely on a suspect and start filtering everything through that presumption of guilt. They in effect think of the case as "solved" before the investigation is complete, and so they stop considering other suspects or possibilities. In that mindset, they tend to discount evidence pointing to innocence while viewing evidence that is even slightly incriminating as strong evidence of guilt.[119]

Another lesson that I learned from studying wrongful convictions was the danger of failing to record police interrogations of suspects – how a suspect's words could be misinterpreted or overstated in court by officers relying solely on their memories and notes. Failure to record interviews had never made sense to me, especially in a system that otherwise seeks to collect and preserve evidence in the most reliable way possible. Why were we settling for second-rate evidence in the context of these interrogations, a choice which often resulted in credibility contests before judges and juries – contests that would be wholly unnecessary if the interviews could simply be recorded and presented in court?

WORKING ON POLICIES TO PREVENT WRONGFUL CONVICTIONS

While I was working on the innocence bill, I learned that a few states had developed "best practice statements" encouraging the recording of interviews of all felony suspects, and I thought we should do the same in Utah. I proposed that the Attorney General's Office set up a committee – the Best Practices Committee – to make recommendations and see what we could do at a policy level to decrease the possibility of wrongful convictions. And so the committee was formed and I was assigned to head it up.

---

[119] In the *Austin* case, highlighted in Chapter 4, officers had tunnel vision. If the case had gone to trial, it also would have had two other risk factors for wrongful convictions – shaky eyewitness identification, and the use of criminal informants.

We started working on a statewide recording policy for law enforcement officers, something that I'd wanted to see happen for a long time. It took some time to get all the law enforcement agencies on board, and at first there was resistance by some officers who liked the status quo and didn't want to have to record interviews. Two things probably helped us in lining up the necessary police support – the threat of possible legislation if nothing was done, and the experiences of officers in other jurisdictions.

A few months earlier at an innocence conference, I had spoken with a police official from Washington, D.C., who told me that, several years before, a recording policy had been imposed on the Washington D.C. police over their objection. He said that the officers had started out in complete opposition – but now, after having the policy in place for several years, they wouldn't ever go back to doing business the old way. Even the hard-liners had come to see the benefits of recording suspect statements. He said that recording had resulted in fewer motions to suppress statements that were allegedly coerced, fewer hearings to determine if suspects' statements should be suppressed, fewer claims of police misconduct, and more guilty pleas.

We were able to take that information to Utah's law enforcement groups and use it to help convince them that the benefits of recording far outweighed any perceived drawbacks. We argued that law enforcement and prosecutors should take the lead on the issue of recording, rather than waiting to have it involuntarily imposed on us.

In the end, we were able to line up the support of the Utah Chiefs of Police Association, the Utah Sheriffs' Association, the Utah Department of Public Safety, and the Statewide Association of Prosecutors. And so, in 2008, the recording policy was instituted. It was, I believe, a much-needed reform to enhance the reliability of confession evidence and guard against inaccuracies, misunderstandings and distortions that could result in innocent people being wrongfully convicted.[120]

At the same time that our Best Practices Committee was developing the recording policy, we were also working on another recommendation supporting procedures to enhance the reliability of eyewitness identification. Since so many exonerations involved cases where mistakes were made in eyewitness identification, we recognized the need to implement policies to help lower the possibility of suggestive identification techniques.

For example, police often show a witness a photo lineup that generally contains a suspect's picture and pictures of several other people with similar characteristics. If the officer conducting the photo lineup knows which person is the suspect, there's always the chance that the officer might cue the witness, even subliminally, toward the "right" choice. Because of that, it's important to have the photo lineup conducted by an officer who does not know which photo is of the suspect.

Another important procedural safeguard is that an officer conducting a photo lineup should emphasize to the witness that the person who committed the crime may or may not be included in the photo spread. Otherwise, the witness might feel pressure to pick out the person who most resembles the suspect, but who may not be the one who actually committed the crime.

When I left the Attorney General's Office in June of 2009, the eye-

---

[120] In April of 2009, just prior to my retirement from the Attorney General's Office, I wrote a letter to President Obama urging him to direct federal law enforcement agencies to record custodial interrogations of suspects. I was encouraged to do so by the fact that when he was in the Illinois Legislature, he had proposed and successfully passed a bill requiring the videotaping of interrogations. I had always been offended by the long-standing policy of the FBI NOT to record their suspect interviews and, with the election of President Obama, I hoped the practice would end.

I received a letter in September of 2009 from the Department of Justice, with the somewhat less-than-reassuring statement that "You can be certain that the Department's law enforcement components are giving your concerns our consideration."

I received no further communication, but in May of 2014, the Department of Justice, without public comment, issued a memorandum entitled "Policy Concerning Electronic Recording of Statements," changing its long-standing policy discouraging the recording of interviews and establishing a presumption that federal agents should electronically record statements of arrestees in their custody. While not as sweeping as Utah's recording policy, it represents a major beneficial policy shift – one that the Justice Department had resisted for decades.

witness identification procedures were still being reviewed by the Best Practices Committee.

THE SEEDS OF INNOCENCE TRAINING

While we were working on getting the new innocence law passed, there was something else I wanted to do. The advent of DNA evidence had brought a unique opportunity, not only to exonerate and free those who had been wrongfully convicted, but also to study how justice had gone awry in those cases.

I had been a member of the Prosecution Council Training Committee for several years, and we regularly planned annual prosecutor training conferences. At a meeting in the spring of 2007, I proposed that we offer as part of our fall conference an ethics presentation on how to avoid prosecuting innocent people. The fall conference was the primary annual training conference, and the one that most prosecutors throughout the state attended. As part of that training, I proposed that we bring in an actual exoneree to speak to the prosecutors.

At first, several other members of the committee were dubious. They had heard the claims of some innocence advocates who had intimated that large numbers of prison inmates were actually innocent, and were aware of some of the heated exchanges between prominent innocence advocates and spokesmen for the nation's prosecutors. In many of these cases, prosecutors had ended up in the position of defending against the claim that our justice system was "broken." These dynamics between the most vocal and prominent members of both sides had set up an "us against them" mentality that tended to frame the debate.

I wanted to avoid that whole area of controversy, and so I said that the point wasn't how many innocent inmates there were – if there were only a handful or even just one, it was still too many, and we should look to see what we could learn from cases where it was clear that the wrong person had been convicted. After all, no one should be more concerned about convicting the wrong people than prosecutors – because if and when it happens, it's not only a nightmare for the innocent, but also a safe haven for the actual criminals, who are never brought to justice and continue to walk the streets.

I told the committee that we would bring in an exoneree whose innocence was beyond doubt – someone who had not only been cleared by DNA, but whose case had also been definitively closed after DNA had identified the real killer. The prosecutors on the committee were all long-standing friends, and with the assurances I gave them, even those who were initially hesitant ultimately agreed to incorporate innocence training into the fall conference.

PROSECUTORIAL ETHICS: BEING MINISTERS OF JUSTICE

The year before, coincidentally, I had volunteered to head up an ethics panel at the Fall Conference on a related topic: the level of certainty prosecutors should have before bringing serious criminal charges against people. I was particularly interested in the topic because a man in my neighborhood had almost been charged with sexual abuse of a child for allegedly improperly touching his six-year-old nephew during a camping trip.

The allegations had arisen in the context of a contentious divorce, and I knew enough about the situation to suspect they weren't true. Had that man been charged, the stigma attached to the charges – charges that would have publicly branded him a child molester – could have followed him for years, and would have affected his life profoundly, even if he had ultimately been acquitted at trial.

Fortunately, the prosecutor reviewing the case was conscientious, and willing to take the time and effort necessary to carefully evaluate all the evidence before making a charging decision. While the police were pushing

312

for criminal charges, and while it appeared at first blush that the man might be guilty, after delving deeper into the facts and circumstances surrounding the allegations, the prosecutor ultimately declined to file charges.

So during the ethics panel, I emphasized that we as prosecutors must take very seriously our responsibility as gatekeepers in making charging decisions. I also said that, while it's true that we can legally bring charges against people on the fairly low standard of "probable cause," my personal view is that that's not enough. We should never take a casual approach – particularly when we are bringing serious charges that can immediately stigmatize the people we charge. Sometimes this means telling the cops no. Always, it means screening our cases carefully, and never taking the casual position that it's OK to charge on a minimum of evidence and let the innocent defendants get sorted out later.

During the ethics panel, I also raised another issue: Since we place our credibility behind what we say, should we as prosecutors be arguing for a defendant's guilt if we are not personally convinced of it ourselves?

It might seem like a strange question. After all, why would a prosecutor argue for guilt under those circumstances? How could a weak case even make it to trial?

There are several reasons why this could happen. Although prosecutors' offices generally have screening standards that say criminal charges should only be filed if there is a reasonable likelihood of conviction, the law allows charges to be filed simply upon "probable cause," a much lower standard than what is required for a conviction – "proof beyond a reasonable doubt."[121] So prosecutors can file on the low threshold of probable cause without violating the law, and end up with a weak case at trial.

There are other ways a weak case could go to trial. Sometimes prosecutors don't require police officers to do a thorough investigation before filing charges, and if they don't, cases can be filed that are inadequately

---

[121] Probable cause, as its name implies, only requires a reasonable likelihood that a defendant may have committed a crime. That's a far cry from proof beyond a reasonable doubt.

investigated.[122] One variant of this occurs when officers induce prosecutors to file charges even though evidence is weak, assuring them that the officers will be able to develop further evidence of a defendant's guilt after charges are filed – evidence that never materializes.[123]

Additionally, some cases that appear solid when they're filed may get weaker afterwards, when new information comes to light or witnesses equivocate.[124] In some of these instances, prosecutors may be disinclined to question their own charging decisions or to dismiss charges, particularly if the case has made its way through the system and is approaching trial.

And there's another dynamic at work that may reinforce a prosecutor's reluctance to re-evaluate a case after filing. We have an adversary system of justice, and prosecutors and defense attorneys regularly square off against each other in court, which can foster a sense of competition and, sometimes, animosity. This dynamic can cause prosecutors to have tunnel vision once charges are filed, preventing them from being open to new information that may come in later – information that may undermine confidence in a defendant's guilt.

In such instances, potentially exculpatory evidence that comes to light after charges are filed might not be enough to motivate a prosecutor to dismiss a case after the battle lines have been drawn and the case is in an adversary posture. And this can be true even though the additional information might have caused the prosecutor to hesitate or decline to file the case in the first place, had it been known when the case was initially screened.

The problem with prosecutors taking this position – that once a case is filed, they won't re-evaluate it – is that it elevates advocacy over justice. While it's true that prosecutors are advocates, they are first and foremost

---

[122] See the *Gladstone* case, Chapter 2.

[123] This is often in situations where officers believe a suspect is dangerous and needs to be arrested quickly, to ensure public safety.

[124] See, for example, the *Rudiger* case in Chapter 3. That case also highlights another circumstance. Knowing that 75% of wrongful convictions occur based on mistaken eyewitness identification, what does a prosecutor do when a victim is certain of her identification, but might be wrong? Is she entitled to her "day in court"?

ministers of justice,[125] and whenever there's a conflict between the two roles, their obligation to seek justice must always trump their role as advocates. That principle requires prosecutors to check their egos at the door, and to be willing to sometimes let defense attorneys "win" by dismissing cases when new information comes to light that casts doubt on a defendant's guilt.[126]

When I introduced these ideas in the ethics panel, the responses of the prosecutors to both the level of certainty needed to file charges and the level of certainty needed to advocate for guilt was interesting. Some of the prosecutors seemed to take the position that they were too busy to agonize about charging decisions. What was wrong with just charging if they had probable cause? After all, that's all the law required. Others seemed to understand the awesome power prosecutors have to bring serious charges against members of their communities, and that such power should be used with great care, even under pressures (including time pressures) that can make it more difficult to do so.

The conference attendees were also divided on the issue of whether prosecutors should argue a defendant's guilt if they themselves are uncertain of it. Some at the conference felt that as long as they were operating in good faith and weren't stepping over the line by offering their personal opinions regarding guilt, there was nothing wrong with advocating for a conviction and letting the jury decide, even if the prosecutor had some ambivalence about the evidence.

While it's true that the law prohibits prosecutors from making personal statements such as, "In my opinion, the evidence clearly shows that the defendant is guilty," how much difference does that prohibition actually make? As a practical matter, I doubt that juries make any meaningful

---

[125] Under Rule 3.8 of the Utah Rules of Professional Conduct, entitled, "Special Responsibilities of a Prosecutor," the comment states, "A prosecutor has the responsibility of a minister of justice and not simply that of an advocate."

[126] I used to make the point in prosecutor training that it's important to try to maintain good relations with defense attorneys, and that if for some reason that's not possible, we as ministers of justice must not treat defendants more harshly just because we don't like their attorneys.

distinction between hearing a prosecutor utter those words and hearing one say, "The evidence is clear, and the State asks you to find the defendant guilty of murder." With the assumption that a trial is not just a debate, wouldn't jurors expect prosecutors to believe what they say? And couldn't that potentially influence a jury's decision?

The ethics panel that fall had sparked an interesting discussion, and started a dialogue I thought was important. Still, I had no idea that the following year, those same issues would be brought home with more force in another training conference – this time in the context of innocence training, where the prosecutors would come face to face with an innocent man convicted of murder.

INNOCENCE TRAINING COMES TO UTAH

Now that I had a green light from the Prosecution Council's Training Committee to bring out an exoneree, I went down to Katie Monroe's office to see what the possibility might be of bringing Kirk Bloodsworth back to Utah to address the prosecutors. Having heard him speak, I really wanted him to be part of the presentation. Katie said she was not sure that was possible, due to both Kirk's busy schedule and the fact that he was based back East and worked for an organization that may not agree to send him out to Utah once again.

Around the same time I was exploring the possibility of bringing Kirk out for the conference, I was also working to line up a non-DNA exoneree to speak to an interim committee of the Legislature. An endorsement by a committee would make our bill a committee bill, and enhance the likelihood of its passage during the 2008 General Session, which would begin the following January. I wanted to put a human face on the problem of wrongful convictions by having an exoneree testify before the Legislature – someone the lawmakers could relate to. I asked for Katie's input on who would be a good choice, and together, we went through a list of possible exonerees.

Pretty quickly, I focused on Scott Hornoff, a former Rhode Island police officer who had been convicted of murder and sent to prison for several years. He had ultimately been released after the true killer came forward and confessed with details only the murderer would know. The real killer was the victim's former boyfriend, and when the police checked out his story, it was clear that the wrong man had been convicted. Scott was released, and the true killer was convicted and went to prison. As was fairly common, Scott had received no compensation or financial assistance when he was released from prison.

I felt Scott was the perfect candidate to bring out to Utah for two reasons: He was a non-DNA exoneree, and he had received no financial assistance whatsoever upon his release from prison. So he was a good fit for both parts of our bill. I also got excited about the possibility of having Scott do police innocence training with me. He could come out to Utah for a few days in June, testify before the Judiciary Interim Committee, and then participate in innocence training at the Utah Peace Officer Association training seminar that was going to be taking place the same week.

Katie also thought Scott would be a good fit, but told me not to get my hopes up. Unlike Kirk, Scott wasn't associated with an innocence or justice program which might foot the bill for him to fly out to Utah. Katie wasn't sure if the Rocky Mountain Innocence Center could afford to bring him out, and she doubted he could come on his own dime. We got Scott on the line and explained what we were trying to do. He caught the vision of it right away, and, to my delight, said he really wanted to come, and together we'd find a way to make it happen.

And it did happen. In fact, both Kirk and Scott came out to Utah that year. Scott testified in support of our bill, and the committee passed it out with a unanimous recommendation of support. He and I then drove up to Logan, where we did a joint presentation at the Utah Peace Officer Association training conference. I figured nothing would have a greater impact on police officers than hearing that one of their own had been wrongfully convicted of murder. If it could happen to a cop, it could happen to anyone. Spending a couple of days with Scott in June of 2007 was a great experience for me, and started a friendship that lasts to this day.

In September of 2007, Kirk Bloodsworth and I did a joint presentation at the Utah Prosecution Council Fall Training Conference. Our presentation included a PowerPoint slideshow highlighting the ethical duty of prosecutors to be careful in bringing criminal charges and to not just rubber-stamp police decisions, and we talked about the lessons that could be learned from exonerations. I called the presentation: "The Atticus Finch Prosecutor: Lessons in How to Avoid Prosecuting an Innocent Person."

To make the point about mistaken identification, I used a personal experience. I played guitar, and had been mistaken for another guitar player by several people, including an investigator I had worked with for more than ten years, and whose office was right across from mine in the State Capitol. While leaving a message on my answering machine, this investigator reported that he had seen me playing guitar with the symphony orchestra the night before. He even mentioned that both he and his wife had looked through binoculars, and they were both certain that it was me.

Since this was about the fourth time someone had told me they'd seen me playing at places I hadn't been performing, I called the symphony and got the name of the guy. They told me his name was Tully Cathey, and that he was a music professor at the University of Utah and a well-known guitarist. I then looked him up on the internet and, sure enough, the resemblance was uncanny. In my PowerPoint presentation, I did a side-by-side comparison by staging a photo of me with a guitar, similar to the one I had found of Tully on the internet. I captioned it, "I sure hope Tully behaves himself."

At the prosecutors' conference, Kirk did a great job recounting, with both humor and emotion, the nightmare he'd lived through, and received a standing ovation from the prosecutors. After he addressed the group, I led a discussion with a panel of experienced prosecutors, which included my old friend and mentor Bob Stott of the Salt Lake County District Attorney's Office, Uintah County Attorney Jo Ann Stringham, and Don Linton of the Cache County Attorney's Office, who had joined Scott Hornoff and me for lunch in Logan back in June, after Scott and I had made our innocence presentation to the Utah Peace Officers' Association.

At the end of the fall conference, we tallied up the surveys the prosecutors had filled out rating the presentations, and were pleased to learn that the innocence training was one of the highest-rated and best-received ethics presentations we had ever put on.

In January of 2008, two years after Rep. David Litvack first introduced his innocence bill, we were finally successful in getting our innocence bill through the Legislature. Senate Bill 16, *Exoneration and Innocence Assistance*, sponsored by Greg Bell,[127] was one of the first bills passed by the Legislature in its 2008 General Session, and it was signed into law by Governor Jon Huntsman in a ceremonial signing. I attended the signing with Katie Monroe and Heather Harris, now a lawyer rather than a law student. I had worked on hundreds of bills through the years, but never was I more pleased to see a bill signed into law.[128]

THE CASE OF BEVERLY MONROE

In May of 2008, it was again my privilege to be involved in innocence training. This time I teamed up with Katie and Beverly Monroe, and we highlighted Beverly's case, describing how, in 1992, a state police officer focused his suspicion on her after her boyfriend committed suicide. While

---

[127] Senator Bell sponsored the bill with the full support of David Litvack, the state representative who had not only sponsored the bill twice before, but who had worked with us on the committee to draft the consensus bill. David felt that the bill had a greater likelihood of passage if it were to be sponsored by a Republican, and he placed the importance of the bill's passage over personal ego. In that, he was a true statesman, and this bill, although it does not bear his name, is part of his legacy as a legislator.

[128] As of the date of this writing, two previously convicted defendants have been exonerated under the new statute – Debra Brown, who had been convicted of murder, and Harry Miller, who had been convicted of aggravated robbery.

the matter was initially investigated as a suicide by the local authorities, the officer got it in his mind that it was not suicide, but murder.

The investigation ended, incredibly, with Beverly being charged with first-degree murder in June of 1992. When Beverly hired a prominent defense attorney to represent her, he told her not to worry – the prosecution had a weak circumstantial case at best.

At the time Beverly was charged, her daughter, Katie, was a young lawyer, just two years out of law school. Katie was working as a law clerk at the Court of Appeals of Virginia, and the clerkship was ending that summer. She had been offered a job at the U.S. Commission on Civil Rights, but deferred taking it so she could go home to support her mother and attend her trial.

Beverly was tried in the fall of 1992, and despite the weakness of the evidence against her, she was convicted of murder and sentenced to prison. Katie knew her mother was innocent, and couldn't believe she had been convicted on such flimsy evidence. So she put her job on hold and started working to free her mother, although at first she had no clue how to go about doing it.

Katie had no office, so she set up camp at the Library of Congress and started researching what to do. She decided that the first step was to get her mother released on bond while her appeal was pending before the Court of Appeals of Virginia. Katie was able to secure Beverly's release on bond in May of 1993, and then took the job with the U.S. Commission on Civil Rights, pending a decision by the Court.

When the Court of Appeals handed down its decision in May of 1995, it was very bad news. The Court upheld Beverly's conviction, and when she filed a petition for appeal, the Supreme Court of Virginia promptly refused to grant it. And so in January of 1996, Beverly was ordered back to prison, where she would spend the next 6 1/2 years.

In the fall of 1995, Katie took a leave of absence from her job to put together a team to work for her mother's exoneration and release. Not long afterwards, Katie gave up her job altogether to work full-time on her mother's case. She contacted everyone she could think of who might be able to help her free her mother, and eventually had a breakthrough. A large law firm in Richmond, inspired by Katie's presentation and conviction of her mother's innocence, agreed to work on the case pro bono, and provide resources to effectively challenge Beverly's conviction. They even provided Katie with an office to work out of.

Together, Katie and her associates worked tirelessly to obtain records and documents relating to Beverly's case, and to interview and depose witnesses. Finally, in April of 1998, they were ready, and filed a comprehensive 165-page federal habeas corpus petition in the Federal District Court in Virginia. Beverly read the petition and supporting documents and said that, whatever the outcome, at least now the truth of what happened was finally going to be presented in court.

Katie's odyssey through the court system in her dogged search for justice for her mother could easily be the subject of an entire book. Suffice it to say that, in the spring of 2002, Federal Judge Richard Williams awarded Beverly a writ of habeas corpus, and ordered her release from prison![129]

While there was jubilation when Beverly was released on bond and allowed to go home, there was also concern, because the State promptly appealed Judge Williams' decision, attempting to preserve the conviction. It was a nerve-racking year for the family, with the specter of Beverly being returned to prison once again, if the court decision went against her.

Then, in April of 2003, wonderful news arrived – the Fourth Circuit Court of Appeals upheld Judge William's granting of the habeas petition! Shortly afterwards, all charges against Beverly were dropped. It was now

---

[129] The writ of habeas corpus was based on the court's finding that Beverly's continued confinement in prison was unlawful, in light of the exculpatory evidence the prosecutor failed to disclose to the defense, which would have weakened the State's case against her and may have resulted in an acquittal instead of a conviction. The judge also noted that the case was based on weak circumstantial evidence and the testimony of an unreliable police informant, or "snitch."

June of 2003, eleven years after Beverly was first charged with murder. Finally, the family's collective nightmare was over.

Fighting for her mother's exoneration and freedom changed the course of Katie's career, and it was Utah's good fortune that, some years later, she accepted an offer by Dan Medwed of the University of Utah College of Law to serve as the first full-time director of the Rocky Mountain Innocence Center.

Like all the innocence presentations I was involved with, the one highlighting Beverly and Katie's incredible story was riveting and well-received by those who attended the conference, and it was another opportunity for me to spend time with people I very much admire. Just as Beverly, Scott Hornoff, and Kirk Bloodsworth probably never imagined themselves becoming friends with prosecutors, I certainly never envisioned becoming so close to people who had been convicted and spent time in prison for murders they didn't commit.

Because of my work promoting both training and legislation to assist the innocent, Katie nominated me to speak at a national innocence conference in New Orleans in June of 2008. It was a great experience, and I was pleased to attend and let those in attendance know that prosecutors could be partners rather than adversaries in working for innocence reform. I also enjoyed getting to know the people involved in the Innocence Movement.

FULL CIRCLE

As I think back on my career as a prosecutor and especially those last few years, it seems fitting to me that my focus turned back to where it was when I began – wanting to be sure that innocent people who might be caught up in the criminal justice system would be able to find their way out, and return home.

I think that this transition wasn't much of a departure for me, because throughout my career, the theme playing in the back of my mind was that, above all, we should not be prosecuting the wrong people, no matter what pressures might be brought to bear to "solve a case" or "reassure the community." It affected the way I approached charging decisions, and made me more willing than many to re-evaluate a case if new evidence surfaced. And, finally, it allowed me to consider the possibility that the system, even with all its safeguards, could still make a mistake and result in an innocent person being convicted and sent to prison.

EPILOGUE

WHEN I THINK BACK ON MY JOURNEY through the criminal justice system, I realize I was lucky.

I was lucky because I got to go to work every day and do meaningful and interesting work, and because there were aspects of my job I was passionate about.

I was lucky because I had good mentors like Paul Boland, George Oakes, Dick Shepherd, Bob Stott and Mike Wims.

I was lucky because when I started my career at the Salt Lake County D.A.'s Office, there was plenty of opportunity to get trial experience quickly.

I was lucky that early in my career, I was randomly assigned to do a presentation at a training conference on how to cross-examine mental health experts in court, and as a result I developed an interest in the interplay between mental health issues and criminal law, and became a specialist in that area.

I was lucky because as an Assistant Attorney General, I was able to travel around the state, assisting county prosecutors with major cases, forging friendships with them, and seeing how justice was administered in the far-flung regions of Utah.

I was lucky because I never had a case go wildly off the rails, never had anyone get away with murder, and, to the best of my knowledge, never convicted or sent an innocent person to prison.

I was lucky because I was able to work to help enact policies and laws to improve the criminal justice system.

I was lucky because for many years, my office was in the State Capitol, near the Legislature, and I got to walk the stately grounds and historic hallways every day.

I was lucky because when I worked as an Assistant Attorney General under Jan Graham and Reed Richards in the 1990s, I had no doubt that I had the best prosecution job in the state.

I was lucky because I got to regularly participate in training conferences – making presentations to lawyers, judges, police officers and mental health experts.

I was lucky because I got to mentor young prosecutors, and to learn from them.

I was lucky because I got to work with great people in both the Salt Lake D.A.'s Office and the Attorney General's Office, many of whom became good friends.

I was lucky because the job wasn't all murder and mayhem, and in between we managed to have fun, whether it was retelling the legendary "lizard with a ladder" story (you had to have been there), singing a fractured version of "Pancho and Lefty" at a prosecutors conference, going up to the cabin in Mt. Air Canyon for annual SWAPLAC and division meetings, or putting on a goofy skit at an office party.

I was lucky to become involved in the Innocence Movement, work for innocence reform, and in the process meet extraordinary people like Katie and Beverly Monroe, Scott Hornoff, Kirk Bloodsworth, and Dennis Fritz.

And finally, when I walked out the door of the Attorney General's Office and retired in 2009, I was lucky that I felt no sense of loss, because being a lawyer wasn't my only passion, and there were other things I wanted to do.

I think Woody Allen once said that 80% of success is just showing up. I was there when some big cases came along, and I did my best with them. I showed up. I never asked to be assigned high-profile cases, and more than once I tried to avoid them, but I got more than my share, and I had my time in the limelight.

But the best days of my career weren't the ones I spent in trial with news reporters and cameras. They were the days I worked quietly at the policy level to try to improve the criminal justice system – to make it more fair and just.

I hope my efforts in seeking justice, both in court and in the Utah Legislature, have made a difference, for I like to think that I was always guided by the spirit of Atticus Finch, whose portrayal in *To Kill a Mockingbird* inspired me to become a lawyer in the first place.

ACKNOWLEDGMENTS

I WISH TO THANK A NUMBER OF PEOPLE for their contributions to this book.

I'm grateful to Rick Whitehouse, my life-long friend, for encouraging me to do what I'd idly talked about doing for some time – putting pen to paper to write about my experiences as a prosecutor. The first sentence of the book came to me late one night after I'd spoken with Rick on the phone, and once I started writing, the book practically wrote itself.

No one could have received more encouragement to publish a book than I received from my good friends Barbara and Phil Oakley. I met them after I received a call from Barb asking if we could meet for lunch, as she was researching a new book about one of the cases I had prosecuted. (She had already written a book about another Utah case.)

A few weeks before Barb contacted me, I had sent a chapter of my book to my friend and former colleague Mike Wims for his input. Mike had asked me if he could forward the chapter to Barb, as he was aware that she was researching a case that Mike and I had prosecuted together, and he felt that the chapter had background information that might be helpful to her. I told him that would be fine, not thinking much about it.

When I met Barb and Phil to discuss the case Barb was researching, she told me how much she'd enjoyed the chapter Mike had forwarded to her, and asked if I had written any others. When I told her I had just finished a draft of the whole book, she asked me if I would send her a copy, and shortly after I did, I heard back from both Barb and Phil. They responded to the manuscript with such enthusiasm that they all but insisted that I publish it. Without their energetic support, I may never have seriously considered publishing the book, which I originally wrote simply because I enjoy the process of writing and had stories I wanted to tell.

I am greatly indebted to Katie Monroe for her review of the book and suggestion that I include more information about my upbringing and formative years, to give the reader better insight into why I was a "reluctant prosecutor."

I also appreciate the contribution of Mike Steffen, who reviewed the manuscript and gave me helpful editorial suggestions.

Special thanks to my daughter Kaely Horton, an amazing writer in her own right, who skillfully edited the book and made invaluable "big-picture" suggestions on how to improve it.

I appreciate the valuable conceptual input I received from Adam Michaud in a general advisory capacity – suggestions about the title, text, and cover.

Thanks too to my brother and best friend, Joseph Horton, and my sister-in-law Ann, who provided their usual insightful input and encouragement throughout the process of my writing the book.

Many thanks to my friends, colleagues, and brothers-in-arms, particularly Bob Stott, Paul Boyden, David Walsh, Rich McKelvie, John Soltis, Dave Schwendiman, Rob Lunnen, Earl Dorius, Dave Blackwell, Pat Nolan, Don Linton, Mike Wims and Fred Voros.

Thanks also to my former colleagues in the Utah Attorney General's Office, Agent Ron Miller and Paralegal Sharon Fleck, who teamed up with me on many high-profile cases through the years, and who made my job easier due to their considerable skills, insights, and professionalism.

I also want to thank Former Utah Attorney General Jan Graham and her chief deputy, Reed Richards, as well as Former Chief Deputy John T. Nielsen of the Salt Lake County Attorney's Office – the best bosses I ever worked for.

And I would like to acknowledge the contributions of my mentor, Richard "Shep" Shepherd, who read the book and gave me input.

Thanks to my multi-talented daughter Eyrie for her keen eye in proofreading the book.

Thanks to my cousin, Joe McMurrin, for his helpful suggestions on ways to improve the text.

Thanks to my nephew Jared Swensen for his help with photography.

Thanks also to Assistant Attorney General Robert Steed, for being the example of a "tough prosecutor" that I refer to in the article at the end of Chapter 2.

For their helpful input on matters on which I sought advice from time to time, thanks to my sisters, Eve Chamberlain Utley and Joan Evans, my nephew Matt Horton and his wife Tori, as well as a number of friends: Mike O'Connor, Jay Munns, Robert "Jimmy" Orr, John Penido, Jack Campbell, Whale Szczepanowski, and Max Glenn.

Thanks also to Craig M. Howard, AKA Juste LeTouvrai, because, … well, just because I wrote a book and wanted to put him in it.

Thanks to Dave Cowden and Johnni Prince, for their support, suggestions and advice.

Thanks to Bobbi Benson, who contributed so much to the production values of the book, designed the front and back book covers and interior features, helped me with strategic decisions, and guided me through the process of self-publication.

Thanks to my wife Jo for keeping the home fires burning while I was traveling around the state assisting local prosecutors with murder cases, living out of motels for weeks at a time; for being a good sounding board when I needed to talk about cases I was handling; and for insisting that we take regular family vacations so our lives would not be consumed by my work.

And, of course, I have dedicated the book to my father, Creighton C. Horton, M.D., and to Paul Boland, my mentor and trial advocacy law professor at UCLA. Without their influence, I would never have become a trial lawyer or written this book.

CREIGHTON C. HORTON II

CREIGHTON WAS BORN AND RAISED in Southern California, went to law school at UCLA, and moved to Utah in the late 1970s. Although he started out with aspirations of being a defense attorney, he was hired by the Salt Lake District Attorney's Office in 1978, and prosecuted cases there for nine years, ending as team leader of the Career Offender Unit, which prosecuted habitual criminals. He was recruited by the Utah Attorney General's Office in 1987, and worked there until he retired in 2009. For seventeen years, he was chief of the Criminal Justice Division, and for two years served as chief of the Violent Crimes and Special Prosecutions Section.

During his career, Creighton handled some of the most noteworthy cases of the day, including capital murder cases and cases involving religious extremists. He specialized in countering mental defenses in homicide cases, where defendants claimed insanity or diminished mental capacity. In addition to his trial work, he worked with the Utah State Legislature, promoting bills to improve the criminal justice system.

Near the end of his career, Creighton became involved in the innocence movement, as DNA testing began exonerating more and more defendants across the country. He promoted legislative reforms in Utah to facilitate DNA testing for inmates who asserted their innocence, and to allow judges to issue orders of exoneration. Later, he worked collaboratively with innocence advocates to pass legislation to allow judges to exonerate defendants in non-DNA cases, where the evidence of innocence was clear. That bill also set up a system to partially compensate wrongfully convicted people for the years they spent in prison.

In addition to innocence legislation, Creighton worked to put in place statewide policies to require police officers to record interviews with suspects, and he spearheaded police and prosecutor training to reduce the possibility of innocent people being caught up in the criminal justice system. In the course of his innocence work, he became friends with several exonerees from around the country – people who had been wrongfully convicted of murders, and later exonerated.

Creighton has come full circle as an author. In college, he was an English Major with a creative writing emphasis. He enjoys the process of writing and telling stories. He has had a lifelong passion for playing music which was sparked by The Beatles' British invasion of America when he was in high school. He currently resides on the West Coast, where he plays music in restaurants and pubs with his buddy Dave, and continues to write when the spirit moves him.